D1224269

The Middle Ages in 50 Objects will appeal to anyone with a passion for history and delight in things. Evocatively bringing the medieval world alive, it unearths buried weapons, de-codes enigmatic images, and rewards the curious with details of materials and makers, myths and movements. An outstanding resource for instructors and visual learners, this volume satisfies both the intellect and the senses.

Maureen C. Miller, University of California

The recent turn to "materiality" among medievalists has paid off handsomely in this informative and beautifully presented study. The book testifies to the added value of collaboration in scholarship and of the utility of integrating different scholarly approaches to the study of objects. The authors obviously experienced great joy in executing the project, and I experienced the same emotion in reading it.

William Chester Jordan, Princeton University

A splendid visual feast, this compelling account of the Middle Ages will fascinate and engage students, specialists and general readers alike. This is Medieval History with a difference – of approach, scope, and content – that is as stimulating as it is enjoyable.

Julia M. H. Smith, University of Oxford

The Middle Ages in 50 Objects, as its name suggests, places objects front and center in the telling of history. Using select works from the rich collections of the Cleveland Museum of Art, the authors present an admirably broad and diverse picture of the medieval era. Written in an engaging, approachable style, and with an authoritative erudition, this work will offer students an excellent introduction to the field.

Christina Maranci, Tufts University

With its focus on carefully selected objects and its attention to material culture, this book is both a masterpiece of methodology and a must-read volume for scholars, students, and interested public alike. Using the objects to address broad interdisciplinary questions concerning Islamic, Byzantine, and European societies, it brings the Middle Ages back to life in a sophisticated and intelligent way.

Claudia Bolgia, University of Edinburgh

The luxury items and ordinary medieval artifacts this volume showcases range across the full chronological and geographical scope of the capacious Middle Ages. They comprise a splendid cabinet of curiosities, a wondrous collection of images and stories, wrapped in rich contextualizations, that allows the reader to assemble a complex, multifaceted image of the Middle Ages.

Asa Simon Mittman, Professor of Art History, California State University, Chico

The Middle Ages in 50 Objects

The extraordinary array of images included in this volume reveals the full and rich history of the Middle Ages. Exploring material objects from the European, Byzantine, and Islamic worlds, the book casts a new light on the cultures that formed them, each culture illuminated by its treasures.

The objects are divided among four topics: The Holy and the Faithful; The Sinful and the Spectral; Daily Life and Its Fictions; and Death and Its Aftermath. Each section is organized chronologically, and every object is accompanied by a penetrating essay that focuses on its visual and cultural significance within the wider context in which the object was made and used. Spot maps add yet another way to visualize and consider the significance of the objects and the history that they reveal. Lavishly illustrated, this is an appealing and original guide to the cultural history of the Middle Ages.

Elina Gertsman is Professor of Medieval Art at Case Western Reserve University. She is the author of *The Dance of Death in the Middle Ages: Image, Text, Performance* (2010) and *Worlds Within: Opening the Medieval Shrine Madonna* (2015), and editor of several books, including *Visualizing Medieval Performance: Perspectives, Histories, Contexts* (2008) and *Crying in the Middle Ages: Tears of History* (2011, 2013). Most recently, with Stephen Fliegel, she published a catalogue that accompanies the focus exhibition they co-curated at the Cleveland Museum of Art, *Myth and Mystique: Cleveland's Gothic Table Fountain* (2016).

Barbara H. Rosenwein, Professor Emerita, Loyola University Chicago, is a medievalist and a recognized authority on the history of emotions. She is the author of *Emotional Communities in the Early Middle Ages* (2006), *Generations of Feeling: A History of Emotions, 600–1700* (2016), and has just completed (with co-author Riccardo Cristiani) *What is the History of Emotions?* Her textbooks, *A Short History of the Middle Ages* and *Reading the Middle Ages: Sources from Europe, Byzantium, and the Islamic World*, are currently going into new editions.

The Middle Ages in 50 Objects

Elina Gertsman

Barbara H. Rosenwein

CAMBRIDGE
UNIVERSITY PRESS

CAMBRIDGE
UNIVERSITY PRESS

University Printing House, Cambridge CB2 8BS, United Kingdom

One Liberty Plaza, 20th Floor, New York, NY 10006, USA

477 Williamstown Road, Port Melbourne, VIC 3207, Australia

314–321, 3rd Floor, Plot 3, Splendor Forum, Jasola District Centre, New Delhi – 110025, India

79 Anson Road, #06–04/06, Singapore 079906

Cambridge University Press is part of the University of Cambridge.

It furthers the University's mission by disseminating knowledge in the pursuit of education, learning, and research at the highest international levels of excellence.

www.cambridge.org
Information on this title: www.cambridge.org/9781107150386
DOI: 10.1017/9781316577189

First published 2018

Printed in China by Clays, St Ives plc

A catalogue record for this publication is available from the British Library.

ISBN 978-1-107-15038-6 Hardback

Cambridge University Press has no responsibility for the persistence or accuracy of URLs for external or third-party internet websites referred to in this publication and does not guarantee that any content on such websites is, or will remain, accurate or appropriate.

Contents

Part IV Death and Its Aftermath

Acknowledgments

We wish to acknowledge the invaluable support of the Cleveland Museum of Art staff: Stephen Fliegel, the Robert P. Bergman Curator of Medieval Art; Sonya Rhie Quintanilla, the George P. Bickford Curator of Indian and Southeast Asian Art and the Interim Curator of Islamic Art; Elizabeth Saluk, the Registrar for Exhibitions and Rights and Reproductions; and the librarians at the Ingalls Library, especially Louis Adrean and Christine Edmonson.

We thank those generous scholars who helped us with translations: Roshi Ahmadian, Mohsen Ashtiany, Sheila Blair, Riccardo Cristiani, Ross Duffin, Nancy Gauthier, and Helen Swift. Special thanks are due to Sheila Blair, who read through and commented with care on all our essays concerning the Islamic world, and to Riccardo Cristiani, who helped with the book at every phase and ably prepared its index. We are grateful to current and former CWRU graduate students Aimee Caya, Dominique DeLuca, and Victoria Hepburn, who proved to be fantastic research assistants, and James Wehn who helped out with the information on the CMA's prints.

Finally, we thank our families, who shared our frustrations, joys, and labors with good humor and steadfast support.

Abbreviations and Conventions

c.	circa
cent.	century
d.	death
r.	ruled

All dates are CE unless otherwise noted.

Introduction

Complex and varied, vibrant and intense, medieval objects demand to be examined closely, to be thought about deeply, to be approached kinesthetically. Extraordinary in the multiplicity of meanings that it harbors and engenders, the material culture of the Middle Ages offers its beholders a rich experience of looking, often multisensory, always rewarding. It offers, too, a glimpse of a vivid society, or rather the many societies that were in constant flux and in intermittent conversations (and, at times, screaming matches) with one another. And yet, each object has its own history. So how do we write history *through* objects?

The premise of our book is that such history requires intense collaboration. Its predicate is a triumvirate of sorts: a nexus of art history, museology, and history. An art historian, perforce, will focus on images themselves, teasing out the network of associations they trigger, visual discourses they tap into, and viewing practices they suggest. A historian will concentrate on the larger context, proposing a set of situations and conditions spun around an object as if an intricate cocoon. Both will want to marshal a wide variety of sources—textual and visual, oral and aural—in order to understand not only the agency of men and women in the objects' creation, but also the objects themselves as active agents in the formation of history. Finally, the museum will serve both as a framework and a guiding force: enriching and constraining all writing efforts, suggesting how collecting practices shape our historical imagination.

Our choice of the collections is quite deliberate. The Cleveland Museum of Art is justly famous, boasting an extraordinarily wide-ranging compendium of medieval objects, acquired over the years for a variety of purposes, by a variety of curators, but always with the viewing public in mind. The collections—with their broad chronology and a geographical reach extending across Eurasia—allow us to glimpse the history of not only the European Middle Ages but also the Byzantine and Islamic worlds. It is true that the museum writes its own version of history through its holdings and display, through what it was willing and able to acquire. The CMA's Christian manuscripts are astonishing, for example, but it has no Jewish books as of yet: medieval Jewish art was scarce at the time of its creation and it is even scarcer now; Christian service books such as Missals greatly outnumbered Jewish service books such as Haggadot, and history was kinder to them. We considered this an appropriate challenge: to make present in word what is

absent in image. Medievalists are faced with the issue of lacunae all the time, even when they have the full run of every library in the world—our sources are often fragmentary, and we learn to make the most of what we have. Here, Judaism is made visible through a variety of objects, including the Jonah sculpture and the illuminated initial that depicts Isaac and Esau, while the threads of Jewish culture are woven into the fabric of many more essays.

And thus we set out to produce a full and rich history of the medieval world based on the 50 objects we chose for the purpose. Historians of every sort are increasingly interested in what material things can tell us about the past. Then, as now, people lived in relation to objects, and objects shaped their practices, ideas, and feelings. Every era tells us much about itself from the items that it creates, uses, prizes, and destroys. But the Middle Ages is particularly illuminated by its material objects because its culture was so attuned to the meanings of things as they were felt, seen, heard, tasted, and even smelled—the incense burning in a mosque, the gleam of light from a garnet brooch, the chanting in a synagogue, the touch of fingers to an ivory mirror, the Eucharistic wafer dissolving in the mouth.

We would like to think that our methods of inquiry are indebted to medieval thinkers who themselves drew on ancient books on rhetoric. In his commentary on the work of Roman rhetorician Martianus Capella, for example, the ninth-century monk Remigius of Auxerre wrote: "First to be considered are the seven topics, that is circumstances, which are established at the beginning of every authentic book: who, what, why, in what manner, where, when, by what faculties." These are the questions that guided us as we tackled each object in turn. For the sculpture of Christ and Saint John, for example, there are two contexts: the one in which the Gospel narrative was written down and then another in which this sculpture was experienced. This brought us to the convent culture of late medieval Swabia, to the world of devotional objects and nuns that levitated before them, to the practices of meditation and to the culture of mystics, to the living sculptures and visionaries that beheld them. But we also wanted to explore the Rhineland more generally—its affluence and its politics—and then widen the horizon still further, to include the plague that swept the region along with the rest of Europe, and finally to come to the issues of reform and Reformation in this turbulent and spiritually vibrant world. To visualize this world and the place of the sculpture within it, we include a small map.

In this manner, each object serves as a point of reference whose significance opens out in ever wider circles, all important to explore. The object is in the first place of keen interest in itself; indeed, that is why it entered the museum's collection. In the second place, it suggests the tastes, concerns, beliefs, prejudices, and practical needs of whoever commissioned or purchased it. Finally, it is part of

a much larger whole: the people immediately interested in or touched by the object may be a minority living in a world largely indifferent to such an object; or they may represent a majority and thus speak for nearly an entire society. Medieval art may—it often does—represent the concerns of elites, for the objects made for the rich are frequently the things that were kept and cherished over time and subsequently purchased by museums. But we have made sure to include non-elite objects as well—a pilgrim's flask, a soldier's helmet—as well as objects seen and used by different classes concurrently. The marble altar front may have stood in a well-endowed church either in Constantinople (today Istanbul) or Ravenna, but the people who entered that church, who saw the altar and perhaps even touched it, came from various walks of life. Similarly, the feline incense burner perfumed the air of a mosque in Khurasan, Iran, that was open to believers of many estates.

The choice of objects was particularly difficult because we wanted to present them in the compass of a compact, rather than dauntingly long, book. We opted for a mix of well-known pieces and those less published to ensure coverage of many, though admittedly not all, important cultural themes of the Middle Ages; the sum total thus adds up to more than the book's four parts. In the first part, "The Holy and the Faithful," we tackle the notion of the sacred. The reader will encounter Jewish prophets and Christian martyrs; the Hebrew scriptures, the New Testament, and the Qur'an; liturgical implements of various kinds; indignant monks and earnest pilgrims; images of the divine and body parts of saints. But then we endeavored to knit entire worlds around those topics: a blood jasper calyx occasions a discussion of medicine and magic as well as of the Eucharist, while an alabaster panel with the Carrying of the Cross provides an avenue for talking about medieval drama and performance. The famous Jonah sculpture lends itself to the discussion of the Old Testament story, to be sure, but also to the brief exploration of the nascent Christian community of the pre-Christian Roman Empire, still intact and seething with religious ferment. The Khurasan incense burner sparks not only engagement with religious culture but also with literary discourses of the rapidly expanding Muslim world. Emperors and noblemen, merchants and bureaucrats make their entrance, too—for there can be no discussion of devotional behaviors without politics, or religious worship without economy. Here, as elsewhere, we engage with a dazzling array of materials: marble and ivory, parchment and silver, wood and terracotta.

Sacred figures reappear in Part II, "The Sinful and the Spectral," but in some very different roles. We see Christ beaten by disfigured and distorted reprobates; we see the Virgin Mary in resounding triumph over Original Sin. But we also see Adam and Eve committing this very sin, and, indeed, an entire set of personified sins arrayed on a metal bowl: Pride, Anger, Envy, and Lust. On an illuminated

page, Acedia, or Sloth, sits stewing in her own boredom, ignoring her lively court. In the well-Islamicized world of fifteenth-century Eurasia, Persian-inspired monstrous demons grimace in their chains on striking album leaves. Monstrosity unravels into the spectral, as beasts and hybrids invade the viewing space: grotesques cavort on manuscript pages, and a basilisk colludes with a lion on a carved column capital. This, too, is a world unto itself, which nonetheless often takes potent social commentary as its subject. The otherness of Christ's tormentors identifies them as the Jews: the image comes from fourteenth-century Venice—that is, a time and place that witnessed mendicant Franciscan preachers vilifying the Jews on Italian city streets. Acedia, in turn, was used to warn a young Genoese heir to a merchant's fortune against the temptations of laziness, which would be directly detrimental to his family occupation.

And so the echoes of the everyday, which whisper across the pages of the first half of the book, come to the fore in Part III. Entitled "Daily Life and Its Fictions," this section gathers objects that allow us to talk not only about the quotidian existence of medieval women and men, but also about the ways that this existence was presented, subverted, and fictionalized. The Parisian ivory mirror purports to be a courtly scene—a game of chess—but just as courtly love was an imaginary construct, so did the game signify much more than an innocent pastime, representing that which could not be represented. Similarly, the Kashan tile exalts love, or rather fictions of love, inscribed with erotic poetry that likens lips to precious stones, black curls to vipers, and gardens to paradise. A gorgeous Gothic fountain, an automaton meant to titillate the senses, not only stands witness to a real entertainment at court, but also appeals to literary tastes, alluding to the magic springs and pure streams that played such a great role in the medieval imaginary. From Frankish noblemen to Venetian warriors, from Byzantine dignitaries to Italian doctors, from Parisian law men to Carolingian monastics—this section of the book casts its net widely, to explore life in Islamic, Byzantine, and European societies. We look at courts and commerce; industry and coinage; power and law; war and conquest; schools and universities. But we know that many of these themes as seen through visual representation are temporally complicated and ideologically fraught—and so we tried to be cognizant of the very nature of the representation and the fictions that it imposes.

Finally, and perhaps inevitably, we come to the subject of death in the last section of the book, "Death and Its Aftermath." Here, we look at the so-called Last Four Things—death, judgment, heaven, and hell—and all sorts of matters that cohere around these topics. We explore instruments of death, such as a knife-like dagger called a scramasax; mourning and burial rituals, both Jewish and Christian; grave markers, European and Islamic; representations of dying and death and of

the Last Judgment; conceptualizations of Death as a personified force; and visions of afterlife—the joys of heaven, the torments of hell, and the uncertainties of purgatory. From the scene of Saint Lawrence roasting on an open-fire grill to the grinning skeletons who have come to collect the Pope, the landscape of life's end unfolds across the long Middle Ages, always terrifying, sometimes hopeful, always inevitable. Here, as in the other parts of the book, the themes that we chose have the advantage of cutting across time periods and geographical boundaries. The objects included reveal people's hopes, fears, joys, and pretensions; their rules, tastes, customs, and habits; their myths, stories, beliefs, and value systems —all treated within the hard facts of political and social developments, and the always abundant, exquisite, and stupendous material culture.

Organized chronologically, each section of the book offers a microcosm for contrast and comparison. The vision of the Middle Ages offered here is lively, active, bustling. Like exquisite treasures in a coffer, the objects presented here are arranged to be rummaged through, to be admired, to be thought about. Readers will no doubt use the book in two main ways. Those wishing to be systematic will start from the beginning and read to the end. Even in that case, they will find themselves whizzing across Europe, landing in Iran, and drawn back again through Constantinople. Those who wish to dip into the book here and there will create their own sort of disorientation, but they will find some bearings in the running heads, which signal both the part they are in and the names of the objects. We imagine readers finding answers to some of their questions, questioning some of our answers, and being propelled to ask still new questions—to set out on all manner of new intellectual explorations, look closely at the images on offer, and seek out others. It is our hope that this book helps its readers to form a rich picture of the medieval world—a world astonishing and frustrating, foreign and familiar, and always laced with wonder and contradiction.

PART I

The Holy and the Faithful

1

Jonah Cast Up, c. 280–290, Asia Minor (?), marble; 41.50 × 36.00 × 18.50 cm (16 ^{5}⁄$_{16}$ × 14 ⅛ × 7 ¼ inches)

IN THE Book of Jonah in the Hebrew Bible, God orders Jonah to go to Nineveh— today a ruin near Mosul in Iraq—and preach against its wickedness. Rather than obey, Jonah tries to flee about as far as he can go on a ship set to cross the Mediterranean Sea. He fails miserably: once the voyage begins, a tempest sent by God threatens to destroy the ship. Realizing that the storm is his fault, Jonah asks the sailors to throw him into the sea. The men oblige, but Jonah does not drown. Instead, he is swallowed by a "great fish," interpreted at times as a sea monster. Jonah remained "in the belly of the fish three days and three nights," singing a psalm of praise and thanksgiving to God, until the fish, commanded by God, "vomited out Jonah upon the dry land" (Jonah 1:17, 2:10).

It is precisely this moment that is commemorated in the marble sculpture of Jonah Cast Up. A strong, muscular man with an abundant beard and wild curly hair, Jonah dives out from the toothy jaws of the beast, arms up, the movement of his torso echoing the direction of the sea creature's pricked-up ears and scrunched snout. The broad-shouldered Jonah, with his copious curls and robust arms, is reminiscent of images of Zeus, the Greek god of thunder and the ruler of Olympus. The monster is highly dynamic, all head and sinuous body, with two small wing-like protrusions. It rests on its powerful forepaws and curls back on itself, its tailfin connecting with Jonah's right hand. Even as the beast disgorges Jonah, it seems unwilling to let him go: its teeth clasp his torso; its fantastic paws dig into the ground; its eyes roll up in its head from the vain effort to hold onto the prophet.

This moment marks the turning point in Jonah's story. Now, obedient to God, Jonah goes to Nineveh to prophesy its end. But when the people there hear his message, they are filled with remorse and abandon their wicked ways. Seeing this, rather than destroy the city, "God repented of the evil which he said he would do to them; and he did not do it" (3:10). Distressed by this change of heart, the indignant Jonah prayed to God: now that his prophesy was undone, it was best for God to kill him, he felt. The divine object lesson soon followed. When, in a pout, Jonah sat down to rest under a shade plant that God created for him, the plant was quickly destroyed. Just as Jonah pitied the plant, so, God explained, should Nineveh's creator pity that city.

In its original context, the story was meant for an audience of monotheists—the Jews—living in a world dominated by polytheists. Although the narrative seems to

take place c. 700 BCE, when Nineveh was a major city in Assyria, the Book of Jonah was probably not written until 350 BCE. That puts its date of composition just before the time of Alexander the Great (d.323 BCE), whose conquests were to destroy the old world order. Assyria no longer existed when Jews of the Persian Empire first read the Book of Jonah. But Nineveh remained for them a symbol of unbelief and wickedness. The moral of the Book, then, was to teach the Jews to accept God as merciful enough to save even the most corrupt of peoples.

But the original readers of the Book of Jonah were not the appreciative audience of Jonah Cast Up. The sculpture seems to have formed part of an ensemble. It was supposedly found buried in a very large jar alongside six paired portrait busts, an image of Christ the Good Shepherd, and three other representations of Jonah: in prayer, under the shade plant, and being swallowed by the sea monster. The patrons, therefore, appear to have had Christian leanings: Christians read the story in the Book of Jonah as a prefiguration of Christ's death and Resurrection. Indeed, Matthew 12:40 told them to do so: "For as Jonah was three days and three nights in the whale's belly, so shall the Son of Man [Christ] be three days and three nights in the heart of the earth." Still, the original purpose of the marbles is unclear. They may have been used in a funerary context, where the subject of Jonah and the theme of salvation would have been especially appropriate. Or perhaps they were made for a domestic setting, as a constant reminder of the hope of redemption. The entire set appears to have been made c. 280–290, probably in Asia Minor, which then was a part of the Roman Empire.

By then, Rome's empire was vast and in crisis, threatened by attacks from people to the north (the so-called "barbarians") and the east (the Persians). Vigorous military action on the part of several emperors late in the century turned the tide. Under Diocletian (d.305) the Empire was reunited, though administratively divided. The major line was drawn between its eastern and western halves. That division would have a very long afterlife: the eastern half became the Byzantine Empire (whose avatars today are Russia and Turkey), and the western half eventually became many of the present-day states of Europe.

While the era of Diocletian was good news for many living in the Empire, it was a difficult time for the nascent Christian community. Its members,

The Roman Empire, c. 300.

scattered among the cities of the Empire, had begun to forget earlier persecutions. They had gained high offices in the civil service and served in the army. However, after c. 300 they confronted the Great Persecution. Soldiers were ordered to sacrifice to the Roman gods or face discharge; Christian churches were destroyed; books of scripture were confiscated and burned; and Christians were stripped of their rank if they did not conform, making them liable to torture or execution. Whether carved before the Great Persecution or at some point during it, the marble image of the rebellious Jonah—not only saved from drowning but also finding himself cast safely ashore—must have been exceptionally reassuring.

Jonah Cast Up thus stands as a perfect witness to the cultural and religious complexity of the late third century. Visually arresting, the image marries a Jewish theme to a Christian purpose, seeing an essential harmony between these two monotheistic religions, a positive view that would persist through the centuries even as another strand of thought would emphasize the perfidy of the Jews and the triumph of the Christians. Its style borrows from that of ancient Greece, with its appreciation of the beauty and weightiness of human and animal forms, and is dependent especially on the emotionality and verve of Hellenistic art. The acceptance of a "pagan" style suggests the sophistication of the Jonah sculpture's patrons, surely a prosperous family that was nostalgic for Hellenistic culture even as its members distanced themselves from paganism through their religion. At the very time that it was made, the original creators of the Jonah story, the Jews, were dispersed throughout the Roman world as well as outside of it. The synagogue—which, like "church," meant the community of believers in addition to being the place of worship—included the Book of Jonah in its services. Jonah's story pointed up God's desire to love, rather than to destroy: a hopeful message in turbulent times for Jews and Christians alike.

2

Altar Front, c. 540–600, Constantinople or Ravenna, marble; 101.00 × 169.50 × 25.50 cm (39 ¾ × 66 ¹¹⁄₁₆ × 10 inches)

J UST before he was expelled from Jerusalem and stoned to death, the very first martyr, Saint Stephen, reportedly cried out: "I see the heavens opened!" (Acts 7:56). To ordinary believers, a similar glimpse of heaven was made possible via a small window—called a "fenestella"—cut into this marble panel that once fronted the altar of a sixth-century church. A small shrine with relics would have been placed just behind or slightly underneath the fenestella. Suffused with God's grace, relics—fragments of a saint's body, or something that had touched that body—had real power in the world. The devout could tap into that grace via the fenestella by lowering a bit of cloth right through it in order to come into contact, albeit indirectly, with the hallowed remains. A pair of pulled-back curtains, carved on both sides of the fenestella, suggests the mystery and wonder that lay behind them.

By the time the panel was made, the Roman Empire had long been Christianized. After Emperor Constantine (d.337) commanded his army to fight under the cross-shaped sign of Christ (the so-called chi-rho), and after he and his co-emperor Licinius agreed to tolerate all the religions in the Empire in 312, Christianity became both acceptable and attractive. Constantine himself favored the Christian Church. Rebuilding the ancient Greek city of Byzantium as Constantinople and deliberately turning it into the New Rome, Constantine made this capital a Roman Christian showcase. As the century wore on, Christianity gained in power and prestige, and by the 390s it was declared the official religion of the Roman Empire, while polytheism was outlawed. Nevertheless, numerous people throughout the Empire were not Christian, notably Jews and rural dwellers (the so-called *pagani*, or pagans).

The quality of this altar carving suggests that it came either from Constantinople or Ravenna, two of the most important cities of the Roman Empire. During the sixth century, that empire was splitting into eastern and western halves. Although Emperor Justinian (d.565) sent his militia to reunite it forcibly, their success was only partial. Soon armies of "barbarians" took over most of the western half. But even then the eastern half, which historians call the "Byzantine Empire" or "Byzantium," held onto an important swath of territory in present-day Italy, with Ravenna as its administrative center.

Both cities boasted lavishly appointed churches. The principal church of Constantinople, Hagia Sophia (Holy Wisdom), was rebuilt in the sixth century for

Emperor Justinian. Architecturally stunning, with a veritable lacework of arches, the church boasts a central dome supported by pendentives (tapering triangular structures) on four colossal piers. Justinian spent lavishly on the church, using 40,000 pounds of silver in its decoration and hiring 10,000 workers to cover its domed ceiling with gold. The dome's base is pierced by 40 windows, and the light that filters through them led court historian Procopius of Caesarea to observe that "[the dome] seems not to rest upon solid masonry, but to [be] suspended from heaven." Mosaic and marble, used with abundance throughout the church, heightened the radiant effect.

Byzantium and the West, c. 600.

The same materials were of equal importance in the roughly contemporary church of San Vitale in Ravenna, also commissioned by Justinian. A particularly stunning pair of mosaics depicts the emperor and his consort, Empress Theodora. Positioned across from one another in the sanctuary, the mosaics show each imperial figure offering the liturgical vessels needed for the celebration of the Eucharist—the ceremony commemorating Christ's Last Supper. Justinian, surrounded by his army men, clerics, and bureaucrats, holds a shallow bowl for the bread; Theodora, followed by her retinue, carries the chalice for the wine. These mosaics are positioned on either side of the altar; in this way, Justinian and Theodora, who never visited the city, were perpetually present in one of the most important churches in Ravenna.

Indeed, the altar was the focal point of every church; it was there that the priest conducted the Mass. The altar's origin lies in the tables used for the re-enactment of the Last Supper, its flat top reflecting this function. Gradually, the Eucharistic bread and wine placed on the table came to be understood as Christ's flesh and blood, and the rite took on a sacramental significance as a vehicle of grace from God to the faithful. Early Christian altars were intimately connected to the martyrs—holy men and women who died for their faith—and were often placed above or in front of their graves, thus connecting Christ's suffering and Resurrection to the martyr's experience. When the persecutions stopped and the Roman Empire became Christianized, the remains of other saints joined those of the martyrs in churches all across the Empire. Every church needed an altar, and many were fitted out with special compartments for relics.

The resemblance of this altar panel to contemporaneous stone sarcophagi, or coffins, is therefore not accidental. Four columns support a triangular pediment and two arches filled with scallop-shell designs. The scallop-shell motif was a traditional feature in ancient Roman funerary imagery, where it was often used as a background for portraits of the deceased. Below the arches, two large crosses frame the fenestella, evoking the Crucifixion and Christ's triumph over death. In the interstices between the pediment and arches, two lambs munch on vegetation, and two small palm trees flank the upper register. The palm trees, ancient symbols of victory, make the concept of eternal life visible: adopted by early Christians as signs of martyrdom, palm fronds also refer to paradise. The lambs signify the earthly Christian flock, whose priests and bishops were called "pastors," and who were supposed to care for the laity, their charges, as shepherds watch over their sheep.

The lambs, however, do double duty. They also allude to Christ as the sacrificial "Lamb of God," who, as John 1:29 puts it, "takes away the sins of the world." The concept was not new; already in the Jewish Torah, the lamb was above all the animal of sacrifice. When God ordered Abraham to tender his son, Isaac, as a burnt offering (Genesis 22:2), Abraham told his son: "God will provide for Himself the lamb." And, indeed, at the last moment, an angel stopped Abraham from delivering the fatal blow, substituting a ram—an adult male lamb—in Isaac's place. The lamb was slain on the eve of Passover, a Jewish festival that celebrated the liberation of the Israelites from Egyptian slavery: by divine order, the sacrificial lamb's blood was sprinkled on the door-posts of Israelites whose first-born were thereby spared by the angel of death (Exodus 12:1–23). The paschal lamb was equated with Christ by Saint Paul (I Corinthians 5:7–8), and this comparison was famously elaborated on by the early Christian philosopher Saint Justin Martyr (d.c.165): "the lamb which God enjoined to be sacrificed as the passover, was a type [foreshadowing] of Christ [. . .] and that lamb which was commanded to be wholly roasted was a symbol of the suffering of the cross which Christ would undergo. For the lamb [. . .] is dressed up in the form of the cross."

The symbolic imagery on this altar thus makes clear the complex connection between a saint's burial, the Eucharistic celebration, Christ's sacrifice, and the faithful's hope of redemption. Small wonder that people longed to be buried as close as possible to the altar of a church or to the saints' shrines, where the bodies of ordinary believers would be close to the remains of people whom God had clearly chosen. Just as Emperor Justinian's courtiers vied to be near him, so the faithful wanted to bask in the glow of men and women who were certain to triumph on the Last Day.

3

Pilgrim's Flask with Saint Menas, sixth–seventh century, Egypt, terracotta; 10.00 × 6.40 cm (3 ⅞ × 2 ½ inches)

MANUFACTURED at a local Egyptian workshop in the sixth or seventh century, this pilgrim's flask, or ampulla, subtly reveals the militaristic world of its place and time. Saint Menas (d.c.300) was, according to his *Passio*, or martyrdom account, an Egyptian by birth. A soldier in the Roman army, he was put to death for his faith during the persecutions of Emperor Diocletian and brought to his burial place at Abu Mena, near Alexandria, Egypt, by camels. This explains why Menas here appears to be dressed in military garb. Surrounded by a circle of dots, he stands in the early Christian pose of prayer, hands raised to God, two Greek crosses flanking his head, and two camels kneeling at his feet on either side. The emphasis on camels is important: miraculously, the animals stopped at Abu Mena of their own accord and refused to move the body of the saint any further. The image is repeated on the other side of the flask. The vessel is far from being unusual: numerous flasks like this one were sold to pilgrims arriving at Abu Mena from all across the Christian world.

Egypt, c. 600.

When Menas was martyred, Christianity was a minority religion. But, later in the fourth century, when it became the official religion of the Roman Empire, Menas proved to be an extremely popular saint. One of the earliest churches in Constantinople was built in his honor. Pilgrims flocked to the modest shrine built over his grave at Abu Mena, and in the fifth century, Emperor Zeno (d.491) sponsored the construction of a grand complex there. Eventually, it included the Martyr Church, later enlarged; another, bigger church built to the east of the first one and connected to it; arcaded streets; and many buildings ranging from a grand palace to baths to modest shelters for the poor. To the south was a semi-circular building probably used as a hospital. In the early seventh century, Sophronius, the patriarch of Jerusalem, had good reason to describe the site as "the pride of all Libya." It was one of the best-known Late Antique pilgrimage spots.

Pilgrimage was integral to the Christian experience in every way. In the early fifth century, Augustine, the North African bishop of Hippo, famously wrote that the very life of the Christian was a pilgrimage. Born into the City of Man, the believer made use of its institutions not to pursue a career or for pleasure or to make money. Rather, the "things of the world"—food, clothing, languages, schools—were to be "used" on life's pilgrimage to the City of God, where peace, friendship, and happiness reigned eternally. The intercession of saints like Menas helped people on this arduous journey to the heavenly city. Saints could intercede with God on behalf of supplicants, especially of those who made an effort to trek to the shrine and make their petition. But this was not easy. By the seventh century, the famous Roman road system was in disrepair and highway robbery was common. Indeed, the hardships of pilgrimage were considered the necessary preparation for access to a holy relic: the effort expended on travel was a sure way to convince a saint of one's true devotion.

What sort of help did Menas give the faithful? Stories about his posthumous miracles, recorded in the seventh and later centuries, were written in several languages, including Coptic, Ethiopian, and Greek. They tell vivid tales of Menas's healings, conversions, and even how he brought about a resurrection from the dead. One amusing story recounts that while at the shrine, a crippled man is encouraged by the saint to climb into bed with a mute woman; the woman awakens screaming, the man flees swiftly in shame; at once they understand that they have been healed of their afflictions. Sometimes, Menas took instant revenge on wrongdoers. In one story, a man who comes to pray to the saint is hacked to pieces by a murderer who covets his gold, only to have Menas appear, revive the dismembered man, and punish the transgressor. Another miracle claims that a woman who was nearly raped by a stranger on her way to the shrine was saved when the saint caused the would-be rapist's horse to drag him to the crowded shrine, where he was shamed before a jeering audience. Still another miracle suggests that in some parts of the early seventh-century Byzantine Empire, Jews were still seen in a positive way, as a people ready for conversion: that story has Menas come to the rescue of an honest Jew who is swindled by his dishonest Christian friend. The Christian seeks forgiveness, and the Jew decides to be baptized. There was, in fact, a baptistery just to the west of the mausoleum housing the tomb of Saint Menas. It had two separate rooms, one probably reserved for the baptism of women, the other for men.

The arrival at the tomb of Saint Menas was carefully orchestrated. In order to reach the shrine, all the pilgrims were obliged to follow a wide, colonnaded avenue that narrowed dramatically until it met a large rectangular space lined with

porticoes and shops. Once at the saint's mausoleum, the pilgrim still had to navigate a steep stairway as well as the dark and circuitous underground passageway to the crypt. But that made the goal all the more welcome. In the vicinity of the tomb, the pilgrim would have seen a stone relief carving of Saint Menas—probably the model for the design on this and other flasks, which were sold by vendors near the shrine. Then, entering the crypt, the petitioner would have arrived at the tomb itself, framed by a hanging dome covered in a gold mosaic that sparkled in the light shed by oil-burning lamps. The shrine's guardian, an archpriest, led the pilgrim to the tomb to experience the "kiss" of the saint, symbolized by a bit of oil from one of the lamps. Many pilgrims planned to stay a night or two by the tomb, a period of "incubation," to be sure that the saint would indeed intervene on their behalf.

Before returning home, the faithful filled the flasks with some substance sanctified by the mere proximity to the revered body: a handful of earth from around the shrine, water from a nearby spring, a bit of oil from the lamps that burned by the tomb or from an alabaster vessel that stood in front of the church altar. The ampulla was then sealed with a stopper that in some cases may also have borne the image of the saint. At some shrines, oil or water was poured through special openings over the holy relics and then collected at another opening, at the bottom, to be stored in flasks. Believers returned from pious pilgrimages wearing the ampullas at their belts or around their necks. Such objects had become eulogiae or "blessings"—and, indeed, some of them were inscribed with the word "blessing" or "gift."

Gifts, indeed, were important for the devout. Pilgrims sought to extend their connection to the saints well after they returned home. Often, they left votive offerings (ex-votos) at the shrines, both in gratitude for the effected cure and in the hope that their virtual presence would continue to assure the saint's assistance. The flasks, too, prolonged the pilgrims' bond with the sacred places they visited, allowing the faithful to recall and re-live their pilgrimage spiritually. No wonder the devout were sometimes buried with their flasks. These objects were far more than souvenirs: they were bits of heaven to take home, expressions of hope that the pilgrim's journey through life would end safely in the City of God.

4

Calyx (Chalice), 900s–1000s, Byzantium, Middle Byzantine,
blood jasper (heliotrope) with gilt-copper mounts;
h: 7.70 cm (3 inches)

THIS exquisite cup is only three inches tall, yet its effect is striking. The bloodstone, also known as heliotrope or blood jasper, is here encased in a finely worked gilt-copper mounting with an intricate design. Its sanguine red is blotched with gray-green, and highly polished to reveal a smooth surface that begs to be touched. The metal catches the light, while the cup's opaque surface seems to absorb it. The effect is one of delicate extravagance. Such luxurious vessels are exceedingly rare, associated primarily with the Byzantine church and court. Byzantine emperors loved to use them as diplomatic gifts; the king of Italy and the emperor in Germany were lucky recipients at different times. The bottom of this chalice carries a punched mark, perhaps of a particular maker, but it cannot be localized with any specificity. Very likely, it was used during the Mass in the ritual of transubstantiation, when, sanctified by the priest, the wine in the chalice was believed to become the blood of Christ.

The calyx was probably a product of the Macedonian Renaissance—a revival and adaptation of the art, philosophy, and literature of Greco-Roman antiquity that took place at Constantinople largely under the rulers of the Macedonian dynasty, who reigned, intermittently, from 867 to 1057. As the eleventh-century Byzantine historian Michael Psellus (d.1078) famously wrote in his *Chronographia*, "I doubt if any other family was ever so favored by God as theirs was—a surprising thing, when one reflects on the unlawful manner in which the family fortune was, so to speak, rooted and planted in the ground with murder and bloodshed." Despite intrigue at the top, this was the time when wealth was pouring into the capital from the Empire's well-oiled tax system as well as from its conquests to the west (in Italy), to the east (in Anatolia and Syria), and to the north (in the Balkans). Some of the techniques to produce cups of hardstone, once known in ancient Rome and Persia, and employed in the Islamic world as well, were now drawn upon by Byzantine artisans ready to respond to wealthy lay and ecclesiastical patrons. Ancient vessels were re-mounted in precious metals, and new ones were made to rival them.

Hardstones had already been greatly valued in antiquity, with jasper emerging as one of the most prized among them. When the Roman poet Lucan (d.65) described the glorious hall of Cleopatra in his poem *Pharsalia*, he marveled at the yellow jasper stones that shone on her couch and coverlet. The Jewish Roman scholar Josephus (d.100), echoing Exodus 28:20, described the garb of the high

priest in his *Antiquities of the Jews* and named jasper as one of the precious stones on the priest's breastplate. The Bible, in fact, has numerous references to jasper, the most remarkable of which is, perhaps, Revelation 21:10, where an angel carries the seer to the "holy city, Jerusalem, coming down out of heaven from God," its walls made from and adorned with jasper.

Both in Byzantium and the West, different kinds of jasper were part of magical and medical learning. Byzantine women wore bloodstone amulets to help with menstrual bleeding and to guarantee a successful birth. In Spain, Isidore, the bishop of Seville (d.636), described the magical relationship between heliotrope and the sun in his comprehensive compendium of universal knowledge, *Etymologies*; the stone, he wrote, receives the sun "as a mirror and detects eclipses and shows the moon stealing in." Much of this information came from the Latin encyclopedia *Natural History*, penned by the Roman philosopher Pliny the Elder (d.79) and well known to medieval authors. When bundled with a heliotrope plant and accompanied by certain prayers, Isidore wrote, blood jasper can render one invisible, although he discounted the superstition that jasper conferred safety upon its owner/wearer. Later, heliotrope was also used in divination, and was thought to ward off bad luck. If quarried under the sign of Virgo, placed next to a wolf's fang, and subsequently wrapped in laurel, heliotrope would prevent nasty gossip; left on the church threshold it would trap adulterers within.

Most important for the liturgical chalice, however, were the material's symbolic virtues. The green of jasper, according to the Venerable Bede (d.735), the most educated man of his day, signified the "unfading verdure of faith," while the red of the heliotrope evoked Christ's blood spilled during the Passion. Some extant Middle Byzantine bloodstone amulets feature the Crucifixion, with crimson splashes spectacularly streaking their surface. Others bring together religious and medical lore, as when the biblical narrative about the woman with the issue of blood (Matthew 9:2–22) on one side is combined with the Crucifixion on the other. The use of a bloodstone calyx for the sacrament of the Eucharist would therefore have been especially appropriate.

Byzantines and Europeans shared not only ideas about therapeutic and symbolic properties of precious materials, but also profound attraction to their opulence—and this, ultimately, informed the subsequent history of relations between the East and the West. After initial expansion under the Macedonian dynasty, Byzantium had to contract and regroup with the coming of the Seljuk Turks, who took over the Islamic heartlands and much of Byzantine Anatolia as well. In response, in the 1090s, the Byzantines sent mercenaries, largely made up of European adventurers, to fight the Seljuks. Finding his army insufficient, Emperor Alexius I (d.1118) thought it well to

supplement them with other Western troops and asked Pope Urban II for help in recruiting more warriors. The pope chose to understand the request very differently: he went on a tour of France to drum up knightly volunteers for an armed pilgrimage to free Jerusalem from the infidel Muslims and subject it to the rule of Christians. The unexpected result of Byzantium's efforts to regain the territory it lost to the Turks was thus the arrival of European knights on its shores, marking the beginning of the event that has come to be called the First Crusade.

The initial, though tentative, cooperation between the Byzantines and the crusaders during this time came to an end when the Crusade leaders started to conquer territories for themselves, setting up four small coastal states in the Levant. New crusades were called to shore up these states. Then, in 1204, fueled by long-simmering religious differences as well as the mutual distrust and disparagement between Europe and Byzantium, came a major turning point: the Venetians, a key player in Byzantine commerce, diverted the army of the Fourth Crusade to attack Constantinople itself in 1204. The crusaders plundered the city, feeling themselves to be the right-

The Byzantine and Seljuk Empires, c. 1090.

eous saviors of Byzantium's precious relics and happy recipients of its finest objects. Nicetas, a Byzantine historian who may have witnessed the plunder firsthand, offers a memorable description of the pillage: "They snatched the precious reliquaries, thrust into their bosoms the ornaments which these contained, and used the broken remnants for pans and drinking cups [...] When the sacred vases and utensils of unsurpassable art and grace and rare material, and the fine silver, wrought with gold, which encircled the screen of the tribunal and the ambo, of admirable workmanship, and the door and many other ornaments, were to be borne away as booty, mules and saddled horses were led to the very sanctuary of the temple." Lavish objects—carved hardstones, gemstones, enamels, and silks—were passionately coveted in the Latin West for centuries: the heliotrope calyx pictured here may have been a generous imperial gift or the casualty of feverish plunder.

5

Christ's Mission to the Apostles, c. 970–980, Ottonian, Milan, Italy, ivory; 18.20 × 9.90 × 1.00 cm (7 1/8 × 3 7/8 × 3/8 inches)

Wᴵᵀᴴ his mouth slightly open and his formidable stare fixed upon the viewer, Christ stands on a thin protruding ledge, his right hand raised in blessing. His commanding presence has clearly mesmerized the twelve apostles, pictured here in bust length. They emerge from the ivory, six on each side, and turn toward Christ, listening to his every word. No inscription indicates what these words might be, but they are likely communicating the ultimate mission given to Christ's disciples: to spread the word of God to distant lands. After his Resurrection, Christ appeared to the apostles to command: "All authority in heaven and on earth has been given to me. Therefore go and make disciples of all nations, baptizing them in the name of the Father and of the Son and of the Holy Spirit, and teaching them to obey everything I have commanded you" (Matthew 28:18–20). These words—the Word, really—is indicated by the book held in Christ's left hand, its beaded cover echoing the beading on Christ's halo and on the frame of the ivory itself. In fact, although its original function is unknown, this ivory may have once been on the cover of a Gospel book.

The style of the ivory is characteristic of the period, called "Ottonian" after the first three successive emperors of the new ruling dynasty: Otto I the Great, Otto II, and Otto III (this last Otto died childless, and so his second cousin, Henry II, became the last Ottonian emperor). The dynasty ruled a large territory that stretched from the north of Germany to Rome during the tenth and early eleventh centuries.

While proud of their local, Saxon heritage, the Ottonians saw themselves as heirs to all the great empires, past and present. Consequently, the art and architecture produced during their rule drew on a heady mix of sources: the much-admired Roman art, ancient and early Christian; imperial Byzantine art, brought to the court from Constantinople by Princess Theophanu, the wife of Otto II; the art of the Germanic past; and, finally, the art of the great Carolingian Empire, recently disintegrated. Ottonian rulers, their families, the churchmen they appointed, and members of the nobility patronized

The Ottonian Empire, c. 1000.

the arts. During their reign, one of the most important European churches was built: Saint Michael in Hildesheim. It was conceived by Bernward, the bishop of Hildesheim (d.1022), who previously had served as a chaplain at the imperial court and tutored the young Otto III. Bernward traveled extensively, and he was impressed by the great monuments he saw in Italy and France. He must have been especially struck by the carved wooden doors on the fifth-century church of Santa Sabina and the second-century Trajan's Column, both in Rome. Upon his return to Germany, Bernward commissioned enormous bronze doors for his church of Saint Michael. Cast in two single pieces and standing over 16 feet tall—a tremendous feat on the part of metalworkers—the doors featured Old and New Testament narratives arranged side-by-side, with scenes from Genesis on the left door coordinated with scenes from Christ's life on the right. In addition, Bernward ordered a monumental column for the church, also bronze-cast, and clearly inspired by Trajan's monument, as suggested by its helical structure, with 28 scenes from Christ's ministry ascending in an upward spiral. At Hildesheim, Christ took the place of the conqueror Emperor Trajan (d.117).

In fact, the Ottonian dynasty identified itself with Christ's rule. Thus, when in 936 the German dukes, counts, and other nobles elected Otto I king in the church at Aachen (built by the Carolingian emperor Charlemagne), the presiding church-man, Archbishop Hildebert of Mainz (d.937), introduced him as "Otto, the elect of God." Hildebert followed this by consecrating the new king in a lengthy ritual that centered on the sacred implements of power, the sword with its belt, the scepter, and the staff. Each had its proper function: "Take this sword with which you shall defeat all of the enemies of Christ, barbarians, and evil Christians. All of the power of the entire empire of the Franks has been granted to you by divine authority so that there will be true peace for all Christians.[...] You are warned by these symbols that it is your responsibility to restrain your subjects with paternal discipline." The kings took these admonitions seriously, repeating their divine mission in official acts. When Otto III gave some property to his treasurer, he styled himself "Otto III, servant of Jesus Christ and August Emperor of the Romans according to the will of God our savior and liberator." Because of their special relationship with Christ, the Ottonians considered themselves fit to appoint and invest the high churchmen of their realm.

Some images of the emperor at the time suggested that he himself was Christ-like, his head in heaven, his feet resting on earth. Others asserted Otto III's global reign: one gospel book depicts the enthroned crowned ruler flanked by members of his court, clerics and soldiers both, with four women—personifications of his provinces—bringing him tribute. The miniature, with its enlarged central figure

attended by the worshiping subjects, is anticipated in this ivory, with its hieratic composition, vivid gestures, and intense gazes. All were hallmarks of Ottonian art, seen both in relief sculpture and in manuscript illumination. These shared traits suggest cultural conversations among the many different workshops active in the empire. Great manuscript centers were established in Trier, Echternach, Cologne, and Reichenau; Trier was also a center for metalsmithing, along with Essen and Hildesheim. It is thought that this ivory was produced in Milan, but definitive attributions are notoriously difficult: ivory carvers may have moved among various monastic workshops or else accompanied the royal court, itself itinerant.

This court depended as much on the emperors' consorts as it did on the emperors themselves. Adelheid of Burgundy, the second wife of Otto I, was considered to be co-emperor with her husband. Theophanu, the spouse of Otto II, similarly held that title. The power of royal and noble Ottonian women extended to religious life as well. Many entered monasteries, living there in comfortable apartments while writing and commissioning books. Their standing was high. Adelheid was praised in an epitaph by Abbot Odilo of Cluny (d.1049) as "steadfast in hope and faith, filled with twofold charity, thoroughly just, strong, prudent, and extremely modest, and she lived prosperously, ruling over worldly affairs with the help of the Lord."

That Odilo, the abbot (head) of a monastery in France, cared about the piety of a German queen and empress is partly explained by the fact that, like the Ottonians, the Cluniacs—the most prestigious monks of their day—meant to reform the world. They considered the emperor an ally in their mission. When Abbot Odilo proclaimed All Souls Day (a Cluniac invention), he singled out the soul of the emperor for special prayer. In part, however, Cluny's support of the Ottonians was not so much ideological as a natural outgrowth of personal ties. Adelheid and Otto lavishly gave Cluny land and even monasteries. The monasteries that they handed over, originally their private property, then became the property of God. But even land donated to Cluny was gifted not to earthly recipients but rather (as one gift from Otto and Adelheid said) to "blessed Apostle Peter." Phrases like this make clear that transactions with Cluny were thought to occur in another world—the heavenly realm of Christ and his apostles on the ivory.

6

Feline Incense Burner, 1100s, eastern Iran,
western Afghanistan, or Turkmenistan, Khurasan,
copper alloy, cast and chased; 35.50 × 11.00 × 32.50 cm
(13 ^{15}/$_{16}$ × 4 ^{5}/$_{16}$ × 12 ^{3}/$_{4}$ inches)

T HIS striking incense burner has been taken to represent a lion but may also be a caracal—a type of lynx well known in Iran and recognizable by its long ears topped by black tufts. Although now darkened with age, the burner originally radiated a warm golden color. Formed in several separate pieces later fused together, the beast has a removable head-and-neck ensemble that allows a container filled with incense and hot coals to be inserted into its body. The rising smoke escaped through the openwork palmettes that pierce its torso and neck. The animal's thighs and shoulders are decorated with elegant arabesques. Its thick, curved, and deeply incised tail extends from his hind quarters to his neck—perhaps to serve as a handle—while its spherical head is crowned by long pointed ears entirely covered with decoration and capped by small orbs. The beast's symmetrical body is highly stylized and densely covered with ornament.

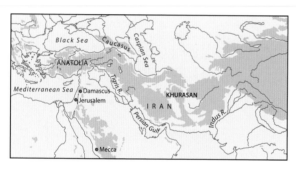

Khurasan and environs.

The burner was made in Khurasan— the home of the Abbasid dynasty that took over much of the Islamic world in 750. Even after most of the inhabitants of this formerly Persian region converted to Islam, it retained many of its older traditions. Above all, the Persian language persisted, though now written in the Arabic alphabet. As Turkic peoples moved into Iran in the tenth century, the mix of ethnicities and traditions there became richer still. The very word "caracal" comes from a Turkic word for "black-ear(ed)," which in turn was a translation of the Persian name for the animal. This linguistic diversity was mirrored in the daily lives of many, as numerous intellectuals and craftspeople traveled from one Islamic princely court to another, sometimes speaking a Persian dialect, writing in Arabic, and communicating with their powerful patrons in Turkic.

Felines constituted some of the most favored themes of ancient Persian art, life, and lore. Caracals, also known as Persian lynxes, were reputed to accompany the

lion in pursuit of food and then eat its leftovers. But they were also recognized for their remarkable speed and prowess, trained to hunt small game, and given the nicknames "guide" and "leader." By contrast, the lion was frequently used as a princely symbol. *Kalila wa Dimna*—a famous text that originated in India but was translated from Pahlavi (Middle Persian) to Arabic in the eighth century by the Persian writer and courtier Ibn al-Muqaffa' (d.c.757)—features a lion as a key figure in its interrelated series of fables. The tales form part of a moralizing "mirror of the princes" genre, which takes up questions of wise rulership to delight, educate, and caution its audience. The great literary achievement of the eleventh century, the *Shahnameh* (*Epic of Kings*), composed by the Persian poet Ferdowsi (d.1025), features lions in a variety of roles: as cruel beasts; as symbols of ferocity; as models of courage.

Lions and lynxes were also important protagonists of medieval Islamic bestiaries—encyclopedias on animals that include moralizing and, at times, religious interpretations of their appearance and behavior. Many such bestiaries derived their material from the early Christian *Physiologus* and from Aristotle's *Generation of Animals*. Among the most famous was the *Kitab al-Hayawan* (*Book on Animals*), written by the ninth-century Arabic Abbasid scholar al-Jahiz. Copied for centuries, it provided a model for many subsequent writers, including the Cairo scholar Kamal al-din al-Damiri (d.1405). In his treatise *The Life of Animals*, al-Damiri describes the lion as the noblest wild beast of prey. The animal is courageous and agile, strong and brave, yet malevolent. Lion cubs are born essentially dead, he writes, lumps of formless flesh, until their fathers breathe life into their mouths on the third day of their existence. This same wondrous fact is found in Christian bestiaries as well, where, however, it is interpreted in Christological terms and seen to symbolize Resurrection. Lynxes, in turn, were believed to possess magical fur that could cure wounds, arouse sexual desire, enhance potency, and even guard against hemorrhoids.

This particular incense burner was one of a large number of copper alloy vessels produced in eastern and northeastern Iran during the eleventh and twelfth centuries. This was the time when Iranian arts flourished, with the creation of stunning glass and ceramic objects, alongside sculpture and painting. Persian culture also gloried in beautiful textiles, used for clothing, wall-hangings, napkins, carpets, and even containers for dry goods. "Robes of honor" were distributed by rulers to their most valued courtiers; and both men's and women's clothing was characterized by bright colors and bold patterns, often featuring encircled animals and decorative calligraphy. Deep color saturation and ornament were highly prized, as were shiny and iridescent fabrics. This blossoming of material culture

must be ascribed, in part, to the rapid urbanization and the rise of a middle class, both of which were nourished by a thriving commerce. Expensive objects of gold and silver were produced for the courts of rulers; bowls, pitchers, candlesticks, buckets, boxes, trays, keys, and lamps were made of various lesser metal alloys for domestic use.

While in the West many churchmen, the moral arbiters of their society, looked with horror on the new commercial economy that was sprouting up at about the same time in centers like the Rhineland, the Netherlands, and northern Italy, Muslims were unabashedly proud of their prosperous urban trade. One of the most influential Persian philosophers and theologians of his time, Muhammad al-Ghazali (d.1111), once compared markets to God's tables and said that an honest merchant was like a warrior involved in a jihad against Satan. Nevertheless, this incense burner preaches against commercial concerns. The elegant Arabic inscriptions that form broad bands down the beast's spine and encircle his neck come from the Qur'an—God's word as revealed to the Prophet Muhammad in the early seventh century—and they warn against mercantile "trafficking." The verses quote the Qur'an sura titled "Congregation," which admonishes: "O believers, when proclamation is made for prayer on / the Day of Congregation [Friday], hasten to God's remembrance / and leave trafficking aside; that is better for you / did you but know. / Then when the prayer is finished, scatter in the land / and seek God's bounty" (62:9–10). As if to stress the Qur'anic origins of this sentiment, the inscription is in Kufic—the angular form of calligraphy that, at least until the eleventh century, was associated with religious texts.

The Qur'anic inscription, which calls the faithful to prayer, suggests that the burner was used inside a mosque. This would make it a highly unusual object. Certainly, incense burners stood in some major mosques: sweet smells were associated with the garden of Eden. But figural representation was discouraged in places of worship; plenty of zoomorphic incense burners exist, but they seem to have been made for secular use. Perhaps the beast's stylized body, covered with a textile-like pattern, somewhat circumvents the prohibition. So does the band of inscription, which further denaturalizes the animal. Moreover, the importance of this particular inscription on the incense burner is underlined by the fact that the very same text from the Qur'an was used in key architectural features of congregational mosques, such as portals and mihrabs—niches in the mosque walls that indicated the direction of Mecca. On the feline, however, it also clearly alludes to the burner's function: as the smoke diffuses through the air, so the devout will "scatter in the land" as they go about their daily tasks.

7

Leaf from a Qur'an, 1100s, Iran, opaque watercolor, ink, and gold on paper; 32.00 × 21.30 cm (12 9/16 × 8 3/8 inches)

I N THE seventh century, a new religious, political, and social force came into being: Islam, meaning "surrender" or "submission" to God in Arabic. Rooted in Christian and Jewish traditions, this monotheistic religion also had a holy book: the Qur'an. The page illustrated here is written in a highly stylized and beautiful Arabic calligraphy called kufic. A variation on the rectangular style of handwriting used for early Qur'an manuscripts, it is here graced with dramatically tall vertical letters set against a ground decorated with foliate arabesques. Ornamental designs such as this heed injunctions formulated both in the Qur'an, which warns against idol-making, and in the later Hadith ("sayings" of the Prophet), which elaborate on that prohibition. Unlike many earlier Qur'an manuscripts, which were formatted horizontally, this one is oriented vertically, as were most of the manuscripts produced after the end of the ninth century. The folio comes from a book of some 2,000 pages, and contains only four lines written in black ink, with vocalizations marked in red and blue. The elaborate script suggests that it was a presentation copy, meant less to be read than to be cherished by those who already knew the text by heart. Gold leaf disks with verse counts act as visual pauses, separating the verses. The elegant frame that encloses the text extends into two delicate half-palmettes in the left margin. The words appear as a fine treasure enclosed in a golden box with exquisite clasps, to be prized and cherished.

By the tenth century, the book—both as a physical object and as an intellectual concept—had become pre-eminent in Islamic culture. Calligraphy was deemed the finest art, a skill worthy of the aristocracy. A treatise by philosopher al-Tawhidi (d.1023) collected sage comments praising penmanship across the centuries, including this by an eighth-century Persian: "Handwriting is the necklace of wisdom. It serves to sort the pearls of wisdom, to bring its dispersed pieces into good order, to put its stray bits together, and to fix its setting."

But in the time of Muhammad, Islam's prophet, Arabic was mainly oral; its prestige came from the stories and poetry recited within the polytheistic tribal culture of Arabia in which Muhammad (d.632) grew up. There were numerous tribes, some nomadic, others semi-nomadic. Still others—farmers and city-dwellers—were sedentary. Muhammad belonged to a tribe at Mecca, a large oasis that boasted not only a flourishing market economy but also a sacred shrine, a cubic building called the Ka'ba. Here the tribes of Arabia came not only to trade but also to worship their

many gods. Muhammad, orphaned as a boy, grew up and married in Mecca. But, spiritually dissatisfied, he sometimes retreated to a nearby mountain to pray.

On one of those retreats, Muhammad heard what would become the opening words of the Qur'an (meaning "recitation"), understood by Muslims as the word of God as transmitted by the angel Gabriel to the prophet himself. Over time, the entire text was revealed and, as later written down and arranged (perhaps as early as a few decades after Muhammad's death), became the book known as the Qur'an. Today often divided into 114 chapters—or suras—of gradually decreasing length from hundreds of verses to just a few, the text covers the gamut of human experience and the life to come. Like all Arabic books, it starts from what English readers consider the "final" page and reads from right to left. This folio contains a portion of sura 4 (Surat al-Nisa, "The Women"). The text corrects some beliefs and practices of both the Jews and the Christians, setting Islam apart from those other religions and yet revealing their close connections as people of the book and worshipers of the one true God.

Finding his message unwelcome in Mecca, in 622 Muhammad fled to Medina, an oasis about 200 miles away. This flight (in Arabic, *hijra*) was later taken to be year 1 of the Islamic calendar, which is based on a solar year of 354 or 355 days. While in Medina, Muhammad converted and allied with numerous nomadic tribes, forging a formidable fighting force. In 630, now accompanied by his followers, the prophet returned triumphantly to Mecca and destroyed the images of the gods at the Ka'ba. Soon Mecca became the place toward which Muslims were told to address their daily prayers, and it remains the destination of thousands of pilgrims. Along with prayers and the *hajj* (pilgrimage to Mecca), the basic tenets of Islam include a declaration of faith, charity-giving, and fasting during the ninth calendar month, Ramadan.

After Muhammad's death, armies led by Muhammad's successors—known as caliphs, or deputies—conquered some Byzantine territory as well as that of the Persians. By the eighth century, Muslims ruled lands stretching from Spain to Central Asia. Often they borrowed from those whom they conquered—for example, issuing coins based on Byzantine and Persian designs and establishing their capital at Damascus (formerly a Byzantine city). Although it is a myth that Muslim conquerors learned about paper from Chinese prisoners of war captured during battles in Transoxiana, the story reveals a larger truth: that paper-making came to the Islamic world from China via shared routes in Central Asia. The use of paper quickly spread for ordinary correspondence and workaday books, but it was only slowly adopted for copying the Qur'an.

The initial caliphs were drawn from a new elite formed around Muhammad himself. The first two succeeded him without controversy, but the third, Uthman (d.656), met bitter opposition. His adversaries supported Ali, the husband of Muhammad's daughter Fatima. Civil war broke out, with Uthman's dynasty, the Umayyads, emerging triumphant. The losing faction formed what would eventually be known as the Shi'ites—often distinguished from Sunnis, who constitute the majority of Muslims today. The Umayyads ruled the Islamic world from Damascus, gathering taxes and paying little attention to the many different regional needs and desires of their empire. In the eastern half, once part of Persia, discontent grew, coalescing around the Abbasid family. In 750 the Abbasids ousted the Umayyads everywhere except in al-Andalus (Islamic Iberia) and moved their capital from Syria to Baghdad in Iraq. The new dynasty ruled an exceptionally prosperous polity that maintained dynamic trade relations with all parts of the known world and supported a notable flowering in scholarship, literary culture, and the arts. However, by the year 1000, regional rulers were threatening Abbasid sovereignty, and many of them were Shi'ites. For a while it seemed that the Islamic world would become Shi'ite, even though the caliph himself remained Sunni.

The arrival in Iran of a Turkic people called the Seljuks changed the face of Islam. Allying themselves with the caliphs at Baghdad, the Seljuk leaders, staunch Sunnis, proclaimed themselves sultans (rulers). In the late eleventh and through the twelfth century they took over much of the Islamic world and part of Byzantine Anatolia as well. The Anatolian Seljuks called their state "Rum"—Rome; it was the ancestor of today's Turkey. During this period, Iran, though politically unstable, was nevertheless wealthy and cultured, as witnessed by striking innovations in architecture, metal-work, and ceramic wares that continued to influence artistic production for centuries. Calligraphy continued to rule supreme, as this folio so amply demonstrates. Indeed, its script is remarkably similar in style to the inscriptions on both ceramics and buildings in Iran and Iraq. Calligraphy heralded excellence, accomplishment, and virtue. As one of al-Tawhidi's sources summed it up: "Handwriting is the tongue of the hand. Style is the tongue of the intellect. The intellect is the tongue of good actions and qualities. And good actions and qualities are the perfection of man."

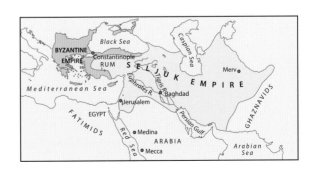

The Seljuk Empire in the twelfth century.

8

Arm Reliquary of the Apostles, c. 1190, Lower Saxony, Hildesheim, Germany, gilt-silver, champlevé enamel, oak; 51.00 × 14.00 × 9.20 cm (20 $\frac{1}{16}$ × 5 $\frac{1}{2}$ × 3 $\frac{9}{16}$ inches)

THIS gilded arm is a so-called "speaking" or body-part reliquary. Often, such vessels contained body parts unrelated to their outward form or even housed contact relics—for example a cloth touched by the saint. But this reliquary indeed holds a lower arm bone that supposedly belonged to one of Christ's apostles. The metal hand is frozen as if in mid-gesture, the open palm suggesting that it is making the sign of the cross. Apostle busts in medallions circle the top and bottom edges of the gilt-silver sleeve, while a decorative band of enamels runs the length of the garment.

The sleeve is shaped to resemble a liturgical vestment, the clothing that the priest wore when he officiated at the Mass. Indeed, arm reliquaries, which first became popular in the twelfth century, were used in religious services and processions. Some stood on altars, the gleaming companions of the transubstantiated Christ. They also played a key role in healing and blessing rituals; like a cyborg arm extending from the bishop's hand, the reliquary harnessed and transmitted the power of the body part within. They were conduits of grace: as an inscription on one arm reliquary clarifies, "The right hand of God transmits saintly power." On some arm reliquaries, the metal fingers are folded in a gesture of blessing; others, like the present example, have fingers extended, as if striving to reach those in need of a miraculous touch. Guibert of Nogent (d.1124), a theologian and Benedictine monk, described the recovery of his cousin, cured by contact with the arm reliquary of Saint Arnoul: the disease was chased by reliquary's touch around the poor man's body until it was at last trapped between his shoulder blades and extinguished.

The Reliquary of the Apostles was likely donated to the cathedral of Saint Blaise in Braunschweig, Germany, by Henry the Lion (d.1180), the Duke of Saxony and Bavaria. Henry's wealth and power rivaled that of the German Emperor of the time, Frederick Barbarossa (d.1190). Less than a century before, however, dukes like Henry had little influence in Germany because the emperors ruled with considerable authority. In large part that imperial power depended on high churchmen—bishops and archbishops—whom they appointed and "invested" with office. Bishop Thietmar of Merseburg (d.1018) described his own investiture: led into a special chapel, he was "commended into the hands

of the king" who "committed the pastoral office to me with the staff." This practice was challenged at the end of the eleventh century by the papacy, who declared it—and the authority of kings over churchmen that it implied— anathema. The so-called Investiture Controversy (1075–1122) began, and with it a long war between imperial forces, the papacy and, siding with the popes, the German nobility. The struggle was officially concluded with a compromise that still allowed the emperor an important say in German Church affairs. But unofficially, and more significantly, it ended with enormous political power in the hands of regional nobles—men like Henry the Lion.

In 1172, at the height of his career, Henry the Lion decided to go on a pilgrimage to Jerusalem, bringing with him a huge retinue: high churchmen, various princes, and perhaps 500 knights. He was greeted in Constantinople by Emperor Manuel himself with the ceremonial—and numerous gifts—that the Byzantine court usually saved for kings. After that splendid reception, he went on to Jerusalem, where the First Crusade (1096–1099) had succeeded in setting up a small Christian kingdom. There he donated money and gifts to many churches, lavishing particular generosity on the Church of the Holy Sepulcher. Back in Constantinople, he received numerous relics from Manuel, including, perhaps, the bone that now resides in the Arm Reliquary of the Apostles.

All this gifting was part and parcel of medieval rulership. While today we look askance at diplomatic gifts if they are too valuable, in the Middle Ages such gifts were signs of generosity, wealth, and power. Rulers would have no followers and no prestige if they did not constantly distribute gifts. These had to go to churches as well as to other powerful people because churches were themselves bulwarks of support—military, religious, and political—of every ruler. Relics were an important part of this economy and fetched a high price. In 1237, to save his sinking empire, the emperor of Constantinople Baldwin II successfully mortgaged the Crown of Thorns to the Venetians; subsequently purchased for a stupendous price by the king of France Louis IX, the Crown (along with other relics) was encased in the French royal chapel (Sainte-Chapelle) built for just this purpose in the shape of a jeweled reliquary box.

And yet, there were dangers inherent both in the beauty of reliquaries and the wealth they represented. Before around 1100, Europe had been quite impoverished, but now that towns had burgeoned, a frankly commercial, money-based economy was widespread. Sensitive churchmen reacted immediately, some fleeing the cities to seek refuge in lonely valleys. New religious orders—for example, Cistercians—emphasized poverty and plainness. Bernard of Clairvaux (d.1153), a Cistercian abbot with a particularly sharp tongue, berated

monks who carried out their religious vocation in splendidly decorated churches and excoriated the laity for revering all the wrong things: "The richer a place is seen to be, the more freely the offerings pour in. When eyes open wide at gold-cased relics, purses do the same. A beautiful image of a saint is on show: the brighter the colors, the holier he or she will be considered. Those who hasten to kiss the image are invited to leave a gift, and wonder more at the beauty than at the holiness they should be venerating." Others, too, were appalled by the conspicuous consumption they saw all around them and were especially aghast at the way their fellow churchmen used their wealth to capitalize on the uneducated and the credulous. Guibert of Nogent may have been grateful for the relic-powered healing of his family member, but he decried the rival monks at Beauvais who, according to him, faked miracles in exchange for pilgrims' gifts.

The cult of saints reached a high pitch in the twelfth century. Relics were bought and sold, gifted and stolen. Efficacious relics brought prosperity to the churches that owned them, and so *furta sacra*, or holy thefts, became common. An astonishing story about the relics of Sainte Foy (Saint Faith), stolen from the church of Agen, is a case in point. The theft, perpetrated by a monk from Conques named Arinisdus, seems to have taken place in the ninth century; some 200 years later the narrative was included in the text of *Translatio* (the account of the relic's relocation), where the holy burglary was justified as being made "for the salvation of the country and the redemption of many people." Salvation aside, Conques was in dire need of a financial boost, as its resources were being siphoned away by the nearby rival monastery at Figeac. Arinisdus, disguised as a priest, gained admittance to the religious community of Agen and, after some years, got himself appointed the guardian of its treasure. One night, he broke into the saint's tomb, took her body, and returned to Conques, where Sainte Foy continued to perform high-profile miracles, thereby making clear that she had wanted to be stolen. Henceforth she brought both glory and prosperity to the monastery. Soon, one of the most striking medieval reliquaries was created to enclose a piece of Sainte Foy's skull: the monumental figure of the saint—with a core of yew wood, made of gold, seated on a silver-gilt throne, and encrusted with gems, cameos, and enamels—remains at Conques to this very day.

9

Virgin and Child, late thirteenth century, Liège (?), wood (oak) with polychromy and gilding; 83.00 × 24.00 × 20.00 cm (32 ⅝ × 9 ⁷⁄₁₆ × 7 ¹³⁄₁₆ inches)

D RAPED in an elegant mantle, her wavy hair framed by a delicate veil, this rare wooden Virgin holding her Child comes from the valley of the Maas (Meuse) River (or Mosan region), perhaps from Liège. Her long, strong fingers grasping the diminutive torso of her son, her eyebrows quizzically arched, Mary seems poised to come to life: to move, to speak. This expectation is less fanciful than it seems: stories that described such instances of enlivening circulated throughout medieval Europe. Earlier in the century, for instance, the abbot (head) of the German abbey at Heisterbach, Caesarius (d.c.1240), compiled his famous *Dialogues on Miracles*, a gathering of some 746 miracle stories, and in its pages one finds a veritable legion of the Virgin's animated statues. In Caesarius's accounts, sculpted Virgins sweat profusely to stop the Second Coming; move their limbs to protect the pious from enemy arrows; and box nuns on their jaws to avert them from lustful temptations. Many of these statues were made of wood, like the one here. And yet, one is hard-pressed to imagine this sculpture lashing out at wayward nuns: Mary stands tall and somber, her face serene, her figure graceful and rarified. At the time of its creation, the statue boasted opulent cabochons—glass, gems, or both—set along the edge of the Virgin's blue-and-gold mantle and around her neck; now only empty holes remain. The small Child is seated cross-legged on his mother's right hip, and below the Virgin's feet writhes a small green dragon. Nearly three feet high, an image such as this could have been placed on an altar, and used in liturgical processions and religious plays.

The medieval diocese of Liège.

In the eleventh century, about 200 years before this sculpture was made, the cult of the Virgin began to grow in Western Europe. Mary, already a focus of pious devotion in Byzantium, became the subject of learned treatises and, as in Caesarius's stories, an active protagonist of miracle stories. By the twelfth and

thirteenth centuries, all Cistercian monastic churches and numerous others were dedicated to the Mother of God, and her image took pride of place on the portals of great cathedrals and atop their many altars. At first, the Virgin was usually represented seated, displaying the Christ Child on her lap. Such a sculpture is called *sedes sapientiae*, or the Seat of Wisdom, where Mary serves in effect as the throne for her son. But soon her appearance changed dramatically: she became a young mother, princess-like, fashionably dressed, lovely and charming, who stands holding the Child in her arms, at times interacting with him affectionately. The transformation continued throughout the later Middle Ages, as Mary's motherhood grew more and more visually pronounced. At the same time, she was made into a central character in representations of Christ's Infancy: the Annunciation and the Visitation, for example, or the Nativity and the Presentation in the Temple. Those scenes changed rapidly, too. By the fourteenth century, the Virgin was shown pregnant already at the moment of the Annunciation, her belly swelling in response to the angel Gabriel's greeting, "Hail, Mary, full of grace." In the Visitation images, the bodies of Mary and her cousin Elizabeth grew transparent, disclosing to the beholders small infants inhabiting their wombs. Images of the breastfeeding Mary appeared, too, and in some exceptional cases she was shown giving birth. The devout also saw the Mother of God as the mother of all humanity, sheltering the pious under her voluminous cloak and interceding on their behalf in her role as the Virgin of Mercy.

One distillation of these traditions was the Shrine Madonna: a statue of the Virgin and Child that split open to reveal complex iconographies painted and carved within. Many of these statues contained the sculpted Trinity in the middle, revealing Mary as the mother of the entire Godhead. The Shrine Madonna was often represented crowned: seconding her role in this world was the Virgin's place in the celestial realm as the Queen of Heaven. Indeed, she was often depicted alongside Christ, receiving a crown from him or his angels. Even though the Virgin here is not crowned, the choice of gold and blue for her garments points to her place in the heavenly hierarchy. The small dragon below her feet functions as a simultaneous allusion to Mary's role as the new Eve who defeats the deceitful serpent, and to her persona as the Woman of the Apocalypse, triumphant over the devil who takes the form of a dragon according to the Book of Revelation.

Even though Mary has lost her right arm, and the Child his head, the sculpture is remarkably well preserved, with original paint and gilding. The geometric designs on the cloak recall the celebrated metalwork produced in the region, known for its enamels, goldsmithing, and jewelry. The valley of the Maas River

was a commercial artery, a major pump—along with the Po Valley of Italy and the Rhine of Germany—of the commercial revolution of the eleventh and twelfth centuries. The area produced some of the most important metalsmiths, including Nicholas of Verdun and Hugo of Oignies. Although the heyday of Mosan metalwork had passed by the time the Virgin and Child were carved, the painted decorations on Mary's mantle and especially the rectangular designs along its hem recall Mosan enamels and finely crafted metal jewelry, and the resemblance would have been even more pronounced when these patterns were set against the now-missing cabochons. This wooden sculpture, in other words, was made to resemble a valuable gold object.

The precious quality of this sculpture points to the wealth of Mosan cities, abbeys, and churches. In the thirteenth century, the Mosan region—roughly equivalent to the diocese of Liège—was in theory part of the Holy Roman Empire. But during the first half of the thirteenth century, the emperor was occupied by battles with the papacy, while during the second half he was the plaything of warring German factions. Stability in the region was only relative. The dukes of Brabant held some power in the west, but the bishop of Liège dominated the east. He was a "prince-bishop," and claimed to rule in the city of Liège itself as well as elsewhere. At the same time, his power was frequently challenged by popular rebellions. In the mid-thirteenth century, for example, the scion of a wealthy banking family, Henri de Dinant, led a revolt of artisans and workers against the rule of the prince-bishop of Liège Henri de Gueldre. For a time, the citizens managed to establish a commune with its own taxation system and army, but soon the bishop put down the revolt.

The thirteenth century saw a vast expansion of international trade; a typical route went from England to the Low Countries and on to Italy. Despite moments of political unrest, the cities of the Maas Valley thrived, like most in the Low Countries. Workers in towns like Maastricht and Liège turned the wool from English sheep into cloth that was widely distributed across all of Europe. Much of this was low quality, but some was luxury fabric. Such lively commerce depended on a growing population, general reliance on credit, and an increasing supply of coined money, the silver for which came from mines in Germany. Mosan cities sold various goods to noble consumers from both the towns and the countryside, and among their customers were wealthy monasteries and churches that flourished in the area: purchasers of brass bells, baptismal fonts, liturgical furnishings—and gilded images of the Virgin and Child.

10

Christ and Saint John the Evangelist, early
fourteenth century, Germany, Swabia, near Bodensee
(Lake Constance), polychromy and gilded oak;
92.71 × 64.45 × 28.84 cm (36 ½ × 25 ⁵/₁₆ × 11 ⁵/₁₆ inches)

ONE day, in the nuns' choir of the Katharinenthal convent, located in what is
now northeastern Switzerland, sister Adelheit Pfefferhartin prayed in front
of a statue of Christ and Saint John the Evangelist. So fervent was Adelheit's prayer
that she was seen levitating above the floor. She was not the only one: according to
the convent chronicle, various nuns were borne aloft or rendered as translucent as
crystal before the sculpture, which must have been much like the one pictured
here. The seated Christ, young and handsome, tenderly embraces the boyish Saint
John. Asleep and trusting, John rests his head on Christ's chest, his face framed by
lush golden curls, a slight smile on his face. Christ, knowing what is to come, stares
straight ahead, his lips slightly parted, his gaze benign but distant. The figures'
delicately painted faces, their bare toes, and their tubular fingers starkly contrast
with the richly gilded surfaces of their mantles. The men's right hands are joined in
an echo of the nuptial gesture, the so-called *dextrarum iunctio*—but theirs is
understood as a mystical marriage, a union of the soul with the divine.

The image is based on the Gospel of John 13:23–26, which describes the shared
meal during which Christ announced that one of his brethren would betray him.
As John, "one of the disciples, whom Jesus loved," leans on Christ's breast, another
disciple, Simon Peter, asks about the identity of the traitor. Christ's answer is
plain: "He it is to whom I shall reach bread dipped." John continues: "And when
he had dipped the bread, he gave it to Judas Iscariot." But neither Peter nor Judas is
present here; indeed, all other apostles are gone and every marker of space is
subtracted except for the bench where the two men are seated. The statue offers its
beholder a hushed, intimate moment shared by the two men in advance of the
terrible events about to unfold. As part of the larger narrative—in this case, the
Last Supper—this type of devotional image, called an *Andachtsbild*, isolates Christ
and his beloved disciple, focusing the beholder's attention on the sacred contact
between the two, inciting the viewers to pious contemplation.

Such contemplation was especially fostered by men and women connected to
the Cistercian monastic order, which encouraged a rich interior life along with the
simplicity of material existence. There were numerous guides for mystical

meditation that came out of this order. One of the earliest was by Aelred (d.1167), the abbot (head) of the English Cistercian monastery of Rievaulx in the twelfth century, who explained to his readers how to contemplate sacred events: "Cast your eyes back [...] to the past. First enter the room of blessed Mary [Mother of Jesus] and with her read the books which prophesy the virginal birth and the coming of Christ." The contemplative was to dwell on every stage of Mary's and Christ's lives, feeling every emotion of all the protagonists in each story. For the theme of Christ and Saint John the Evangelist, Aelred told the meditator to imaginatively accompany Christ to the upper room where the Supper would take place and to stay there a while: "Do you see? What is that, I ask, who is reclining on his breast and bends back his head to lay it in his bosom? Happy is he, whoever he may be. O, I see: his name is John. O John, tell us what sweetness, what grace and tenderness, what light and devotion you are imbibing from that fountain. [...] What have you done to deserve all this, John? [...] This is the special privilege of virginity: you were chosen to be a virgin by the Lord and therefore loved more than the rest." Saint John, who was frequently identified with the bride from the biblical Song of Songs (or Song of Solomon), provided a perfect model of the mystical union of the soul with Christ, especially for female devotees. The sculpture here, with its emphasis on what is essentially connubial imagery, makes it clear that John does not merely sleep on his Savior's breast: rather, he communicates with Christ's Sacred Heart, soaking up its grace.

Books like Aelred's proliferated in the thirteenth and fourteenth centuries, many penned by Dominican friars, who focused on preaching and pastoral care. Material culture, at least from the last decades of the thirteenth century, also played an important role in affective devotion. Monasteries such as the Dominican Katharinenthal made special use of images to induce visionary experiences. Another Katharinenthaler nun, Sister Berta von Herten, is said to have had a vision of the seated Christ, who invited Berta to join him and lovingly tilted her head toward himself—a miraculous encounter clearly spurred on by the sculpture of Christ and his disciple. Even when we cannot definitively locate the visionary before a particular statue, the mystical experience itself often suggests the use of images. When the Dominican mystic Margareta Ebner remembers "how my lord, Saint John, rested upon the dear heart of my Lord Jesus Christ" and thinks about "the sweet drink he drank and sucked from the sweet breast of Christ," one cannot help but imagine Margareta before the sculpted pair, sitting "there with delight and desire so that [she] would have gladly died of love." Margareta's confessor, Heinrich von Nördlingen (d.after 1356), was instrumental in encouraging her visionary

experiences; indeed, many Dominicans became spiritual guides to cloistered and semi-cloistered women.

Among them was Henry Suso (d.1366), who spent most of his life not far from Katharinenthal and wrote an autobiographical account in the simple southern German of his day. Calling himself the "Servant of Eternal Wisdom," he reported that during the first eighteen years of his life he was restless, even though he had already joined a Dominican convent and dedicated himself to preaching God's word. But his life changed when he wandered into the convent's church: "As he stood there, disconsolate and solitary, he went into an ecstasy and saw and heard what is ineffable. [. . .] His heart was hungry and yet satisfied, his mind joyous and happy, his wishes were calmed and his desires had died out." Soon after that, he bound himself to Eternal Wisdom—the essence of the divine—in a mystical marriage, not unlike that of John and Christ.

The rise of mysticism in the Rhineland, espe-cially toward the southern region of Swabia and Lake Constance, coincided with the area's rising affluence. Wealthy from trade, especially of salt and cloth, the Rhineland had flourishing cities, and Swabia itself was key to the power of a new imperial dynasty, the Habsburgs. After a long period of civil war, Rudolf I (d.1291) was elected unanimously by the German princes. His dynasty laid the foundations of the Austro-Hungarian Empire that lasted until the twenti-eth century. But in the fourteenth century, Habsburg power was challenged by many princes, not least those from the Lake

Southwest Germany, c. 1300.

Constance region. At the same time, the Black Death—the great plague that swept Europe 1346–1353—came to the area, hitting the cities with particular fury. While many of the clergy in churches and monasteries suffered greatly, pious benefac-tions made the surviving religious houses rich. Paradoxically, this very wealth made the region a particular focus of later reform movements, including the Reformation. When establishing his "Protestant Rome" at Geneva, not far from Katharinenthal, John Calvin (d.1564), a French theologian and a fervent reformer, rejected images of saints—images much like those of Christ and Saint John—as the stuff of idolatry.

11

Master of Rubielos de Mora, The Coronation of the Virgin with the Trinity, c. 1400, Spain, oil on panel; 144.60 × 91.40 cm (56 ⅞ × 35 ¹⁵⁄₁₆ inches)

DRESSED in blue, arms crossed, the Virgin kneels to accept her crown as the Queen of Heaven. A starry diadem is placed on her head by the three persons of the Trinity. On her right is God the Father, bearded and gray-haired, seated on a golden rainbow. On her left is Christ, holding the cross, with the Crown of Thorns on his head and wounds that pour out gravity-defying blood. Issuing from their mouths, bridging them with wings that touch their lips, is the dove of the Holy Spirit, who holds one of the points of the crown in its long, sharp beak. Mary's pallid countenance is emphasized by her white wimple and pale blue robes, all of which seem to gleam, set as they are against the golden background—the heavenly realm where the Coronation unfolds. Representation of the Holy Spirit as a dove was inspired by John 1:32: "I saw the Spirit descending from heaven like a dove, and it abode in him." In many ways, the painting seems to echo the Constitutions of the Second Council of Lyon (1274), which declared that "the Holy Spirit proceeds eternally from the Father and the Son, not as from two principles but as from one, not by two spirations [divine breaths] but by one." The dove, here, is the embodied form of the life-giving spirations.

Representing the Trinity was fraught with difficulties. Textual sources were of no help, even though the earliest evocations of the triune God appear already in the New Testament; Matthew does just that while prescribing the rite of baptism "in the name of the Father and the Son, and the Holy Spirit" (28:19). Debates on the nature of the Trinity raged throughout the early centuries of Christianity, long after the Council of Nicaea confirmed the orthodoxy of the Trinitarian doctrine in 325. But before the ninth century, images of the Trinity were few and far between, and the triune God was suggested rather than directly represented. However, in the following centuries, several visual formulas developed. Among the most widespread was the Throne of Mercy, which featured God the Father holding the crucified Christ between his knees, and accompanied by the dove of the Holy Spirit. Immensely popular in a variety of media and often used to preface the Canon of the Mass, this image stemmed from Hebrews 4:16: "Let us go therefore with confidence to the throne of grace: that we may obtain mercy, and find grace in seasonable aid." Psalm 109:1, "The Lord said to my Lord: 'Sit thou at my right hand'," inspired another iconographic type: Father and Son placed side by side

with the dove between them. The Trinity could also take the form of identical triplets, or else twist this figuration into monstrosity: one body with three heads, a disembodied head with three faces. The great twelfth-century visionary Hildegard of Bingen (d.1179) imagined a man of sapphire surrounded by rings of fire and light: "And that bright light bathes the whole of the glowing fire, and the glowing fire bathes the bright light; and the bright light and the glowing fire pour over the whole human figure, so that the three are one light in one power of potential."

Late medieval images of the Trinity grew more and more inventive, and they began to include the Virgin as well: God holds his dead son under the armpits, in the presence of Mary and the dove of the Holy Spirit; Christ and his mother beseech God the Judge for mercy on behalf of humanity in the scene of the Double Intercession; the three members of the Trinity—two men with the dove between them—crown Mary as the Queen of Heaven. This last type, to which the painting shown here belongs, appeared toward the end of the fourteenth century and, it would seem, enriched the relationships among the members of the Trinity by including the Virgin into their midst. Here, the hands of the anthropomorphized divinity that place the crown on Mary's head visually echo the form of the dove's wings: the Father and the Son are linked as much by the wings of the dove as by the twinkling crown and therefore by the Virgin herself. But because her halo does not bear the cruciform mark that unifies the persons of the Trinity and because she kneels below them, it is clear that Mary is the creature of a different order. She seems, indeed, more akin to the angelic host that crowds in from behind, below, and all around in the flutter of many-colored wings: some playing instruments, some looking out of the painting at the viewer.

Little is known about the artist, called the Master of Rubielos de Mora because he painted an altarpiece for the church there. Around 1400, when the Coronation panel was created, Spain was just emerging from a long period of militant Christian conquest. Against the Muslims—known as the Moors—who had conquered most of the Iberian Peninsula in the seventh century, Christian warriors from the north fought in wars collectively known as the *reconquista* (reconquest). As early as the eleventh century, those who participated in the conquest of the Moors were accorded the same spiritual privileges as crusaders to Jerusalem: absolution of all their sins. By 1212, the *reconquista* had taken the whole of Spain except for a small crescent around Granada. But Christian Spain was far from unified. In 1400, in addition to the four competing Christian king-doms—Portugal, Castile, Navarre, and Aragon (which had taken over Valencia and thus the city of Rubielos de Mora)—there were numerous conflicting regional

entities. At the same time, two men claimed the papal tiara, one at Avignon and the other at Rome. This development, known as the Great Western Schism (1378–1417), was profoundly destabilizing. Aragon, Castile, and Navarre supported the Avignon pope, while Portugal chose the Roman one.

As the papacy weakened, kings increasingly subordinated the Church and churchmen to their control. Accusations of corruption among the clergy proliferated. Many prelates came from noble families and continued to live lives of luxury. Satirists were merciless: "In the whole village there is no one so well situated / Nor so well made up as his [the priest's] mistress," wrote Castilian courtier Pedro López de Ayala (d.1407). Only one new monastery was founded during this period and, since the *reconquista* had effectively reached its end, the militant orders made up of knight-monks lost their purpose. Pilgrims flocked to shrines of the Virgin. While some of the faithful sought spiritual balm in mysticism or heresy, others fortified their faith by reaffirming their adherence to Church doctrines.

Spain, c. 1400.

The doctrine of the Trinity remained among the most problematic, even after it was worked out in the thirteenth century by the famed scholastic Thomas Aquinas and proclaimed at the Council of Lyon. Still, it was embraced by such learned men as the Dominican friar Saint Vincent Ferrer (d.1419), professor of theology at Valencia and one of the most popular preachers of his day. In a sermon given on Trinity Sunday, Ferrer asked: "How therefore can we grasp that the Father and Son and Holy Spirit are three persons, and undivided in substance, nature and essence?" His answer: the Trinity "exceeds human genius." He resorted to all the old authorities—Saint Bernard, Thomas Aquinas, canon law—to shore up this doctrinal truth. In the face of doubt, heresy, schism, and clerical corruption, this panel vigorously reaffirmed traditional doctrine.

12

Christ Carrying the Cross (panel from an altarpiece),
1400s, England, Nottingham, painted and gilded alabaster;
47 × 28.3 cm (18 ½ × 11 ⅛ inches)

G RASPING an immense cross with spindly flat hands, a tall, emaciated Christ makes his way to Calvary through a crowd of onlookers. He is naked but for his loincloth, his ribs visible, his elbows and knees sharp. Christ is led by a rope tied around his waist, the other end of which is held in the hands of one of his tormentors. The figure on the left likely bore a bill—a staff topped with a hooked blade that here has broken off. A man on the top right carries a hammer and three nails; the man in the middle may have held a halberd. These figures all have blackened and pitted faces, to identify them as evil and sinful. They also wear short tunics and don exotic hats that mark them as Jews, or at least as the malevolent other. One places a proprietary hand on the cross, as if to push it down against those who try to hold it up: the Virgin Mary and a man who is, perhaps, Simon of Cyrene. In the upper left corner, Saint John the Evangelist peers out from the crowd. To the right of the cross, Veronica holds up a piece of cloth for Christ to wipe off his sweat and blood; the imprint of his face will become one of the more remarkable relics in the medieval West—an *acheiropoieton*, an image made without human hands. While the executioners have been darkened, the good, including Christ, are left gleamingly white: alabaster's texture, pliant and polishable, was particularly well suited for rendering flesh.

Gypsum alabaster is a highly unusual stone. It tends to be found just below the soil—two or three feet, no more. In some places, it rests above ground, like "a smooth table," to quote the sixteenth-century scholar John Leland. It becomes malleable when warm: it can be easily scratched, even with a fingernail, and is heat-sensitive and even water-soluble. For that reason, alabaster should not be used on the exterior of buildings, as the elements would easily damage it. But as a material for devotional panels it is strikingly appropriate: when properly polished, it becomes translucent, softly filtering light through its surfaces and suffusing objects carved from it with an ethereal glow. Unlike the much harder and more expensive marble, alabaster quarried in the English Midlands was easily accessible: only small teams of workmen were needed to extract the stone—an important feature in the period after the Black Death (1346–1353), which devastated the European population and decimated its work force. Because alabaster would break easily when quarried, panels like this one were much more common

than, for example, alabaster tombs, which required that large chunks of the stone remain intact when extracted from the ground. But for smaller devotional objects, alabaster proved to be a perfect material: it was relatively cheap, is fairly easy to carve and drill, and readily accepts paint and gilding. Paint is still visible in the Carrying of the Cross, although it has been rubbed off and dirtied (alabaster absorbs not only pigment but also dust and smoke), and gilding is still discernable in the hair and the forked beard of Christ, as well as in the background. Alabaster panels such as this one became extremely popular in the fourteenth and fifteenth centuries, especially in England, where they figured as parts of shrines in prosperous homes and of altarpieces in churches. In fact, this panel likely belonged to one such altarpiece, forming part of several narrative scenes of the Passion of Christ.

Scenes like this may have been inspired by woodcuts, which were in active circulation in Europe by the fifteenth century. Prints were commonly used by sculptors as models for carving in wood, bone, or stone—still extant are caskets, misericords, and altarpieces clearly based on woodcuts and engravings. Alabaster was no exception: many panels bear obvious similarities to contemporaneous prints, some of which were found in the *Biblia Pauperum* (the so-called "Paupers' Bible"), a picture-book Bible that visually related the Old Testament subjects to the life of Christ.

The alabaster narratives recall not only woodcuts, but also lively dramas performed on the streets and in open fields, inn courtyards, and other places suitable for people to congregate. Medieval plays were drawn only in part from biblical accounts; they also depended on apocryphal New Testament gospels, lives of Saints, and vernacular literature. England in particular was famous for its medieval cycle dramas—the Chester, York, and Wakefield (Towneley) cycles among them. Several details in the Carrying of the Cross panel seem to reference such plays: the York cycle alludes to Christ being dragged to Calvary by ropes, while in the Wakefield cycle the Virgin Mary helps Christ lift the cross. Other visual aspects of the image appear to be theatrical: the protagonists' gestures are exaggerated; the faces of the executioners are blackened and ridged, as if covered with make-up or masks; and the cross, covered with a daisy pattern (also visible on the ground), suggests a stage prop. The affective sentiments of the panel, with its focus on Christ's emaciation, the heaviness of the cross, and the wickedness of the tormentors, also find their counterparts in medieval plays. The Chester cycle, for instance (itself indebted to the Middle English poem *A Stanzaic Life of Christ*), dramatized the carrying of the cross with one of the characters, Annas, enjoining the reluctant Simon of Cyrene to aid Christ in his task: "Him seems weary of his way. / Some help to get I will assay, / for this cross, truly, / so far he may not bear. /

Come hither, Simon of Surrey [Cyrene], / and take this cross anon in hie [immediately]. / Unto the mount of Calvary / help that it were borne." This scene appears in the seventeenth play of the cycle, "The Passion and Death of Christ," sponsored by the guild of ironmongers. Specific guilds were entrusted with specific parts of the cycle, often deemed related to their profession: in Chester, for example, the bakers were benefactors of the Last Supper play that involved the bread-breaking, while the cooks were responsible for the production of the Harrowing of Hell and the attendant smoke. The ironmongers' guild, which manufactured nails, frequently staged Passion plays that involved the nailing of Christ to the cross.

The city of Chester lay not far from Nottingham, where this alabaster was made. Nottingham was small, but its location made it a key player in the English Midlands, one of the wealthiest regions in England. The city's Friday and Saturday markets were almost unrivaled, and it sponsored fairs as well. Indeed, Nottingham had to impose traffic regulations on the herds of beasts driven to its markets. Not far from the place where the Trent River first became navigable, Nottingham was also near coal seams that were mined already in the medieval period. Above all, Nottingham was known for its alabaster objects, which were popular locally and admired abroad. Many were made for export, and, in fact, one finds surviving pieces all over Europe and Scandinavia—from France to Iceland, from Spain to Norway— some of which must have been smuggled out of England during the Reformation.

But by the time this panel was carved, Nottingham was declining economically. Like many other late medieval English cities, its elites came increasingly to monopolize government offices. No wonder that the story of Robin Hood, the outlaw who stole from the rich to give to the poor, placed him in Sherwood Forest, just outside Nottingham, and delighted in how he outwitted Nottingham's powerful sheriff.

The English Midlands.

13 Leaf from an Antiphonary, Initial H with the Nativity, c. 1480, south Germany, Augsburg (?), ink, tempera, and gold on vellum; leaf 62.50 × 41.00 cm (24 ⁹⁄₁₆ × 16 ⅛ inches)

L IKE the Jewish synagogue service, Christian worship involved chant, a form of music. With the development of monasticism—a mode of life in retreat from the world, dedicated to obedience and prayer—the day became marked by the Divine Office with its eight "hours" of prayer. Lauds were sung at dawn; Prime, Terce, Sext, and None were evenly spaced throughout the morning and the afternoon; then Vespers were performed at dusk, and Compline at the close of the day. In the middle of the night (about 2 a.m.) the monks rose for the night service originally called "Nocturnes" or "Vigils" but today known as "Matins." The scene on the page illustrated here, painted within a giant H (the first letter of the first word), is a fitting opening for the Matins service of Christmas Day, since it shows the Nativity, or the birth of Christ.

The core of the Divine Office was the Psalter, a book of poetry in the Old Testament and believed during the Middle Ages to have been written by King David, known as a great musician. Monks were expected to sing all 150 psalms in the course of a week. Nor were the psalms the only texts that they sang: there were also "canticles"—biblical songs of praise. Special verses were composed to introduce and to close each psalm or canticle. Numerous books were created to contain the chants, the special verses, and their music; antiphonaries contained the verses sung before or after each psalm or canticle. Such books are usually quite large—as witnessed by this folio—so that the whole choir could see the pages.

The image inhabiting the large initial H begins the phrase "Hodie nobis celorum rex" ("Today for us the King of Heaven"). Because this text is meant to echo the angelic voices that proclaimed Christ's birth to the shepherds, it was sometimes sung by young boys, who stood up in the church gallery. The monks and the lay worshipers (who were often present in the church on great feast days) heard these voices sung on high, just as the shepherds heard them at the very moment of Christ's birth. It is only appropriate, then, that this birth is pictured in the accompanying initial. Decorated with elegant leaves, the "H" fits snugly into a multicolored frame with a golden background; within its curve, Mary and Joseph adore their newborn son. The haloed infant Christ lies on his back atop the Virgin's deep blue cloak as his parents kneel before him, with Mary's hands clasped in prayer. The scene seems to be taking place in a walled garden, or

a *hortus conclusus*—a symbol of Mary's purity. A city looms in the background, behind the shed that consists of a brick roofed fortification whose gaping doorway is filled by Mary's figure: here, then, she appears in her role as a doorway to Christ.

Intricate flowery vines grow out of the frame that encloses the initial; they sprawl into the margins, blossoming into a riotous arrangement of vegetation at the bottom of the page. Among the foliage, a rooster perches on one of the creepers, an owl alights on a flower, and another bird pecks at a pomegranate— an emblem of both fertility and resurrection. A small putto—a Cupid-like figure— sits astride a branch, echoing the nude form of the child in the initial, and above him looms a great blue peacock. Peacock imagery was often chosen to accompany Nativity scenes: the bird was believed to have incorruptible flesh, and so was symbolic of the Virgin Mary who was bodily assumed to heaven.

The music is written on a four-line staff, using "neumes" to indicate the notes. Musical notation began in the ninth century in the West, as small dots and dashes were written above liturgical texts to remind singers who already knew the music whether the tune went up or down the scale. Occasionally lines were drawn so that notes with the same pitch would appear on the same line. Sometimes a yellow or green line was used to signify middle "C," while a red line beneath that indicated the pitch of "F." The four-line staff may have been the invention of Guido of Arezzo in the early eleventh century, though it was not widely adopted until about 200 years later. Guido also introduced the familiar syllables ut (or do), re, mi, fa, sol, and la. Armed with these tools, singers could learn a melody just by looking at a piece of music rather than by hearing and then memorizing it. Here, on this page, a C clef sign sits astride the first line, right after the H of "Hodie." That means that the first three notes have the same pitch—that of middle C. Like the text, the notes are read from left to right, but when two notes are written directly on top of one another, the singer sounds the bottom one first, then the top note. Notation like this suggests that there were no musical instruments to accompany the singers. Yet medieval writers, painters, and sculptors make clear that there were many such instruments, and they were used for worship as well as entertainment.

This antiphonary must have belonged to a Franciscan community, as some of its texts and images refer to Clare, the first female saint of that order. The founder of the order was Francis of Assisi (d.1226), whose colorful legend recounts his conversion by a speaking crucifix, his preaching to birds and fish, his travels to foreign lands, and the imprinting of his body by stigmata—a corporeal echo of the wounds of Christ. Francis's order, the *ordo fratrum minorum* (or "the Order of Lesser Brothers"), differed dramatically from other monastic orders, such as Cistercians and Cluniacs. Franciscans were mendicants, and therefore not

bound to any monastery: rather, like Dominicans—another order that came together at roughly the same time—they lived in cities, preached, begged, and busied themselves with pastoral care. The Franciscan community, in fact, contains three orders: the first order consists of priests and lay brothers; the second order—that of Poor Clares—comprises nuns; and the third, or tertiary, order includes laywomen and laymen who live in the world and may marry, but who devote themselves to charitable work and prayer. The Franciscan rule includes directives "to travel about the world," to "appropriate neither house, nor place, nor anything for themselves," and to preach in words that are "studied and chaste." In the late Middle Ages, both Franciscans and Dominicans were among the most important university professors, scholars, and inquisitors charged with combating heresy.

But none of this worldly activity prevented the Franciscans from spending much of their day in their churches singing the psalms. Augsburg was a center of such activity. David of Augsburg (d.1272), a master of novices (newcomers under probation) in the Franciscan cloisters at Regensburg and then Augsburg had, long before this antiphonary was made, written a book that told the friars how to behave during the Divine Office. In it, he enjoined the novices: "do not be lazy or disdainful; rather, make your body serve the spirit and stand reverently and sing with alacrity and devotion in the church among the angels, who are present there right next to you." Mature friars, however, had to go beyond this, keeping in mind that their prayers were weapons against the demons, to be sung with understanding, concentration, and delight. David's book was wildly popular: most of its copies were made in the fourteenth and fifteenth centuries, coinciding with the production of this manuscript page.

PART II

The Sinful and the Spectral

14

Adam and Eve, Fragment of a Floor Mosaic, late 400s
to early 500s, northern Syria, marble and stone tesserae;
142.90 × 107.30 × 5.72 cm (56 ¼ × 42 ³⁄₁₆ × 2 ¼ inches)

G RASPING a tiny apple as they hold hands, Adam and Eve stare straight at the
viewer. This is the moment of Original Sin, the transgression of transgres-
sions—the tasting of the fruit from the forbidden tree of knowledge. Once part of
a much larger mosaic found in a northern Syrian church, this fragment represents
the various episodes in the Fall of mankind as a single event. Eve proffers the apple
to Adam, who has already accepted it; in fact, they have already tasted the fruit and
become ashamed of their nakedness, as the Greek inscription above their heads
confirms: "And they ate and they realized they were naked." Both Adam and Eve
press ample fig leaves to their genitals, all the better to hide their nudity from each
other and the viewer. The scene and the inscription refer to Genesis 3:7: "And the
eyes of them both were opened: and when they perceived themselves to be naked,
they sewed together fig leaves, and made themselves aprons." As the representation of the most terrible sin of all, this was a particularly appropriate image to tread
underfoot.

Created from Adam's rib, Eve was, throughout the Middle Ages and with a very
few exceptions, seen as a subservient, inferior creature, the guilty party who
seduced Adam into doing the one thing that God had forbidden him to do.
In Genesis, God tells Adam: "You may freely eat of every tree of the garden; but
of the tree of the knowledge of good and evil you shall not eat, for in the day that
you eat of it you shall die." But Eve, tempted by the serpent—the devil—tasted the
delicious fruit and gave it to her husband. Perceiving for the first time their
nakedness, Adam and Eve hid from the gaze of their creator, who sent the two
out of the garden, cursing them and their descendants—all of humanity—with
a life of hard toil, the pains of childbirth, and death.

All women were seen as daughters of Eve, their monthly issue of blood a potent
reminder of the punishment visited upon humanity. In the third century, the
Christian theologian Tertullian asked his female audience rhetorically: "Do you
not believe that you are [each] an Eve? The sentence of God on this sex of yours
lives on even in our times and so it is necessary that the guilt should live on, also.
You are the one who opened the door to the Devil, you are the one who first
plucked the fruit of the forbidden tree, you are the first who deserted the divine

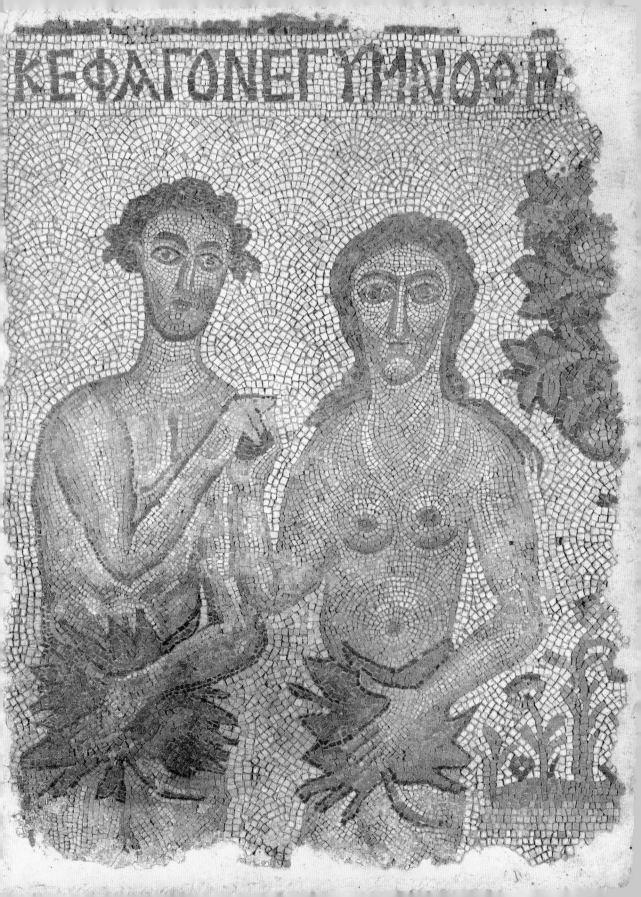
ΚΕΦΑΓΟΝΕΤΥΜΝΟΘΗ

law; you are the one who persuaded him [Adam] whom the devil was not strong enough to attack. All too easily you destroyed the image of God, man. Because of your desert, that is, death, even the Son of God had to die." But other theologians, from Saint Augustine (d.430) to Thomas Aquinas (d.1274), praised the Fall as the so-called *felix culpa* (the happy fault) because of the great good (Christ's Incarnation and redemption of the Original Sin) that was brought out of the great evil. At the close of the Middle Ages, the popular devout imagination came to glorify Eve's transgression precisely because it was responsible for the creation of the Virgin Mary; we read in one fifteenth-century Middle English poem: "Had the apple never taken been, / The apple taken been, / Never'd have our Lady / Been heaven's queen. / Blessed be the time / That apple taken was! / So that we may sing / 'Deo Gratias!'"

Still, fault was placed squarely on Eve's shoulders, and the Syrian mosaic assigns her blame. Even though Adam is the taller of the two, Eve dominates the image: she is larger than Adam, as if positioned closest to the viewer; her facial features are more dramatic than his; and her body—her breasts and her belly—is made up of circles that visually echo the background pattern. The gentle gradation of color suggests a certain three-dimensionality. The carefully modeled flesh of both Adam and Eve calls attention to what they attempt, in vain, to conceal: their newly recognized nakedness. Judging by the fragmentary tree and some vegetation to the right of Eve, one can guess that the rest of the pavement represented the Garden of Eden. Syria was part of the Byzantine, or Eastern, half of the later Roman Empire and the two frontal figures exhibit typical features associated with early Byzantine art: large, eyes, full eyebrows, long and straight noses, and small mouths. Adam appears to stare directly at the viewer, but Eve's gaze seems trained on something invisible, as if she already perceives the future of her children, filled with suffering and pain.

Long before the arrival of Christianity, Syria was one of the wealthiest regions of the Roman Empire. After the Jewish revolt against Roman rule during the time of Emperor Hadrian in the second century, only short—and limited—outbreaks of indigenous violence disrupted an era of peace that lasted until the seventh century in much of the Middle East. True, the Persians invaded in the third century and again in the early sixth. But on the whole the region escaped both invasions and civil wars. Its internal calm was due to an easy-going tolerance that supported a mix of cultures and religions. Arabs (not yet Muslim), Jews, and Roman pagans were equally influenced by the Hellenistic culture spread long before this time by Alexander the Great and his heirs. Mosaics—images made out of tiny stone, marble, and glass tesserae (tiles)—were popular throughout the empire, and

many examples remain from the Middle East, where the well-to-do commissioned them to adorn the floors of their homes. After Christianity became the official religion of the Empire at the end of the fourth century, mosaics took pride of place on pavements as well as on the walls and ceilings of the new churches. At that time, too, mosaic floors began appearing in synagogues—mainly in the region of modern-day Israel, but also in the areas of the diaspora, including Syria. Among a variety of surviving synagogue mosaics—and in addition to geometrical, animal, and vegetal motifs—are images of the zodiac, sacred Temple implements, and biblical scenes such as Noah's Ark. But this image of the Fall finds no parallels among contemporaneous Syrian mosaics, perhaps because so much has been lost to changing religious doctrines.

When Syria came under the control of Muslim troops led by men from Arabia (today Saudi Arabia) in the seventh century, many Byzantine churches were converted into mosques. Nevertheless, even the walls of newly built mosques teemed with mosaic cityscapes, landscapes, trees, and flowers. Representations of living beings were avoided in mosques, to be sure, but they were welcome adornments in the private homes of Muslim leaders. It was only in the eighth century that the so-called iconoclastic movement seized both the Byzantine and Muslim worlds, and many mosaics that featured religious

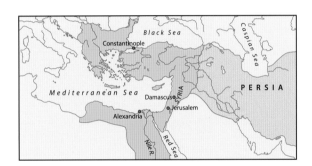

The Eastern Roman Empire, c. 500.

subjects were considered idolatrous and subsequently defaced. Sometimes the defacement was complete and damage irreparable; sometimes, it was done carefully and selectively, likely by the members of the very community that worshiped in churches and synagogues. At times, the original tesserae were chipped out and then inelegantly filled with non-figurative motifs, a fate that this Adam and Eve panel was lucky to escape.

15

Curtain Panel with Scenes of Merrymaking, sixth century, Egypt, tapestry weave with supplementary weft wrapping, undyed linen and dyed wool; 144.20 × 26.70 cm (56 ¾ × 10 ½ inches)

Even though Christianity came very quickly to Egypt, pagan subjects continued to be featured in its visual culture for centuries to come. In this magnificent panel, where undyed linen is intricately woven with dyed wool to produce a complicated set of images, the central part of the design features dancing maenads in diaphanous garb, centaurs, the Greek hero Hercules, and the god of wine, Dionysus. The panel is edged by a frame of roundels that contain various animals including a donkey, a dog, a stag, lions, and bulls. In the bottom panel, a nude Hercules leans on his club, while a dancer lifts and opens her chiton. In the middle square, a barefoot maenad clutches a tambourine and dances with a wine cup held out toward Dionysus, who is grasping two grapevines. In the top square is a nude man with a shepherd's staff on his shoulder; he takes leave of a dancer, who is shod in pointy red footwear and makes music with clappers. This man, too, is likely to be Hercules, as both the shepherd's staff and the club are his attributes: the former refers to his youth as a mountain shepherd, while the latter is a sign of his maturity and the twelve labors (heroic deeds) he had to undertake in order to atone for an unthinkable crime committed during a bout of madness— the murder of his own children.

In each of the two large roundels stands a centaur. Centaurs were believed to be a race of half-men, half-horses. They were depicted as wild and savage beasts, although a few were considered kind and wise. Indeed, both Hercules and Dionysus were supposed to have been pupils of Chiron, a gentle and intelligent centaur whose lineage differed from that of the other centaurs. Here these creatures are visually linked to the images in the squares by the attributes that they carry: in the top roundel, a centaur carries a club (both as the weapon of choice for his kin and as a reference to Hercules); in the bottom one, the centaur holds a shepherd's staff and stands on what appears to be a lion—perhaps an allusion to the unconquerable Nemean lion whom Hercules slew as part of his first labor.

At first glance, the images suggest merrymaking, and in fact there is a little-known story about Hercules and Dionysus engaging in a drinking contest. But more profoundly, these seemingly whimsical figures are bound together by

narratives of revenge, madness, and death. Both Hercules and Dionysus were illegitimate children that Zeus, the ruler of Olympus, had with mortal women. Overcome by jealousy, Zeus's wife, Hera, attempted to stop Hercules's birth and to murder Dionysus *in utero*. When her ploys failed, she visited insanity upon both men, as a result of which Hercules committed infanticide, while Dionysus was overcome by wild wanderlust. The centaurs, in turn, were believed to be descendants of Ixion, the mad and murderous king of the Lapiths—a legendary people living in Thessaly. Invited to Olympus, Ixion fell in love with Hera but was tricked by Zeus into copulating with Nephele—a cloud-woman made in the form of his beloved. Their child, the deformed Centaurus, mated with mares on Mount Pelion, and from those unions half-beasts, prone to drinking and violence, descended. Centaurs figure prominently in many stories about Hercules's feats, telling both of his friendship with some of them and his battles with others.

All this perhaps sounds very far from Christianity, but in fact both Hercules and Dionysus were reinterpreted in the Middle Ages as Christological figures. The comparison between these protagonists of ancient myths and the Christian god appears as early as the second century in the writings of Justin Martyr. Dionysus was associated with grapes and winemaking, and therefore with the Eucharistic wine of the altar. In turn, Hercules's descent into Hades (the Greek Underworld), from which he released his friend Theseus, was likened to Christ's release of souls from hell; moreover, when Hercules died he was raised to Olympus, an end that resembled Christ's ascension. The centaurs, who in the Middle Ages were identified with the constellation of Sagittarius, did not fare so well and eventually came to be considered members of an adulterous, lustful race, both pagan and heretical. They were featured in medieval bestiaries—books that used animals to point up a religious moral—to illustrate the sin of hypocrisy because they combined two natures, one human, the other beastly. In his *Divine Comedy*, Dante relegated centaurs to purgatory (among the gluttons) and hell (among thieves and murderers).

Egypt had an early claim on Christianity: the Gospel of Matthew, composed in the late first century, describes Joseph, Mary, and Jesus fleeing to Egypt to escape King Herod's decree to kill all male infants in and around Bethlehem (Matthew 2: 13–15). Bishop Eusebius of Caesarea (d.c.340) reported a later tradition that linked Egypt's Christianity to the evangelist Saint Mark: "And they say that this Mark was the first that was sent to Egypt, and that he proclaimed the Gospel which he had written, and first established churches in Alexandria." But Christianity did not quickly conquer all of Egypt. Traditional religions and festivals continued; we infer their persistence from the opposition they engendered. For example,

Shenoute (d.466), the abbot of the Egyptian White Monastery, marched into villages to destroy temples and to inveigh against local celebrations. He saw evidence of the devil everywhere: in "unnatural sex," in snakes, in images of the gods still worshiped in various Egyptian communities, and in one particular local landowner, Gesios, who claimed to be Christian but whom Shenoute saw as a "closet pagan."

After the seventh century, when Muslims conquered Egypt and Christians of every sort were subject to the same poll tax, the Christian view there became more or less uniform and was dubbed "Coptic," from the Arab word *Qibt*, meaning non-Muslim. But in Shenoute's era, Christianity was experiencing growing pains and was anything but uniform, especially in Egypt. There, the differences were particularly sharp because of the influence of the Gnostic prophet Mani (d.276). Born in Persia, Mani assumed the title of "apostle of Jesus Christ" and publicized his doctrine throughout his homeland and in the outlying regions of central Asia and the Roman Empire, including Egypt. Mani preached that there were two cosmic principles, Light and Darkness. Light was godly and spiritual; Darkness was evil and material. The followers of Mani, known as Manichees, considered Jesus's human nature, his suffering on the Cross, and his very flesh to be only apparent rather than real. Human beings could free themselves of the shackles of their own flesh through fasting, renouncing sex, disdaining all forms of property, and clinging to the special knowledge brought to mankind by Christ's apostles.

By the sixth century, when this curtain was made, Manichaeism itself had been stamped out. But its influence may be felt in one of the main divisions within Byzantine Christianity regarding the nature of Christ. As part of the Byzantine Empire, Egyptian Christians were supposed to adhere to the view at Constantinople, which claimed (in brief) that Christ had two indivisible natures, one human, the other divine. Many Egyptians, however, took the Monophysite position—close in spirit to what the Manichees believed—that holds Christ's nature to be fully divine. A tapestry with Hercules and centaurs, therefore, tapped into a complex set of traditions that pitted Good against Evil but also was willing to see the good in evil and the evil in good. Small wonder it focused on a hero, Hercules, who had committed the most terrible of sins and yet was elevated to heaven.

16

Plaque from a Portable Altar Showing the Crucifixion, 1050–1100, Germany, Lower Rhine Valley, walrus ivory; 5.10 × 9.55 cm (2 × 3 ¾ inches)

THIS tiny walrus ivory plaque, one of four, was part of a portable altar from western Germany's Rhineland region. An eerily peaceful scene—the calm and serene crucified Christ, the oversized figures of St. John and the Virgin clasping their hands in restrained anguish—is disrupted by the spastic movements of two men pictured in profile on either side of the cross. Directly above them, the personifications of the sun and the moon emerge from the sky. One man thrusts a long sharp lance into Christ's side, while another, his knees bending under the weight of the bucket he holds, proffers a reed topped with a vinegar-soaked sponge. These are the soldiers who come into intimate, if not direct, contact with Christ's body, one before his death, one just after. One man will soon convert and repent, while the other will remain a sinner.

The man with the lance is a Roman centurion named Longinus—a name, derived from the Greek word for "spear," that appears nowhere in the gospel narratives. The elaboration of Longinus's story comes from the apocryphal Gospel of Nicodemus, compiled in the fourth century and based on John 19:34. When soldiers came to break the legs of Christ and of the two thieves crucified alongside him, seeking to hasten their deaths, wrote John, they discovered that Christ was already dead. One of the soldiers—Nicodemus calls him Longinus—pierced Christ's side, and a stream of blood and water flowed down upon him. According to the legend, the issue of water and blood cured the centurion's failing sight. Mark 15:39 tells the story differently: "And the centurion who stood over against him, seeing that crying out in this manner he had given up the ghost, said: Indeed this man was the son of God." It is likely that Longinus is actually a conflation of three different men: one who pierced Christ's breast, one who witnessed the Crucifixion, and one who was in charge of guarding Christ's tomb.

A pagan soldier in service to Pontius Pilate, Longinus is the archetypal sinner turned convert. In the ivory, the centurion's position on Christ's right suggests that he will ultimately be saved. The configuration takes its inspiration from Matthew 25:33–34, 41: "And he shall set the sheep on his right hand, but the goats on his left. Then shall the king say to them that shall be on his right hand: Come, ye blessed of my Father, possess you the kingdom prepared for you from

the foundation of the world. [. . .] Then he shall say to them also that shall be on his left hand: Depart from me, you cursed, into everlasting fire which was prepared for the devil and his angels." Longinus's placement directly under the sun, the symbol of the New Testament, confirms his eventual salvation. In the end, the legend goes, the centurion abandoned his military pursuits to lead the life of a Christian proselytizer, and his spear became the relic of the Holy Lance.

But the man standing on the left side of Christ in the altar panel remains a sinner in the gospel accounts. He stands under the moon, the symbol of the Old Testament. Legend calls him Stephaton; some writings explicitly (and only) refer to him as "the Jew." He is the one who responds to Christ's anguished demand to know why God has forsaken him ("Eloi, Eloi, lama sabachthani?") by mocking the suffering man: "Let us see if Elias come to take him down" (Mark 15:36). This, too, is the same man who answers Christ's admission of thirst by bringing him a vinegar-filled sponge, thus inflicting further agony. The ninth-century theologian Pascasius Radbertus (d.865) saw the vinegar-and-gall mixture

as a symbol of faithlessness, of corrupted human nature. Christ accepts the vinegar and dies.

The users of the altar plaque would have recognized Stephaton as the unrepentant Jew. The Lower Rhine Valley in Germany, where the altar was made, was ahead of its time commercially, and the Jews of the Rhineland both contributed to and benefited from its prosperity. Protected by the cities' bishops (who found them handy to borrow from) and often boasting special royal privileges as well, the Jews were deeply involved in all sorts of commercial activities. At the same time, and perhaps precisely due to their social and economic successes, Jews in this region were the first in Europe to be formally set apart from their Christian neighbors. In Mainz, the Jewish quarter was in the center of the city; at Worms, it was to the northeast. At Speyer, there were two hubs—the one to the north was set up by the city's bishop and had walls; the other was in the city center. Despite the attempt by the bishop to enclose the Jews at Speyer, some of them there—as elsewhere—lived in predominately Christian neighborhoods, while some Christians lived in the Jewish part of town. Jewish communities functioned not only religiously but also politically, acting as self-governing bodies. While Jews still spoke the same language as the Christian community, many affirmed their separate identity by opening schools in which Jewish children would learn Hebrew.

When the First Crusade was called by Pope Urban II in 1095, he pointedly called on Christians to "let your quarrels end, let wars cease. [. . .] Enter upon the road to the Holy Sepulcher; wrest that land from the wicked race [the Muslims], and subject it to yourselves." But, as the official armies gathered to fulfill Urban's call, more informal armies sprang up, inspired by the teaching of the charismatic Peter the Hermit and others like him. Consisting of peasants alongside knights, these armies did not go straight to the Holy Land. Rather, they took a Rhineland detour, looking to kill the Jews, whom they considered to be as bad as the Muslims. Joined by local townsmen, they rounded up the Jews of each city and gave them the choice of conversion or death. Thus in 1096, William, viscount of Melun, attacked Speyer, but many Jews were saved by the local bishop; undeterred, William went on to Worms, where, despite the rescue attempts of the bishop, most of the Jews were massacred. A week later, another army, this time led by Emico, a German knight, arrived at Mainz, where many Jews martyred themselves rather than submit to baptism. Later, a Jewish chronicler, Solomon bar Samson, writing around 1140, wrote that some of the Jews cried out in unison, "There is nothing better than for us to offer our lives as a sacrifice." Regensburg, Cologne, Trier, and Metz soon had their turns. A stirring description of the murders and

suicide-martyrdoms both was composed as a liturgical poem by Rabbi Eliezer ben Nathan (d.1170): "They slaughtered them, they wrung their necks. No household was spared. / They piled together infants and women, young and old. [...] Their lips moved as they made their peace with heaven: / 'There is a God who judges the earth'."

The judgment intimated on the ivory altar is hardly the one the Jews were expecting. Its three other plaques show, symmetrically arranged, the 12 apostles, along with Christ in Majesty surrounded by the four beasts of the Apocalypse and flanked by two angels. This is the Second Coming, the time when all souls will be judged. As Longinus was positioned on the right—*the right*—side of the cross, so he will stand on the right side of Christ on Judgment Day. He will be saved, but his companion, the man with the vinegar sponge standing on Christ's left, will undoubtedly burn in the fires of hell.

Rhineland cities, c. 1100.

17

Dragon's Head, 1100–1150, Anglo-Norman (?), walrus ivory; height 6.40 cm (2 ½ inches)

A⊤ first glance, this dragon's head would not be out of place on the prow of a Viking ship. Its bulging eyes are dominated by a formidable brow, and its scrunched-up snout opens into a frightening snarl. The dragon's maw is toothy and its fangs are sharp. The eyes become all but invisible when the dragon is confronted head-on, lost in the wrinkled folds of skin. The flews around its mouth hang down, and it seems that the beast emits a terrifying sound, a growl perhaps, or a thunderous roar. The neck of the monster is still more astonishing, decorated with stylized acanthus leaves, and on the back of the neck a mask-like face is carved, sprouting foliage everywhere. The creature, in other words, has two faces, both equally distressing. The high polish of the walrus bone from which it is carved endows the beast with translucency and gleam, almost as if it should be seen from far away, perhaps by enemy ships. Indeed, the gaping mouth of the dragon, the ornamental design on its neck, the round bulging eyes, and the curving snout would be at home on any Scandinavian animal-head post. Because dragons so often decorated the longship prows, the English used to call Viking vessels dragonships.

But the head is actually very small: it stands at about 2.5 inches. Its likely provenance is not a ship, but a chair, on which it would have served as an ornamental finial. In Scandinavia, dragon heads were often carved on everyday objects, such as the heads of pins, while swords and belt buckles regularly sported dragon or snake motifs. They were associated with warlike powers, and so would have been appropriate to decorate an important piece of furniture such as a chair, which, in the first half of the twelfth century, was generally reserved for figures of authority. This was especially true of the so-called *sellae curules* or X-shaped seats, used in the past by Roman imperial officials. They were designed to be portable and foldable, with leather or canvas seats stretched across metal or wooden frames, and they often featured animal-head finials, such as the one here.

Three centuries before this ivory was carved, Viking ships began plying the seas. Their earliest contact with the British Isles consisted of hit-and-run attacks, but by the mid-ninth century the Norse invaders were establishing permanent fortifications. At first, these camps were meant simply for stashing their plunder, storing supplies, and protecting their ships. But soon the Northmen were settling in for

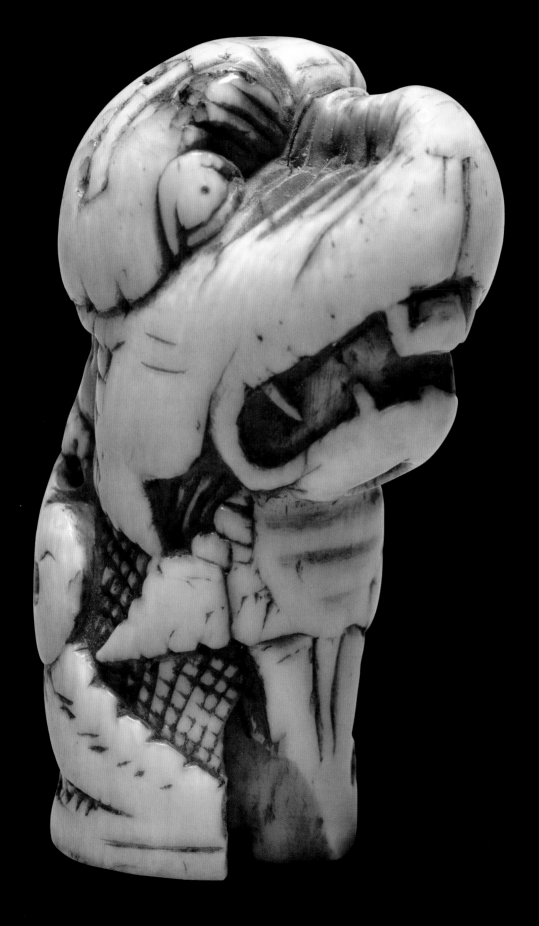

the winter, sometimes as whole families. An entire region later called the Danelaw was settled by a large Scandinavian army mainly from Denmark. The size of this area is much debated, as is its impact on the indigenous Anglo-Saxon population, but Scandinavian place names in a region stretching from Yorkshire to Leicestershire are witness to the fact that Nordic farmers, arriving under the cover of the armies, established real settlements in England. By c. 1000, both Scandinavia itself and its outliers, such as the Danelaw, were Christianized and largely absorbed into the European model: kings, supported by churchmen, ruled and supported churchmen in turn. Thus, Cnut (d.1035), king of both Denmark and England, lavished gifts and privileges on English churches after initially despoiling them. As the Scandinavian elites became part of the economic, political, and religious life of England, they played an active role in regional and Church government and in the patronage of art.

The Anglo-Norman world, c. 1100.

While some Vikings were establishing themselves in England, others were settling in part of northwest France, which came to be called "Normandy" (from "Northmen"). In 1066 the duke of Normandy, William the Conqueror, famously subjugated England, creating the Anglo-Norman kingdom. His dynasty lasted through the first third of the twelfth century, but in 1135 two different claimants to the throne waged a civil war that did not end until the reign of Henry II (d.1189), who ushered in the "Angevin" period of English rule.

William's other nickname, "the Bastard," speaks to his illegitimate status: he was the son of Robert I of Normandy and one Herleva, a tanner's daughter from the town of Falaise. Herleva's other son by her eventual husband, Viscount Herluin, was named Odo. He became the bishop of Bayeux in 1049—appointed to the post, in fact, by William. Odo, it is believed, commissioned the Bayeux Embroidery (often wrongly called a tapestry), a singular piece of Norman propaganda that extolled the virtues of William and vividly described the political and moral inferiority of Harold, the English claimant to the throne. According to the Norman side, Harold, the brother-in-law of the recently deceased king of England, seized the throne unlawfully, a fact confirmed by the appearance of the unusual celestial body: Halley's comet. Produced c. 1070, the Bayeux Embroidery includes an image

of Harold seated on an ornate chair with the comet passing in heaven above. The chair is decorated with several snarling dragon heads much like the one here. Such ornaments, perhaps, were not simply markers of authority but also, in this context, signs of evil: dragons were creatures associated with the devil, who was a liar and a deceiver.

Dragons were prominently featured in bestiaries, which in turn drew from Roman and medieval authorities. The Aberdeen Bestiary, an English manuscript roughly contemporary with this dragon head, claims that dragons, which belong to the snake family, are frequently found in India and Ethiopia. The didactic commentary continues: "The Devil is like the dragon. He is the most monstrous serpent of all; he is often aroused from his cave and causes the air to shine because, emerging from the depths, he transforms himself into the angel of light and deceives the foolish with hopes of vainglory and worldly pleasure. The dragon is said to be crested, [just] as the Devil wears the crown of the king of pride. The dragon's strength lies not in its teeth but its tail, as the Devil, deprived of his strength, deceives with lies those whom he draws to him. The dragon lurks around paths along which elephants pass, [just] as the Devil entangles with the knots of sin the way of those bound for heaven and, like the dragon, kills them by suffocation. [For] anyone who dies fettered in the chains of his offences is condemned without doubt to hell."

Sacred narratives are full of dragon-slayers. In the Book of Revelation 12:7, Archangel Michael and the heavenly host fight together against a seven-headed dragon—the embodiment of evil. Saint Margaret defeats the devil in the shape of a dragon by making the sign of the cross. The story of Saint George and his conquest of the man-eating poisonous dragon goes back to the tenth century. In the eleventh-century *Life* of Saint Vigor, a Norman bishop of Bayeux, the saint is called to the town of Cerisy, which suffers from a terrible serpent. Like Margaret, Vigor overcomes the dragon with the sign of the cross and sends it back to the sea. In the earliest *Life* of Saint Gildas, this British monk saves the people of Rome from a plague by killing a dragon. Saint Siward (d.1055) was said to have fought two dragons as he made his way from his father's house in Denmark to gain several earldoms from the king of England. Some of these stories may well explain why a chair with dragon-headed finials was commissioned by a rich Englishman. A sign of evil as well as a symbol of power, the figure of the dragon could have served apotropaic functions: a malevolent beast repelling malevolent influence.

18

Bowl with Engraved Figures of Vices, 1150–1200, Germany, bronze, spun, hammered, chased, and punched; 6.05 × 28.95 cm (2 ³⁄₈ × 11 ³⁄₈ inches)

FIVE women, engraved in profile on this bronze bowl, seem almost adrift in a sea of words and ornament. At the center is a full-length figure holding mirrors in both hands. The inscription identifies her as the personification of the vice of Pride (*superbia*). Her four companions, pictured bust-length, include Idolatry (*idolatria*), represented just above Pride's head; Anger (*ira*) placed below her feet; and Envy (*invidia*) and Lust (*luxuria*) at either side. The notion of personification was dear to medieval visual culture: it allowed an idea or abstraction to be symbolized by a human being. Latin is a gendered language, and most of its abstract nouns—wisdom as well as stupidity, the New Law (the Church) as well as the Old Law (the Synagogue), the virtues as well as the vices— are of feminine gender and thus were commonly represented as women. Here, the five personifications look alike, distinguishable by inscription only. Only Pride stands out by her full size, suggesting her crucial place in the Western medieval hierarchy of sin.

Pride was not always the main villain. In the fourth century, a hermit named Evagrius (d.399) identified eight bad thoughts that were also impulses, desires, and feelings: pride was but one of many, listed alongside gluttony, lust, avarice, distress, anger, sloth, and vanity. Evagrius's disciple, John Cassian (d.435), adopted most of these, but, by exchanging sadness for distress and anxiety for sloth, emphasized their emotional nature. In the fourth century, the Christian poet Prudentius (d.c.405) wrote a highly influential work called the *Psychomachia* (*Battle of the Soul*), an allegorical poem about the battle of virtues and vices, all specifically personified as women. Here, most of the bowl's protagonists appear: at first, Faith fights Idolatry (called *Cultura Veterum Deorum*, or the Worship of Old Gods), then Chastity attacks Lust, Pride attempts to conquer Humility and Hope, and Wrath succumbs to Patience. As Faith ultimately triumphs after the last-ditch attempt by Discord, or Heresy, to wound the virtue of Concord, it is Idolatry who emerges as the main antagonist, not Pride. But when Pope Gregory the Great (d.604) systematized the vices into the scheme well known today, he made pride the "root" of all the rest, leaving seven—vanity, envy, anger, sadness, avarice, gluttony, and lust—as its evil outgrowths.

Why would Gregory make pride the chief sin? He had scriptural authority to do so. Pride is denounced in Sirach 10:15 as "the beginning of all sin: he that holdeth it, shall be filled with maledictions, and it shall ruin him in the end." Numerous early Christian theologians concurred, chief among them Saint Augustine (d.430), who held pride to be responsible for denying the divine. Instead of seeking God, Pride seeks herself: hence the pair of mirrors—here, symbols of vanity—she holds in her hands, admiring her face in one of them. In fact, these mirrors would not be out of place next to Lust, the sin of unbridled desire, of uncontrolled sexual acts, of lecherous passions; famously, in his *Inferno*, Dante committed the lustful to be forever at the whim of the tempests that are as uncontrolled as the souls that have succumbed to desire. Both Anger and Envy, the two other vices represented on the bowl, were closely linked to Lust: anger through the notion of lost control, envy through the concept of the insatiable desire to possess. Pride, too, seeks to possess, in this case her own reflection—another object of wrong-headed desire. "Mirrors," said Peter Abelard, a twelfth-century theologian, signify "those corporeal acts from which the shame and the comeliness of the soul is discerned just as the character of a human face is [seen] in a mirror." By looking into her mirror, Pride sees her own vileness—that is, the image of herself.

This is, perhaps, why Idolatry, rather than Lust, was incised directly above Pride's head. Indeed, on the bowl Idolatry subsumed many of the other familiar vices—gluttony, avarice, and sloth—that Gregory named. We might see here the echoes of *Psychomachia*, which remained popular throughout the Middle Ages and was extensively glossed—commented on—in those later centuries. But Prudentius was not the first to highlight the perils of idolatry. As early as the third century, Tertullian of Carthage called idolatry "the chief crime of mankind, the supreme guilt of the world" because, in fact, each sin "is committed within idolatry." Two centuries after the bowl was made, the great scholastic Thomas Aquinas (d.1274) would comment on idolatry as "the cause, beginning, and goal of every sin." The presence of Idolatry—the personification of improper worship, of devotion to man-made idols rather than God—unsettles and complicates the meaning of the bowl: it is an image that implicitly critiques improper use of other images.

But their proper use, at least as specific to such a vessel, remains elusive. Over 200 bronze bowls made around this time are still in existence in various shapes and sizes, the corpus visually united only by their uniformly wide, flat rims. They are composed of a variety of metal alloys, and, when decorated, are engraved with many different themes. There are bowls incised with mythological stories about Achilles or Hercules or other famous classical heroes and heroines. Some feature

Ovid's story of Pyramus and Thisbe, a pair of hapless lovers whose secret tryst by the fountain ended in the deaths of both. Other bowls retell the biblical tales of Solomon, Samson, and Susanna, while still others recount the lives of saints. Bowls with the personifications of Wisdom, Philosophy, and the Liberal Arts exist. But Vices and their opposite, Virtues, remained the most popular themes for such vessels, likely because of their moralizing meaning.

Though generally found scattered in the region of the North and Baltic Seas, almost all of the bowls were created in twelfth-century Germany. Their uses were probably as varied as their themes. Undecorated vessels were buried with the dead in the Baltic East, where Christianity was only beginning to spread. In the south of Europe, they may have taken on a liturgical function, for priests had to wash their hands before saying Mass. Some of the bowls were probably used by monks or nuns in penitential rituals. Still others may have been part of classroom settings, where many sorts of objects served as tools for teaching. If today's teachers employ a variety of visual aids and learning devices to help pupils acquire information, so in the Middle Ages school instructors used board games and leather belts, astrolabes and bowls engraved with the alphabet for similar reasons: to catch students' attention, to get them to think, and to stamp their memories. The liberal arts, which included rhetoric, were taught both at cathedral and monastic schools, which were traditional in Europe since the ninth century, and at universities, which were just coming into being in the twelfth century. We know that some students were given the task of writing poems about the tragic tale of Pyramus and Thisbe, learning the arts of poetic composition and persuasive argument in the process. A bowl designed as a diagram of the ill-fated love affair would have encouraged close study of Ovid's story and of images both. The vessel with Vices, conversely, could have spurred students to meditate on the corruption of human nature and its inclination to sin. The absence of the Virtues—the triumphant victors of Prudentius's allegory—would have made this meditation all the more potent and troubling.

19

Engaged Capital with a Lion and a Basilisk, 1175–1200, Northern Italy, Emilia (Bologna?), marble; 30.20 × 33.00 × 29.25 cm (11 $\frac{7}{8}$ × 12 $\frac{15}{16}$ × 11 $\frac{1}{2}$ inches)

T HIS deceptively lovable rooster—with its sharp beak, finely carved feathers, jagged comb, and single wattle—is no ordinary bird. Instead of tail feathers, it features a long, curved, and pointed appendage, drilled with sizable holes. It is not a rooster at all, in fact, but, as the inscription above it says, a fearsome basilisk, a hybrid beast, a cross between a rooster and a serpent—the very symbol of evil itself. Called "the king of crawling things" by medieval bestiaries (moral treatises that used animals as exemplars), the basilisk was said to be capable of slaughtering living creatures by its scent, breath, bodily vapors, gaze, and even by its smile; it could destroy vegetation and explode rocks. The seventh-century bishop Isidore of Seville claimed that the basilisk killed with a hiss. Those who were attacked but survived were made hydrophobic and driven insane. According to the ancient Roman naturalist Pliny the Elder, the poison of a basilisk was so powerful that once, when a man on horseback speared the beast, the poison went up the spear and killed both the rider and his horse. An astonishing tale from the *Gesta Romanorum*, an early fourteenth-century collection of anecdotes, told of deaths suffered by the armies of Alexander the Great near an Egyptian city where a basilisk was hidden in the walls; the monster's gaze had to be deflected by a mirror. Indeed, a mirror was one of the few defenses against the basilisk; another was a weasel that could conquer it simply through its own stench; another was a cockerel. Two hundred years after the capital was carved in the region of Bologna, Bolognese physician and scholar Niccolò Bertruccio (d.1347) claimed that any death without an obvious cause, especially in a deserted place, was caused by a basilisk.

No wonder the great scholar and bishop of Caesarea, Eusebius (d.339), conjectured that the basilisk might be the animal that tempted and seduced Eve to sin. It was symbolic of the devil, who was overcome by Christ at the Incarnation, and will be overcome again at the Last Judgment. Or so, at least, Christian theologians understood the biblical prophesies: Jeremiah 8:17 ("For behold I will send among you serpents, basilisks, against which there is no charm: and they shall bite you, saith the Lord") and Isaiah 11:8 ("And the sucking child shall play on the hole of the asp: and the weaned child shall thrust his hand into the den of the basilisk"). Together with its companion the lion—in this context, another unclean, evil

BASILISC̄

animal drawn from Psalm 91:13 ("Thou shalt walk upon the asp and the basilisk: and thou shalt trample underfoot the lion and the dragon")—the basilisk here hugs the capital of a column that once stood in a church or cloister. Its clawed foot meets the lion's paw at the corner, its beak touches the lion's mane.

Beasts like this basilisk populated monastic cloisters and church naves in great numbers. Certainly, other images were carved on the capitals as well—most notably, stories from the life of Christ and the saints—but many veritably teemed with grotesques and hybrid monsters. These lavishly decorated edifices were often built for the Cluniac order of monks—an order known as much for its political power as for its love of sumptuous building decoration. The acerbic words of Bernard (d.1153), the abbot of the monastery at Clairvaux that belonged to the rival Cistercian order, provide a withering yet obsessive description of such carvings: "in cloisters, where the brothers are reading, what is the point of this ridiculous monstrosity, this shapely misshapenness, this misshapen shapeliness? What is the point of those unclean apes, fierce lions, monstrous centaurs, half-men, striped tigers, fighting soldiers and hunters blowing their horns? In one place you see many bodies under a single head, in another several heads on a single body. Here on a quadruped we see the tail of a serpent. Over there on a fish we see the head of a quadruped." Bernard found such carvings to be not only expensive but also distracting: "so many and so marvelous are the various shapes surrounding us that it is more pleasant to read the marble than the books, and to spend the whole day marveling over these things rather than meditating on the law of God."

But the images of monsters were hardly out of place in monastic communities, for the monks were in fact engaged in a never-ending battle against sin and vice. The standard rule for monks in the West, the sixth-century *Rule of Saint Benedict*, said that every monk must renounce "his own will in order to fight for the Lord Christ." Indeed, the monks were the chief warriors in this struggle of epic proportions carried out between heaven and hell. The *Rule* ordered each monk to take up "the brilliant and mighty weapons of obedience." Prayers and works of charity offered a particularly powerful defense against the devil; the eleventh-century Cluniac monk Jotsaldus wrote that even as the demons tormented the souls of deceased sinners, they were losing their hold on many "due to the prayers of religious men and almsgiving to the poor." Hardy warriors against those demons, the Cluniac monks spent most of their daylight hours (and some hours at night as well) in prayer, which was itself a form of charity. For the monks prayed not only for themselves but also for others. They prayed for the lay benefactors and friends of the monastery; they prayed for monks elsewhere; they prayed for the kings; they prayed for all Christian believers. These were the efficacious acts by

which the souls of sinners were released to rise to heaven. In an era before purgatory was clearly defined, it was believed that souls could move from one spiritual realm to another freely and easily, with the monks oiling the heavenly elevator.

The Cluniac order and houses following the Cluniac model without technical affiliation were legion in France, far less numerous in Italy. Yet quite near Bologna, where the capital was likely made, was one important monastery of the Cluniac type: San Benedetto in Polirone. Nor was it necessary for monks to be connected with Cluny to feel part of the cosmic order that made their vocation essential to the afterlife.

Northern Italy, c. 1200.

Northern Italy in the late twelfth century was a hotbed of religious fervor. There was really no unified Italy at the time, only city-states anxious to be independent of the emperor, who was also the king of Germany. Frederick Barbarossa (d.1190) had conquered northern Italy in his quest to make good his imperial title, but the cities banded together with the help of the pope, and in 1176 Frederick was defeated. Part of the peace agreement involved setting up the Third Lateran Council in 1178, convened to address the problems of the Church. Its most pressing concern was presented by heretics.

Heretics, the council representatives said, were infesting the entire Christian community: "The loathsome heresy of those whom some call the Cathars, others the Patarenes, others the Publicani, and others by different names, has grown so strong that they no longer practice their wickedness in secret [. . .] but proclaim their error publicly and draw the simple and weak to join them." In effect, heretics were akin to venomous basilisks, their teachings spreading through the body of the Church like poison, infecting the minds of the faithful and condemning them to spiritual death. A few years later another council held at Verona specified that heretics and their supporters were to be excommunicated and handed over to the secular authorities to be punished. Thus the *inquisitio*—known later as the Inquisition—was born.

20

Leaf from a Cocharelli Treatise on the Vices, Acedia and Her
Court, c. 1330, Genoa, ink, tempera, and gold on vellum;
sheet 16.30 × 10.30 cm (6 ⅜ × 4 inches)

PROBABLY sometime before 1324, a member of the Genoese Cocharelli family
wrote a Latin treatise on the seven capital vices, followed by a poem on the
history of Sicily in the thirteenth century. Unique in its conception, the
treatise was meant for Cocharelli's children, and particularly for one son,
Johannes. Although quite small—the size of a modern paperback—the book
was sumptuously illuminated. Unfortunately, only six pages of the original
manuscript remain today, scattered among several archives. This leaf, astonishing in its detail, features Acedia, or Sloth, personified as an apathetic and
melancholy woman who refuses to leave her bed. Surrounded by all manner
of diversions, Acedia remains indifferent, reclining on the opulent divan in
her lavish chamber with its bright patterned walls and intricately woven
carpets.

Her diversions are many. There are birds of various kinds; there are
miniature dogs running around the bedcovers. Five young women along
with Johannes himself—much amused by a little bird on his finger—sit
around a gaming table playing at dice. They are wearing complex, luxuriant
textiles and jewelry, and the women's hair is carefully coiffed under bejeweled headdresses. Their surroundings are exotic, drawn from the artist's
intimate knowledge of the Islamic world and its artistic traditions: the space
of the miniature is flattened, structured as if a splendid Iranian carpet.
Genoa, where the manuscript was made, was extraordinarily prosperous,
with far-flung trade relations across both the Byzantine and Islamic worlds.
We know a bit about the Cocharelli family; it moved from France to Genoa
at the beginning of the thirteenth century and found financial success in
one of the Genoese colonies on Cyprus. Cyprus was a way station for luxury
goods from the Islamic world—decorated vessels from Syria, gold-work and
ceramics from Egypt and Iran. From there the merchandise went on to
continental Europe, not least to Genoa itself. By then, the Islamic world was
largely dominated by the Mongols who, under Chinghis (or Genghis) Khan
(d.1227) and his progeny, conquered much of the Islamic world. Those
Mongols who took over Islamic regions soon adopted the religion of their

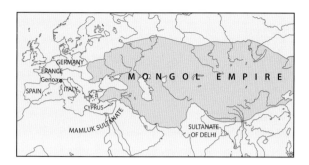

The Mongol Empire, c. 1300.

subjects. The ladies surrounding Acedia are dressed in fabrics and sit on carpets inspired by that Mongol-Islamic world.

The moral of the miniature was not to luxuriate in such splendors but to realize that the world in which Sloth lived was the very world that allowed for the massacre of the last remnant of the Crusader States when Acre was taken by the Muslims in 1291. Little Johannes, who was soon to confront that reality, was meant to learn from the picture's very temptations all the things he had to avoid to ensure his salvation. He came from a wealthy family and was expected to multiply this wealth. While in the past theologians gave prosperous people little chance of going to heaven, in the thirteenth century Franciscan and Dominican friars worked out, with the help of the logical arguments so popular in the schools of the time, a way to be rich ethically. The Dominican scholar Thomas Aquinas (d.1274), in particular, made clear how to make money—even a lot of money—honestly. As Thomas wrote in his grand compendium, *Summa Theologiae*, "Gain which is the end of trading, though not implying, by its nature, anything virtuous or necessary, does not, in itself, connote anything sinful or contrary to virtue: wherefore nothing prevents gain from being directed to some necessary or even virtuous end, and thus trading becomes lawful." Already in the thirteenth century, the idea of the "virtuous merchant" had become a tradition at Genoa, where family fortune, the common good, and Christianity were reconciled to the satisfaction of all. Cocharelli's manuscript stands as a perfect witness to this tradition.

A virtuous merchant must not be slothful, a point made clear in the folio by the various craftsmen who work within and outside the small turreted loggia at the top of the page. They provide both a contrast to the wasteful idleness below and a distraction for Sloth, who points toward the workmen with her left hand. But that, too, does not rouse her: even as she gestures at the workers, she turns away listlessly, heedless even of her male attendant, who holds a falcon released from its enormous multicolored cage. For Sloth—one of the capital vices, or seven deadly sins, as defined by the sixth-century pope Gregory the Great—was also an emotion: sadness. In Cocharelli's manuscript, Sloth is not only lethargic but dejected and forlorn. Although she presides over all, she herself has the least luxurious of garments and wears a plain bonnet, as if demonstrating by her dress her own despair. And indeed, Gregory made despair one of Sloth's "daughters." When

Aquinas considered Acedia, he called it an "oppressive sorrow," which "so weighs upon a person's mind that he or she wants to do nothing." Writing in 1333, friar preacher Domenico Cavalca claimed it was sadness that made people fall into Acedia and boredom. Incapacitated by their lethargy, they stopped "going to church and saying the usual prayers, doing charity work and other good acts." They lived "as if in despair."

In his vision of hell, purgatory, and heaven in the *Divine Comedy*, completed at roughly the same time as Cocharelli's book, Dante Alighieri describes a terrace in purgatory where he feels drowsy and can hardly walk. Behind him come a great throng of people running; "two in front were shouting in tears, 'Mary ran with haste to the hill country,' [. . .] and 'Swift, swift! let no time be lost through little love'." They are the souls of the penitent slothful, running fast to make up for their previous listlessness and recalling the model of the Virgin Mary, who ran to tell Elizabeth her good news from the angel Gabriel. They were the lucky slothful; the unlucky ones were in hell, right in the Stygian marsh. Dante's guide, Virgil, explained, drawing on the ideas of Thomas: "Down under the water are people who sigh and make it bubble at the surface, as your eye tells you wherever it turns. Fixed in the slime they say, 'We were sullen in the sweet air that is gladdened by the sun, bearing within us the sluggish fumes; now we are sullen in the black mire.' This hymn they gurgle in their throats, for they cannot speak it in full words." Their sloth and sorrow rob them of language.

To be sure, for Thomas, some sorrows were useful: sorrow for your own sins or those of others, for example, was a good sort. But even that good sorrow must not become overwhelming, lest it transform into the sinful Acedia that draws one away from the good and from God, who was the source of all good. In fact, Sloth was, according to Thomas, a "special vice" because it not only denied the good (like all the other vices) but was also the opposite of the joy of spiritual charity, which was the highest good. But was Acedia really a capital vice—a vice that led to other vices—if, rather than commit something, it withdrew itself from action? Yes, said Thomas, because those who are slothful not only shun "whatever causes sorrow," but also pass on "to other things that give pleasure." The fleshly, sensual delights that await Acedia in the Cocharelli miniature thus stand in opposition to the spiritual delights of God, and their failure to satisfy suggests the wicked kind of sorrow that overtakes the soul and damns it, finally, to Hell.

21

Miniature from a Mariegola, The Flagellation, 1359–1360, Venice, workshop of Lorenzo Veneziano, tempera and gold on parchment; sheet 29.50 × 21.00 cm (11 ⁹/₁₆ × 8 ¼ inches)

THIS gruesome scene comes from a Venetian book of statutes, a *mariegola*. It evokes the Gospel narratives that tell of Christ's Passion. Arrested and brought to the high priest of the temple, Jesus was subsequently condemned to death. With this condemnation came torture and mockery: "Then did they spit in his face, and buffeted him: and others struck his face with the palms of their hands" (Matthew 26:67). In this miniature, Christ, tied to a column and beaten with reeds, stares out directly at the viewers, engaging their gaze and their pity. Profuse streamlets of blood cascade down Christ's skin and soak his loincloth, and the fine red lines that outline his halo—the same color as blood—stand out against the golden background. Angels above lament as the two torturers, intent on their task, raise their reeds to lash Christ again and again. The use of gold for the background implies that the scene is taking place outside of ordinary time and space, and yet Christ's foot transgresses the ornate frame that surrounds the folio, bringing the torment directly into the realm of the beholders.

Mariegole were the rule books of Venetian *scuole* or "schools"—that is, guilds and lay associations. Whether organized for trades, crafts, or purely religious purposes, all Venetian *scuole* had compendia of rules, often decorated. They covered charitable works and prayers, financial obligations, the association's main purposes and laws, and various tasks assigned to its members. In Venice, five *scuole* were associations of flagellants, and one of them—the Scuola di Santa Maria de Valverde Madre de Misericordia (The *Scuola* of Saint Mary of Valverde, Mother of Mercy), founded in 1308—commissioned the miniature pictured here. The facing page depicts the Virgin Mary sheltering under her mantle a group of flagellants on their knees, their somber habits cut at the back, ready to receive the blows of their whips. The bleeding body of Christ would have served as a model for the scarred and bleeding bodies of the members of the *scuola*.

The practice of flagellation was a way to imitate Christ and do penance. As one *mariegola* put it, "miserable human beings are so continually struck by agitation, so tied by the bonds of diabolical subjection, and always so wrapped in sins that their fragility openly teaches and demonstrates how feeble and fleeting this present life is." As a mode of self-discipline and mortification, flagellation was integral to the pious Christian religious life. The monks of Cluny in twelfth-century France

were advised to beat themselves with whips (*flagelli*) to increase the value of their penance. A movement of flagellants began in Perugia in 1260: the so-called Disciplinati di Cristo. Similar groups sprang up across much of Italy, and the practice spread into France, Austria, Germany, and even the Netherlands and Poland.

New groups of flagellants spontaneously appeared in the wake of the Black Death, an outbreak of plague that devastated Europe between 1346 and 1353, with recurrences for centuries thereafter. The papacy condemned some of these for their heretical views, but flagellation itself remained a respected practice. During the years 1359–1360, when this *mariegola* was created, the Italian flagellants were organized into confraternities, regulated by the Church, and protected by the major mendicant orders. They included many different social classes and involved the pious of both sexes: the men flagellated themselves, while the women practiced acts of charity.

But the men holding whips in this *mariegola* miniature are not pious: instead of inflicting harm upon themselves in imitation of Christ, they inflict harm on Christ. They are, indeed, the very opposite of the man they torture: where he is fair, they are dark; where he faces the viewer, they look away; where he is still, they are in constant motion. One, staring at Christ fixedly from under dark furrowed brows, raises his right arm to strike, the tilt of his head a mirror image—an inversion—of Christ's. The other tormentor turns his back to the beholder and looks up at the angelic host, his arm raised as if to scatter them. While Christ wears nothing but a loincloth, his tormentors are dressed in the finest garb of the period. One sports a small purse hanging from his waist, a mocking echo of the knot that holds together Christ's loincloth. The other dons a hood that trails down his back, an accessory considered particularly stylish in the 1360s. Their exaggerated features—large noses, black curly hair, and bushy beards—mark them as the ethnically different, and so dangerous, Other.

Such ethnic and economic "otherness" suggests, in part, an anti-Semitic sentiment. This was certainly the case with some flagellant groups, who blamed the Jews for the Black Death epidemic. By the middle of the fourteenth century the Jews, barred in many parts of Europe from all professions except money-lending, became firmly associated with usury and so with wealth gained iniquitously. When Venice found itself in financial straits, the city often borrowed money from the Jews, who offered their loans at fixed rates controlled by the city. Popular hostility against usury was exacerbated in Italy due to the preaching of the Franciscan friars, who called usury a grave stain on the purity of the faith.

The order's founder, Saint Francis (d.1226), was the son of a wealthy cloth merchant in the Italian town of Assisi. Taking Christ's admonition that "it is easier

for a camel to pass through the eye of a needle than for a rich man to enter the kingdom of God" (Matthew 19:24), Francis stripped himself naked and vowed thenceforth to follow a life of poverty, begging for his food and lodging. In 1224, he received the stigmata—the five wounds of the crucified Christ—and thereafter increasingly suffered pain throughout his body. His followers, the Franciscans, practiced flagellation and praised its penitential benefits. Just as Francis himself imitated Christ, so the flagellants of Venice, as elsewhere, took Christ's physical suffering and poverty as their model. It is no accident that on the page facing the Flagellation scene, they huddle under the mantle of the Virgin in garb that contrasts starkly with the fancy clothes worn by Christ's persecutors.

Venice was particularly sensitive to the moral issues that riches posed. In the thirteenth century, at the bidding of the city, the Fourth Crusade captured Constantinople, and Venice benefited not only from the extraordinary plunder it amassed but also from its control over part of Constantinople itself as well as crucial territories along the Adriatic coast, Negroponte, and Crete. Its economic hegemony was threatened only by Genoa. Throughout the fourteenth century the two cities fought one another and, not long after the Flagellation scene was painted, Venice

Venetian territories, c. 1400.

essentially destroyed its rival in the War of Chioggia (1378–1381). The city was, in effect, a vast emporium, with its government in the hands of the moneyed and its state-regulated merchant ships plying the entire Mediterranean Sea. Gold, silver, pepper, wool, spices, cotton, sugar, and slaves passed through the Venetian ports, and plenty of people there got very wealthy indeed. But for that they paid a moral price, and the *mariegola* illumination serves as a potent commentary on the dangers of financial prosperity, pitting Christ—the very embodiment of poverty—against his richly attired persecutors. It is ironic, then, that this miniature, which implicitly condemns the evils of wealth, is itself unabashedly and conspicuously lavish, unfolding the Flagellation drama against the sumptuous background of gold leaf.

22

The Madonna of Humility with the Temptation of Eve, c. 1400, Italy, tempera and gold on wood panel; framed 191.50 × 99.00 × 11.00 cm (75 ³⁄₈ × 38 ¹⁵⁄₁₆ × 4 ⁵⁄₁₆ inches)

T HREE women dominate this unsettling altarpiece, two of them tucked away in the darkness at the bottom of the panel. At the center, aglow in light, is the Virgin. At her feet is the moon, above is the sun, and her own halo radiates twelve more sunbursts, with Christ's apostles painted within. Here, then, Mary appears in her guise as the Woman of the Apocalypse, an identification made by a wide range of exegetical and devotional texts. Because in the Book of Revelation the Woman of the Apocalypse is attacked by Satan in the form of a dragon, two dragon-slayers—Saint George and Saint Michael—stand at the Virgin's left. Angel Gabriel kneels before her on the other side. Mary, often depicted enthroned, is here shown as the Madonna of Humility, atop a pillow placed directly on the ground. Her Child turns to the beholder, his mother's breast clasped firmly in his left hand, the nipple between his lips. He is drinking the milk of salvation.

Separated from them by a thick golden band is another woman, a mirror image of the first, or rather an inversion. Her facial features and wavy hair are just like the Virgin's; her right breast is exposed as well. This is Eve, the first woman, and one who, according to the Judeo-Christian tradition, brought death into the world. She is the antithesis of Mary: almost naked rather than dressed, reclining in tomb-like darkness rather than sitting in the radiant light, holding the fruit of damnation. It was not unusual to link Eve and Mary as utter opposites: the Latin AVE, the "Hail" with which Gabriel greeted the Virgin when announcing her pregnancy with Christ (in Luke 1:26–38), was often paired with EVA, Eve's name in Latin. The inverted letters signified the way in which Mary reversed Eve's original sin. Bound by brown vines, seemingly pinned down by the animal skin wrapped around her waist, quite literally rooted to the ground by a small tree that rises before and through her, Eve looks up at Mary with a mixture of regret and defiance. Just as the Virgin is chaste and modest, so is Eve unabashedly sexy: the soft curves of her body and the suppleness of her skin are lovingly rendered, as are her golden locks, one of which outlines her right shoulder and breast.

Eve's inappropriate sexuality is underscored by the tree—the Tree of Knowledge—that grows upward between her thighs. Coiled around this desic-cated tree is the serpent: the evil temptress. It is yet another likeness of Mary and Eve: its thick twisting body ends with a woman's head crowned by the already-

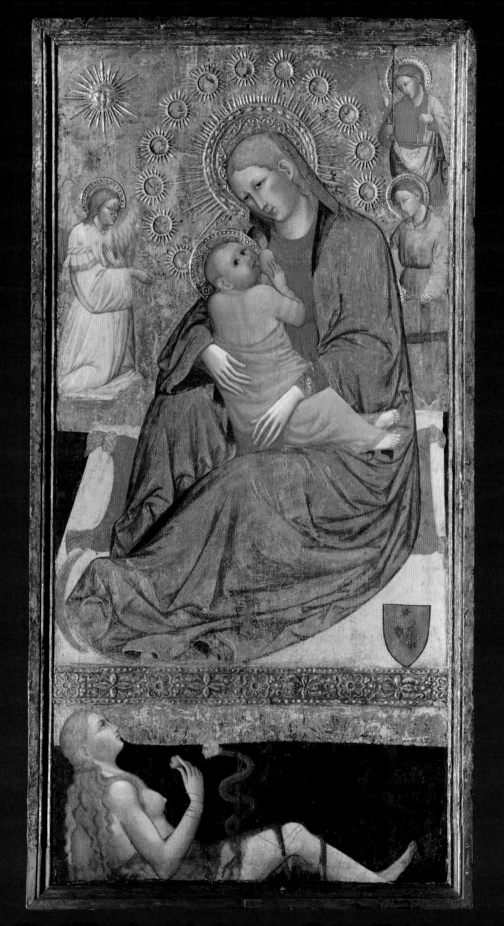

familiar golden hair. Together with Eve, the serpent is confined to the darkness of the lower part of the panel, a potent reminder that although she may look like the Virgin, she belongs in Eve's realm. Devotional panels that feature the Virgin and Child were produced in Italy throughout the Middle Ages, but this altarpiece's focus on Eve is unusual. By virtue of the painting's placement on the altar, Eve was positioned in the closest proximity to the worshipers in the church. That the viewers had a visceral and violent reaction to the panel is amply witnessed by the severe damage that the serpent's human head and Eve's wrist sustained at some point in the painting's existence: intentional damage, no doubt, an attack on the wicked and the immoral, the root of all human sin.

The identity of the painter is uncertain; the altarpiece was formerly attributed to one Carlo da Camerino, but the very existence of such a painter has been cast into serious doubt. A more likely contender is Olivuccio di Ceccarello (d.1439), born in Camerino and active in Ancona. The patron's name is more certain: a heraldic shield poised on the decorative band that separates the women reveals him to be friar Agostino Rogeroli, who may have commissioned the piece for the church of Sant'Agostino at Fermo, along with a precious reliquary.

The disquiet that pervades the altarpiece gestures to the turbulent internal confrontations that shook northern Italian cities since the eleventh century. The most famous of them was between the Guelfs, nominally the supporters of the papacy, and the Ghibellines, nominally partisans of the emperor (who was also king of Germany). The Italian Marche, the region in which the altarpiece was made, was claimed by the papacy, but around 1400 there were *two* popes, both claiming the other to be false.

The underlying cause of the Great Western Schism (as historians dub it) was the rising power of the French crown. But the immediate cause was the legacy of the Avignon papacy: from 1309 to 1377, the popes resided at Avignon, a city in Provence then ruled by the house of Naples but in fact largely controlled by the king of France. The scandal was felt most keenly by Italians. The celebrated poet Petrarch

North-central Italy, c. 1400.

(d.1374) famously called the Avignon Papacy the "Babylonian Captivity," making reference to 2 Kings 25:11, which recorded the captivity of the ancient Hebrews by

Nebuchadnezzar, king of Babylon. The outcry grew deafening enough for Pope Gregory XI (1370–1378) to return to Rome in 1377. But his successor, Urban VI (1378–1389), was chosen under the pressure of a "Roman mob," as the accounts would have it, and soon the French cardinals elected the man known to history as Antipope Clement VII, who eventually fled to Avignon. The two popes fought wars against one another and their supporters, as did their successors.

In this tense situation, the cities of Marche tried to maintain a certain independence, but without much success. The Malatesta family, which came to power in Rimini in the mid-fourteenth century, took over several other cities in the region. In 1353, Pope Innocent VI (1352–1362) sent his legate, Cardinal Albornoz, to Marche with an army, and by 1355 the papacy had excommunicated the Malatesta and retaken many of the cities. Soon Albornoz drew up an official document—the *Constitutions of the Holy Mother Church*—that reorganized the papal states under the administration of the papacy. Even so, some of the cities were granted a measure of independence under their own communal government. The situation at Ancona, where the altarpiece was probably painted, was typical: although ruled by their local communal statutes, the citizens were staunchly behind the "official" pope at Rome. When, in the early fifteenth century, the Malatesta and the Sforza family of Milan tried to conquer the city, the citizens soundly defeated them.

The specter of calamity is keenly felt in many visual and literary sources from the turn of the fifteenth century. A particularly poignant example is found in a Venetian convent chronicle penned by Bartolomea Riccoboni. She reported that the nuns' allegiances were divided between the two popes, and they feared damnation should they accidentally make the wrong choice. Bartolomea tried to calm their fears, claiming that their "consciences remained unblemished and untroubled by any vexing pricks, because both of the parties acted with good intentions." The altarpiece similarly suggests both tension and hope. The serpent stares at Eve, as if willing her to take a bite of the apple; Eve, her profile highlighted against the golden band, looks up at the Virgin; the Virgin gazes out of the panel at the beholder, whose own gaze is brought back to the serpent—a viewing dynamic that implicates the audience in the narrative of humanity's Fall. But it also allows them to gain, "with good intentions," the protection of the Virgin and her son.

23

Zebo (Zecho) da Firenze, Grotesques from the Hours of Charles the Noble, c. 1404, France, folio 22, ink, tempera, and gold on vellum; codex 20.32 × 15.71 × 6.98 cm (8 × 6 ⅛ × 2 ¹¹⁄₁₆ inches)

Mediaeval monsters, anthropomorphic and bestial, were thought to live in extreme geographical loci—on the edges of the known world, in Africa, India, and Ethiopia. Monstrous races—the hairy mouthless Astomi, Panotii with giant ears, the dog-headed Cynocephali, Blemmyae with faces on their chests, web-footed Sciopods—all inhabited the far sides of medieval maps. Animal–human hybrids were found in every direction: the famous Hereford *mappa mundi*, the largest of its kind, includes a sphinx and a centaur, a stork-person and a cynocephalus. At the center was Jerusalem, the holy city; the deformed lurked in the terrifying margins. Their distance from Jerusalem also implied their distance from humanity, morality, and the goodness of the sacred; they were liminal creatures, chimeras physically and spiritually. Monsters lived on the periphery of the world and Christianity both.

And yet they insistently appeared close to home as well. Carved monsters cavorted on column capitals on the edges of the cloisters, stone chimeras dotted the exteriors of churches. They haunted the naves of monastic churches and sat on the finials of monastic and church choir stalls. Demons were thought to enter homes and bodies through marginal, threshold spaces: doors, windows, mouths. Hybrid creatures inhabited corners of ivory mirrors, borders of stained glass windows, and, most riotously, the margins of illuminated books.

So it is with this Book of Hours—a devotional book that belonged to the French-born Navarrese king Charles the Noble (d.1425). At the center of this folio is part of the calendar for November, recording major feast days as well as local saints' days. This is the space of holiness, populated with the names of various saints written in alternating blue and red: among them are Saint Cecilia and Saint Vitalis, Saint Genevieve and Saint Fauste. Some of the most important names—those of Andrew, Catherine, and Clement—are here written out in gold. In the first column are Roman numerals called "Golden Numbers," and in the second column are Dominical letters (the seven letters A through G standing for the days of the week); together they were used to calculate the dates of movable feasts, most importantly Easter. "A" appears as a capital letter to help mark the sequence. The third column contains Roman calendrical dates: here, all are Kalends, or the

ix.	e	kl'	sainte fauste.
	f	kl'	saint aignien
xbi	g	kl'	saint mondain
vj.	A	kl'	saint emon.
	b	kl'	saint seurin.
xiiij	c	kl'	saint columbain.
iij	d	kl'	sainte cecille
	e	kl'	saint climent
xi.	f	kl'	saint grisogone.
xix.	g	kl'	sainte katherine.
	A	kl'	sainte geneuieue
vuj	b	kl'	saint uital.
	c	kl'	saint russin. S
xbi	d	kl'	Vigille.
v	e	kl'	saint andrieu.

first of the month. Enclosed by magnificent vines filled with flowers, birds, and butterflies, the saints' names are nestled cozily at the center of a protected world.

But among the vines, at the margins of this sacred space, are two hybrid creatures, one flying and another galloping in dangerous proximity to this safe enclosure. Opposite the names of Saints Cecilia and Catherine is a green dragon, his head that of an old man wearing a flaccid red headdress. Likened to the devil, dragons were believed to lie in wait for their victims and drain them of blood upon attack. While the dragon's body turns inward, its head looks outward and away from the center of the page, mimicking the bird perched above. In the lower margin, charging among the vines, is a centaur-like beast with a pink lower body, holding a shield and a spear. Mid-gallop, he turns away from the beholder, his red attire flapping in the wind, his blue hat obscuring his head. This hybrid is surely a reference to the Zodiac sign of Sagittarius that appears on the preceding folio, although that Sagittarius is a much more benevolent creature, whose face, framed with golden locks, is visible to the viewer. This beast, in full tilt yet jousting with nothing at all, might also be read as a parody of knightly sport, for centaurs were known for their hypocrisy. Indeed, monsters often functioned as anti-models: cynocephali, according to medieval moralizers, were sowers of discord, while the giants were symbolic of excessive pride. Didactic interpretations of the monstrous were found in all kinds of literature, from various encyclopedias to works on natural philosophy. The consensus of the experts was clear. Monsters were liars, backstabbers, cannibals, deceivers; margins were a fitting place for them.

Books of Hours were meant to accompany their owners throughout the day. Most of their pages did not offer lists of saints, but rather contained the prayers— or reminders of the prayers—that pious laypeople were supposed to repeat daily. The idea was borrowed from the monastic world: the sixth-century Benedictine Rule specified that monks were to chant the "Divine Offices" seven times a day and once at night. As lay piety deepened in the course of the Middle Ages, and as the friars preached the Gospel to townspeople, laymen and laywomen became increasingly keen to incorporate active forms of piety into their own daily habits, even as they married, had children, and went about their ordinary daily tasks. The echo of the monastery in their lives remained not only in the prayers in their devotional books, but also in the way these books were decorated. Saint Bernard famously railed against the "monsters" that the monks gazed at in church and in cloister; but those very monsters adorned, as here, the margins of Books of Hours, offering diversion, a sober reminder of the fragility of virtue, and a taste of the exotic and the transgressive.

For this Book of Hours, at least three artists worked on the margins. One—the man who painted the grotesques on folio 22 pictured here—was Zebo da Firenze, who even signed one of his pages (some read this signature as "Zecho"). Zebo's grotesques are elegant and graceful, fitting neatly into the vine scrolls among equally elegant birds and flowers. In general, in late medieval art monsters become more tame. By the time Zebo was painting, they had been transformed from alien sinners into objects of fascination, their exoticism played up in treatises on travels or world marvels read by lay rather than monastic audiences. This book, too, was made for a lay reader, and not even a specific one. Just as the "pious life" was no longer confined to the cloister, neither was literacy. The result was that by the fifteenth century, manuscript production was often in the hands of entrepreneurs who opened up shops and catered to rich lay customers. Charles did not commission the manuscript, but rather purchased it ready-made from a Parisian book seller. The illuminators reserved room for the buyer to add his or her coat of arms at the bottom of twenty-four pages, and Charles took full advantage of the opportunity, advertising his ownership.

Previously considered to be incomprehensible and occasionally embarrassing doodles that marred sacred texts, medieval margins can be seen as a potent commentary on the central texts and images. Originally, these images ranged widely in content—from mundane scenes to scatological acts, from animals impersonating human beings to hybrid monsters such as the ones on this folio—at times expanding and reinforcing the meaning of the center, at times putting it on its head. But Zebo's images suggest new meanings for the marginal figures: he tended to depict genre scenes, such as a peasant warming his feet by a hearth; landscapes; and miniatures of sacred moments, especially in the life of the Virgin. On this page, Zebo's lively interest in nature is evidenced by the butterflies and the birds nestled among flowers and vines. This was a sign of the times: by the fifteenth century, margins were beginning to empty of monstrous hybrids, giving way to the illusionistic borders and architectural frames that enclosed and revealed the image within, but no longer played with or subverted it.

24

Günther Zainer, The Virgin Mary Overcoming a Devil, from *Speculum Humanae Salvationis/Spiegel menschlicher Behältnis*, c. 1473, Germany, Augsburg, hand-colored woodcut; 7.4 × 12.0 cm (2 $^{15}/_{16}$ × 4 $^{3}/_{4}$ inches)

T HIS woodcut comes from an incunabulum—an early printed book—that contained the German version of the *Speculum Humanae Salvationis* (*Mirror of Human Salvation*). The art of printing was then in its infancy, and the nineteenth-century term "incunabulum" reflects just that, referring to the swaddling clothes and cradle of a baby. On this page, the text begins in Latin, invoking the moment when Simeon blessed the Virgin Mary and her Child, telling her that Christ will be the cause of the rise and the fall of many, "and a sword will pierce your soul as well" (Luke 2:35). Then it continues in German, explaining the conquest of the devil, "our enemy," by Mary and her son. The image, which represents Mary as a warrior trampling the devil underfoot, comes from a chapter that compares Mary and Christ: just as Christ defeated the devil and redeemed mankind through his Passion, so the Virgin continues to save mankind from Satan through her compassion. The devil, with his skull-like head, hoofed feet, and curling tail, is here a sinister mixture of a man, a demon, and a wild animal. As formidable a foe as he may have been, Mary proves to be stronger, striking at his body with the cross and the lance. Both are the so-called *arma Christi*: the instruments or, more literally, the weapons of Christ's Passion, associated with his torture and death. Other *arma* float around the Virgin: the column of the Flagellation, the flail, reeds, and whip; the pincers, crown of thorns, and dice; and a hand tugging at Christ's hair or beard. These are the munitions of the devout, the arms of the pious Christian.

The devil's appearance in this woodcut is fairly typical for the late Middle Ages, but his form had fluctuated greatly over time. The fallen angel who defied God, Satan—or Beelzebub, or Lucifer, whose name means "light"—was not always the deformed creature here crushed by the Virgin. Indeed, the blue angel who appears on Christ's left side in the sixth-century mosaic of Sant'Apollinare Nuovo in Ravenna, might represent Satan since the scene prefigures the Last Judgment and the separation of the blessed (on Christ's right) from the damned (on his left). But already in the illustrated dream-vision of Barontus, drawn in the late seventh century, the demon, while sporting a man's body, has flaming hair and claws for feet. By the eleventh century, when Satan and his minor devils began to

Maria p̃ ꝯpaſſionem vint aduerſariũ nm̃ dpablm̃
portans crucem ꝗ omnia ſigna xp̃i. Crlſo·ꝗ alij todo
res ſup illo verbo Sym̃onis· Et tuam ipius animã
ptranſibit gladius· Lu·ij·   Maria durch ir mutter
lich mitleyten mit irem Sun uberwand ſy vnſern
veindt den teuffel· tragendt mit dem herren dz kreücz
vnd alle ſeyne waffen·

appear above the portals of Romanesque churches, the demonic horde acquired
distinctly bestial, monstrous characteristics. For example, on the tympanum above
the portal of the twelfth-century church of Saint-Lazare in Autun, France, the
devils are deformed, emaciated beings with distended faces and gaping mouths.

In Giotto's Last Judgment fresco in the Scrovegni chapel at Padua, Italy, Satan—blue, enormous, puffy, and horned—devours sinners at the same time as he defecates them. One person half disappears into the monster's mouth, his legs still hanging out; another emerges head first between the devil's legs; still others are clutched in his hands like limp dolls, awaiting their terrifying turn.

In the later Middle Ages, the nature of Satan was much discussed by Dominican and Franciscan scholars. For the Dominican friar Thomas Aquinas (d.1274), the devil's sin was not the everyday sort, such as fornication or drunkenness. Rather, it was pride and envy. Thomas quoted Augustine: "inflated with pride [the devil] wished to be called God." Once Lucifer sinned, he induced some of the others angels to sin as well "by a kind of exhortation." The punishment for their sins was hell, with its "darksome atmosphere." Theologians started to develop the "science" of demonology in the fourteenth century. In the late 1430s witch hunts began, their early victims largely men. Although the witch craze did not gain full momentum until the next two centuries, the late Middle Ages did produce a classic manual, *Malleus Maleficarum* (*The Hammer of Witches*), penned in 1486 by two German Dominicans, Heinrich Kramer and Jacob Sprenger. Witches, according to them, were everywhere, ripe to be apprehended, interrogated, and convicted.

The Church itself paved the way for the obsession with all things demonic as early as the thirteenth century. Already in 1215, the Fourth Lateran Council outlined the role of the devil in Christian theology: "The devil and the other demons were indeed created by God good by nature but they became bad through themselves; man, however, sinned at the suggestion of the devil." The council then made clear what strict observances Christians were to practice to avoid "eternal punishment with the devil." It declared "excommunicated"—cut off from the Church and its salvific grace—"every heresy that raises against the holy, orthodox and Catholic faith which we have above explained; condemning all heretics under whatever names they may be known, for while they have different faces they are nevertheless bound to each other by their tails, since in all of them vanity is a common element." Vanity was thus metaphorically refashioned into a demonic attribute. The same council set up the machinery that in time would come to be known as the Inquisition. A century later, in 1320, John XXII had a special commission determine whether magic "and the invocation of the devil" should be considered heretical. Indeed, the authors of *Malleus Maleficarum* were inquisitors for the Church.

The *Mirror of Human Salvation* was compiled in the fourteenth century. Its popularity is clear from the great number of manuscripts and printed books that

contain its texts (and almost always images), and by the fact that translations from Latin were made into English, French, German, Dutch, and Czech. It contained a mix of elements. Apart from biblical quotes, it incorporated commentaries by such illustrious scholars as Peter Comestor, Jacobus de Voragine, and Thomas Aquinas. It also drew heavily on the Apocrypha. *Mirrors* were organized to show how the events of the Hebrew Bible were "reflected" or "mirrored"—and given their full meaning—in the New Testament. The image of the Virgin conquering the devil, for example, was paired with scenes of Judith decapitating Holofernes, Jael piercing Sisera's temples, and Queen Thamarys beheading King Cyrus. The prologue of the book explained that the text was to be used by the learned, but the images were to edify the ignorant. This referred to Pope Gregory the Great's famous dictum from the sixth century that pictures are the books of the illiterate.

Originally, the *Mirror of Human Salvation* was conceived as a preaching aid for pastoral care, providing ready narratives to include in sermons. The passage in German here was very likely meant to be used in a popular homily. While in the earlier Middle Ages sermons were the prerogative of bishops and were offered mainly during church services, the increasing piety of laypeople in the course of the Middle Ages led to a demand to hear the word of God more often, even on the streets of the towns. The Franciscans and Dominicans, among others, were authorized to preach in the vernacular, although they were trained in Latin by university professors of their orders. Even heretics took to the streets, despite the threat of persecution. Townspeople eagerly awaited the arrival of wandering preachers; they set up stages for the sermonizer and positioned themselves in the direction of the wind to best hear his (and occasionally her) words. Some preachers were famous for speaking for days and inciting the crowds to throw their gaming paraphernalia and extravagant clothing into a bonfire—an act of contrition and a compelling spectacle also meant, in their own way, to conquer the devil.

25

Demon in Chains, illustrated single page manuscript, c. 1453, style of Muhammad Siyah Qalam (Iran?), opaque watercolor and gold on paper; 25.70 × 34.40 cm (10 ¹⁄₁₆ × 13 ½ inches)

Two ferocious-looking people, a man and a woman, flank a demon—a *div* in Persian, *jinn* in Arabic—who is secured by a chain. The man wears a tasseled hat with a rosette, knee-length trousers, a long-sleeved jacket, and soft shoes. He holds one end of the chain in his right hand and raises his left arm as if to strike the demon with his club. The whites of his eyes, and his light gray beard and moustache, gleam against his dark skin. The woman, on the other side of the demon, appears to be a hybrid, half-human and half-animal, her physiognomy not much less grotesque than that of the *div* she has captured. She holds a length of the chain in both hands, raising it close to her face and particularly her mouth, as if to examine it or even gnaw at it. Her long, narrow red mouth with pale lips echoes her eyes: the red of the irises and the white of the sclera. Dressed in a long cloak and dark red scarf, she nonetheless remains barefoot, and her feet have huge toenails, just like the demon's. The demon himself towers above his captors, with the chain part of a gold ring encircling his neck, and with other rings around his forearms and ankles. Nude except for a short skirt, he turns his great fleshy head toward the man. His crescent-shaped eyes express deep grief, his fanged mouth is downturned, his face lined with wrinkles; the pointed ears, deer-like horns, a trunk-like protrusion extending down from his chin, and the long tail wrapped around his right leg leave no doubt about the monstrous identity of the captive.

The painting comes from one of two albums formerly owned by the early Ottoman sultans and now in the Topkapı Palace library in Istanbul. Sixty-five of the paintings and drawings were later inscribed with the name Muhammad Siyah Qalam, or Muhammad Black Pen. Perhaps the name refers to one artist, or perhaps it was a sobriquet for a group of them. The albums themselves are a miscellany and contain images that hark back to a wide variety of styles, showing Persian, Mongolian, and Chinese sources alike. No textual parallels exist for these images, which appear to be independent creations—neither parts of a particular manuscript nor illustrations of a recognizable story. Siyah Qalam mainly painted demons, monsters, dervishes, shamans, and so-called "nomads" or "wanderers" (also variously identified as Kipchaks, Russians, Mongols, and Turks). The images are dominated by dark colors and heavy lines and feature highly animated figures set against blank ground on unsized, unpolished paper, and painted in a limited

range of colors. This is precisely the style of this painting, which, however, does not bear the artist's name.

Miscellanies like the Istanbul albums are not as curious as they seem. In the thirteenth century, under the leadership of Chinghis (or Genghis) Khan (d.1227), various tribes in Mongolia came together to create the largest contiguous empire ever known. Conquering China by 1279 and southern Rus' (from today's Kazakhstan through Ukraine) in the 1230s, the Mongols proceeded on to Poland and Hungary, where they finally stopped. Another branch of the Mongols took over the Islamic world, moving across Iran all the way into Anatolia (Turkey) and

Iraq. Only the Mamluks of Egypt halted their westward push. Violent and sudden as the Mongol drive was, it ultimately opened up lively trade and travel routes between the west and far east. When the Mongols began to rule in China, they brought with them Muslim artists and craftsmen, who both adopted and transformed Chinese motifs. While the Chinese branch of the Mongol Empire ended c. 1350 with the Ming dynasty, Iran remained under Mongol rule—the Timurids, heirs of Timur the Lame or Tamerlane (d.1405)—until the beginning of the sixteenth century.

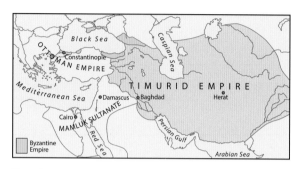

Eurasia, c. 1400.

Venetian and Genoese traders made it their business to frequent the region, which was enormously prosperous. Already by the early fourteenth century the Iranian Mongol rulers had converted to Islam. The art that they and their contemporary elites supported drew on the traditions of the whole Eurasian continent. The arts also flourished in the late fourteenth and fifteenth centuries under the rule of the Timurids, known for their architecture, metalwork, and especially for their astonishing book production that included enormous Qur'an manuscripts, historical chronicles, and collections of fables and poems. Among these manuscripts are sumptuous versions of *Kalila wa Dimna*, a cycle of fables that originated in India; the tenth-century Ferdowsi's mytho-historical epic *Shahnameh*; and Nizami Ganjavi's poetic masterpiece *Khamsa*. Some of the finest workshops were located in Herat. It was perhaps there or in nearby Central Asia that the demon in chains was painted.

Demons hold pride of place in the medieval Islamic imaginary, and they became a particularly popular subject matter in painting in the later Middle Ages. The ideas about these supernatural creatures were inherited from pre-Islamic Persia—where the *div* could be not only a demon but also a giant and sometimes even Satan himself—and Arabia, where the demons were believed to have been shapeless and invisible. Islamic demonology of the era described two sorts of angels: the loyal ones who guided people to God, and the disobedient, who seduced them away. The fallen angels married human women, producing children knowledgeable in sorcery. Somewhere between the good and the evil spirits were the Peris; beautiful and beneficent, akin to the "fairies" of European folklore, they

could be fierce and change form, to look like monsters and demons. Their main enemies were the true demons, the *divs*, as well as sorcerers and witches, who contained them within magic circles and chained them up. The origin of *divs* was not always clear; Persian philosopher al-Razi (d.925) conjectured that evil spirits, or the souls of the wicked, turn into demons.

But the *jinns* were not just folk inventions or subjects of philosophical meditation; they are mentioned throughout the Qur'an, and an entire sura, or chapter, is dedicated to them. There the *jinns* are allowed to speak for themselves:

"We have indeed heard a Qur'an wonderful, / guiding to rectitude. We believe in it, [...] / And we stretched towards heaven, but we found it filled with terrible guards and meteors. / [...] And some of us have surrendered, and some of us have deviated. Those who have surrendered sought rectitude; / but as for those who have deviated, they have become firewood for Gehenna!" (Sura "The Jinn" [72]: 1–2, 8, 14–15)

Demonic presence is striking in manuscripts that recount the Prophet Muhammad's mystical journey to hell, or Jahannam (derived from the Hebrew word *Gehenna*). The Qur'an describes the blazing fires and boiling waters, the smoke and the winds of hell, which is composed of seven levels. At times, the place is styled as if a living monster: also called "the Crusher" (*al-hutama*), it sighs and speaks. Hadith, the gathering of the Prophet Muhammad's sayings and teachings, elaborates on Jahannam's punishments, and mentions a section of it that is freezing cold rather than hot. Further taxonomy of hell's environment and punishments comes from a variety of the so-called eschatological manuals. Jahannam, the complete opposite of al-Janna, the garden of paradise, was seen as the post-Judgment destination for sinful people and *jinns* alike. The wicked *jinns* will be the first to enter Jahannam and will be relegated to its lowest level— the most terrifying one of all. There, these naturally fiery creatures will be fettered together by chains and, some commentators suggest, will be punished by extreme cold. Chief among them will be Iblis—the fallen angel, Satan himself.

PART III

Daily Life and Its Fictions

26

S-Shaped Fibula, sixth century, Frankish, silver with garnets; 2.20 × 2.80 × 0.80 cm ($^{13}/_{16}$ × 1 $^{1}/_{16}$ × $^{5}/_{16}$ inches)

T HIS small fibula, or brooch, gleams with garnets contrasted with matte silver. Seemingly an exercise in abstraction—two circles, two triangles, one square, all linked by striated metal grooves—the fibula is actually zoomorphic in nature. Its sinuous shape, arranged around a symmetrical axis, is formed by two birds, their beaks curving outward from the round garnets that serve as their heads. The fibula is created in the cloisonné technique: thin compartments are soldered on top of a metal base to form discrete cells that are then filled with precious or semi-precious stones or a glass paste and subsequently fired. Sometimes the cells were lined with gold foil so that the stones on top would shine even more luminously. Garnets were particularly prized, not only for their aesthetic but also for their apotropaic and healing powers. Men and women in the sixth century wore such pins during their lives and were sometimes buried with them as well.

This fibula is associated with "the Franks," a name that came to be attached to one of the many peoples whom the Romans called "barbarians." But similar jewelry—animal-shaped and richly ornamented polychrome brooches, buckles, sword-hilts, hairpins, necklaces—was popular among many different early medieval groups living north and east of the Danube and Rhine rivers. Amorphous groups at first, which dissolved and came together in new ways in the course of the centuries, they were organized under kings and took on the structure of tribes under the pressure of the Romans, who wanted to trade and treat with them. In turn, the barbarians wanted to emulate the Romans. Slowly, they took on names: the Lombards, the Goths (later divided into Ostrogoths and Visigoths), the Avars, the Franks. These names did not signify biological ethnicities: rather, their tribal names, along with their clothing, jewelry, and hairstyles, were ways for them to assert their particular cultural identities.

In the fourth century, the barbarians were sometimes enemies and at other times allies of the Romans. Many of them fought in the Roman army. In fact, by the end of that century whole tribes were incorporated into Roman units, fighting as "federates" of the Romans. That peaceful accommodation fell apart when the Huns—Turkic-speaking nomads from the steppes of west-central Asia—entered the Black Sea region and caused the Visigoths to petition Emperor Valens (d.378) to let them settle within the borders of the Empire. Valens agreed, but the Goths

overwhelmed Roman resources; resentments grew on both sides, and in 378 the Goths turned on the Romans, defeated the imperial army, and began a long march through the western half of the Empire. That date is taken by some historians as the "end" of the Roman Empire; others adopt 410, when the Visigoths sacked Rome. Other barbarian tribes followed in the wake of the Visigoths, and by the 500s, when this fibula was made, much of the western half of the Roman Empire was composed of barbarian kingdoms. But at the time no one spoke of the end of Rome, and indeed the eastern half of the Empire continued to call itself Roman until the Ottomans toppled it in 1453.

Barbarian successor kingdoms, c. 500.

The tribes prized portability in their material culture, and precious items possessed during life were often buried with their owners upon their deaths. Such burials serve as potent reminders of daily life: one anonymous tomb in Normandy, dating to the sixth or seventh century, was clearly the grave of a craftsman. It contained tools useful for a jeweler and a smithy—hammers, chisels, a balance, whetstones—and raw materials, including two pieces of glass, coins to be melted down and reused, and a vial of mercury, used in the gilding process. Childeric (d.481/482), the last Frankish king to die a pagan, was buried with, among other jewelry, his own royal signet ring, a gilded silver bracelet, and a cruciform fibula of a type worn by high Roman officials on their right shoulder. The great Anglo-Saxon poem *Beowulf*, set in the sixth century, describes the lure of such buried treasure, the woes it might bring, and the ultimate futility of possessing it. The theft of a golden cup from a dragon's lair provokes the beast's rage and causes him to destroy the land with fire; Beowulf, the hero, defeats the dragon but is mortally wounded in battle. Much of his treasure is interred with him: "And they buried torques in the barrow, and jewels / and a trove of such things as trespassing men / had once dared to drag from the hoard. / They let the ground keep that ancestral treasure, / gold under gravel, gone to earth, / as useless to men now as it ever was."

"Franks" in the 500s meant Gallo-Romans as well as tribesmen of Frankish origin—insofar as such distinctions held any longer. By then the Franks had converted to Christianity, a transformation generally credited to Childeric's son

Clovis (d.511). In fact, most of the barbarians who entered the empire were already Christian, although many had adopted Arian Christianity, a variant that viewed Christ as subordinate to the Father and that was therefore considered heretical by the Romans. The Franks, too, may have flirted with Arianism, but by the sixth century, they were Roman Catholic. Bishops presided over their flocks in the hulks of former Roman cities, and the tombs of saints and martyrs in the countryside served as focal points for pious pilgrimages. Objects like brooches began appearing in ecclesiastical treasuries, offered as gifts and endowments. Their styles came to influence Christian art production—reliquaries and especially Insular gospel books created in and after the seventh century. These manuscripts were given to abstraction and vivid palettes, haunted by geometric and zoomorphic motifs, their luscious pages drowning in a profusion of ornament. Bird-shaped fibulae, in particular, found their visual echoes in the image of Saint John, whose symbol was an eagle.

The fibula shown here may have been produced in a city such as Trier, at a princely court, or in the countryside. Frankish laws suggest a largely rural society. One of the law codes, the *Pactus Legis Salicae* (drawn up around 500 by Clovis) begins with penalties for the theft of pigs, cattle, sheep, goats, dogs, birds, and bees, and then turns to "damage to a cultivated field or some other enclosure." While it does not mention brooches, this law code does have a penalty for the person who "steals a woman's belt." Although we do not know who made this fibula, we do know the name of one seventh-century jeweler: Eligius. He became a royal courtier, then a bishop, and eventually a saint. The garnets used in much of his and other jewelry came from southwest Bohemia and were cut and mounted by a variety of production centers. Indeed, precious fibulae retained their currency for hundreds of years: even in the ninth century, Charlemagne (d.814), king of the Franks and crowned emperor by the pope, was described by one biographer, Einhard, as wearing "clothes of gold, bejeweled shoes and a cloak bound by a gold fibula." Later in the ninth century another biographer, Notker, claimed that a Byzantine envoy who visited the royal court was dazzled by the king, "radiant as the rising sun, striking in gems and gold." Another writer from around the same time, a young monk, showed off his ascetic bona fides by ridiculing the entire kingdom of the Franks as a woman dressed up in sandals, a bejeweled belt, and a golden cloak fastened by a golden fibula.

27

Button, 500s, Byzantium, rock crystal, garnet, granulated gold; diameter: 3.05 cm (1 ³/₁₆ inches)

Eᴀʀʟʏ Byzantine clothing is one of the main casualties of the passing of time. We see it depicted in mosaics and in illuminated manuscripts, but the textiles themselves, heavily used, rarely survive. They were worn out, used and reused, cut into pieces, employed for wrapping other objects. What does survive is the adornment made of hardier materials, such as this button, carved out of rock crystal, which encloses a round garnet set into a star of granulated gold. Other pieces of extant ornament include earrings, brooches, bracelets, necklaces, rings, and belt-fittings. Rock crystal (natural quartz) jewelry was especially prized because the crystal was believed to be petrified ice—water that had lost its liquid, changeable form, and taken on the permanence of eternity. In turn, gems sparkling with light were understood as dim echoes of the Divine Light.

Rock crystal is found nearly everywhere, and in the sixth century the Byzantine Empire had access to much of the Eurasian land mass. While the West had become a mosaic of separate kingships, the eastern half of the former Roman Empire was under the firm control of Emperor Justinian (d.565), whose conquests garnered him North Africa, a bit of the southern Iberian Peninsula, and even Italy. As a result, the Byzantine Empire could, for a time, claim the Mediterranean basin as its own. Economic exchange was easy, not only in the Mediterranean but as far northwest as England and as far east as India. Roads linking regions in Anatolia (Asia Minor) were restored, and Justinian built bridges and barriers against floods.

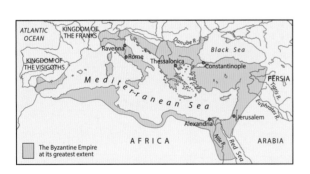

The Empire of Justinian, c. 565.

Although during this period most people lived on rural farmsteads, far from the centers where fine ornaments like this button were manufactured, some cities—Constantinople itself, Alexandria, Thessalonica, Jerusalem—flourished. There were also smaller commercial centers throughout the empire where textile makers, blacksmiths, goldsmiths, and stone carvers plied their trades.

The button may have been produced at such an emporium, or perhaps it was made in Constantinople, which thrived under the reign of Justinian and his wife Theodora (d.548). The craftsman who made this button followed a "new style" borrowed from Persia that featured a flat, abstract pattern and colorful gemstones. But the granulated gold that forms the six-pointed star followed a traditional technique of Etruscan, Greek, and Roman jewelers. While it is impossible to know the original context for the production and use of this button, little doubt exists about its value—and about the attendant value of the garment it adorned.

Garments, in Byzantium, could be precious commodities. They were given as presents and used to settle debts, they functioned as salary payments and security deposits. Clothing was a definitive marker of identity—the type of material, the type of design, and the type of adornment all contributed to defining the wearer's socio-economic status. Difficult-to-obtain materials and dyes were restricted to particular classes. The color purple, for example—made from the eastern Mediterranean shellfish called murex—was especially costly to make. Because of its prestige, the color came to be associated with the imperial family.

Judging by extant images, a rich variety of ornament and the artful layering of material were especially prized by the Byzantines. By Justinian's day, the Roman toga had been abandoned. Now the wealthy layered their garments, some of which were richly ornamented, draping their bodies in cotton, wool, linen, or silk. Atop an undergarment they wore a tunic, sometimes two, and atop that, a cloak. The second tunic, called the dalmatic, might be knee-length and have short sleeves to allow the first, longer tunic to show. The cloak was parted in the center or at the shoulder to reveal the garment underneath. One article of women's clothing was the high-belted *stola*, which essentially consisted of a folded textile rectangle that could also be used to cover her hair. Or a woman could wear a *maphorion*—a mantle to cover her head and shoulders. Men sometimes wore such head-coverings as well. Jewels, too, communicated the wearer's social standing. Cloaks were fastened by pins—fibulae—while tunics might be sewn with gems at the hem and collar and gathered at the waist by jeweled belts. The wealthy particularly treasured silk, often woven into another fabric: under Justinian's reign, the empire was introduced to sericulture, or silk farming.

Silk was, however, expensive; commoners likely wore wool clothing or, in hotter climates, linen. Women donned full-length tunics, men wore shorter ones. Only outsiders wore pants or leggings; Byzantine writers called those garments "Gothic"—that is, barbaric. But barbarian fashions must have been gaining currency because the Theodosian Code, which was compiled in 438 and codified various Roman laws, took great pains to set out a series of garment-related prescriptions. These were

unmistakably xenophobic. The Code was especially unforgiving of the pants-wearers: "Within the venerable City no person shall be allowed to appropriate to himself the use of boots or trousers. But if any man should attempt to contravene this sanction, we command that in accordance with the sentence of the illustrious prefect, the offender shall be stripped of all his resources and delivered into perpetual exile." Pelts were also forbidden: "no one, not even a slave, shall be allowed to wear garments made of skins within our most sacred City" as well as "in the neighboring districts." Proper Romans did not wear pants or pelts; foreigners did.

Clothing and ornaments were as important to the clergy as to everyone else. By the sixth century, Christian churchmen were in agreement: they should wear garb that distinguished them from ordinary worshipers. This was especially the case when they officiated at sacred functions—when they performed the Mass, for example. The choice of clothing evolved alongside the formation of the clergy itself. By the fourth century there were many grades of churchmen: bishops, priests, deacons, subdeacons, and so forth. Each was to wear a distinctive vestment that reinforced the clerical hierarchy. Thus, the late fourth-century Council of Laodicea in Anatolia forbade subdeacons from wearing a particular kind of stole— the *orarium*, which was allowed only to deacons. Christian churchmen took their models for dress not from the attire of pagan religious officials but rather from the fashions of Roman civil authorities, and the *orarium* is one example of this appropriation: it may have derived from the late Roman consular insignia.

Nevertheless, because Christ was their ultimate model, sixth-century churchmen wanted to avoid the appearance of luxury. They refused to wear the color purple, for example: it was too indissolubly connected with the emperor as well as with soldiers and members of the Roman pagan priesthood. A Christian priest wore a chasuble, a poncho-like cape, over his under-tunic. Made of linen, usually white, this became the priestly alb. Deacons, by contrast, wore the dalmatic—the same over-tunic that laymen wore. It was distinguished from other tunics by narrow stripes of colored fabric running from the shoulder to the hem.

Fashions changed, of course, throughout the years. Western historian Odo of Deuil (d.1162), writing in the twelfth century, commented on the tight-fitting clothes he saw worn by some Byzantine imperial messengers: "the wealthy are clad in silky garments that are short, tight-sleeved, and sewn up on all sides"; he compared their wearers to athletes. Trousers came into fashion at the same time: David Comnenus, the governor of Thessalonica, wore them, much to the disapproval of his Archbishop Eustathius. But the love of luxury remained, with sumptuous textiles and opulent jewelry orna-ments continuously witnessing the keen desire of the Byzantines to signal their status, function, and moral worth through their outward appearance.

28 Solidus with Busts of Constans II and Constantine IV (obverse), 659–661, Byzantium, gold; diameter 1.90 cm ($^{11}/_{16}$ inches)

BYZANTINE coins, which survive in great numbers, provide important insights into the social fabric of the empire: its trading networks, its tax structure, and its perception of imperial authority. Gold coins served as a material manifestation of imperial identity and power, disseminating the image of the rulers to the far corners of the empire. Soldiers were paid in gold coins, and imperial subjects used the same coins to pay their taxes. It was the emperor's responsibility to control the mints, to assure the purity of the gold and the proper weight of the coins.

This coin is a solidus, a standard coin struck in 24-carat gold. On the obverse are the portrait busts of Byzantine Emperor Constans II (d.668) and his son Constantine IV (d.685) who ruled (after 654) as his father's co-emperor, and, eventually, as the sole emperor after Constans II died. The coins offer a fair idea of the appearance of the two men—their sometime predecessor, the usurper of the Byzantine throne named Phocas (d.610) who briefly ruled the empire between 602 and 610, introduced portraiture to coinage. A solidus could therefore record the changing physique of a given emperor: Constans II appears as a young boy on early issues (he was only 11 when he became sole emperor) and then acquires his formidable facial hair on later coins like this one. Here he is distinguished by his long beard and rather dramatic moustache. He wears a chlamys and sports a plumed helmet topped with a cross. Constantine IV, also in a chlamys, is shown to the right and slightly behind his father; he wears a crown similarly surmounted by a cross. A third cross floats between their heads. Together, the pair's attributes represent military, civic, and religious authority.

On the reverse are full-body figures of Heraclius and Tiberius, the younger brothers of Constantine IV crowned as Augusti during the reign of Constans II. The Latin inscription, VICTORIA AVGU (abbreviation of AVGUSTORUM), translates as "the Victory of the emperors." Crowned and beardless, Heraclius and Tiberius stand on either side of a cross mounted on three steps. The two each wear a chlamys, and hold a cross-topped globe. By associating the father and his three sons, the coin asserted dynastic authority, broadcasting the robust family of Constans II and his plentiful male heirs. It is instructive to know, then, that after the death of his father, Constantine IV had his brothers mutilated—he wished to rule alone and to leave the throne to his youngest son, Justinian II (d.695).

But what was the imperial throne worth by then? The high and mighty preten-sions of such coins corresponded to reality in the glory days of Justinian (d.565), when the Byzantine Empire stretched from today's Turkey across North Africa and took in parts of Italy, while extending northward in the Balkans up to the Danube River. In the seventh century, however, little of this remained. War, first with the Sasanid Persians, then with formidable newcomers to the region—Muslim armies from Arabia inspired by their new religion—transformed not only the geography but also the very culture of the Byzantine Empire. Shortly thereafter, the Bulgars, mainly a farming and peasant population, moved into the Balkans from the north.

With the Persians the war was fairly brief. Taking advantage of a weak moment in the reign of Phocas, the Persian King of Kings marched into Byzantine territory, taking Damascus, Jerusalem, and all of Egypt. Although by 630 the Byzantines had retaken all, they (and the Persians) were exhausted, easy prey for Islamic armies inspired by a militant notion of "striving" (the root meaning of jihad). By 661, around the time that the solidus shown here was struck, the Arabs had rolled over Persia and the southern half of the Byzantine Empire. In the 670s, in the time of Constantine IV, the Bulgars began to take over the Balkans. By this time, the Empire was a shadow of its former self, focused mainly on Anatolia, with a few outposts in Italy and Greece.

The Byzantine Empire, c. 700.

The urban fabric of the Empire shrank as well. Cities were depopulated, their buildings and public spaces turned to rubble. New walls were some-times built, but they embraced a much smaller area than the originals. Some people built houses within the rubble, and bishops (where there were bishops) built churches. Some urban settlements turned into simple fortresses, bastions against military onslaughts. But many cities were abandoned altogether. Byzantium's foundations shifted to the countryside—with the important excep-tion of the imperial capital. The loss of Antioch, Alexandria, Carthage, and Jerusalem meant that Constantinople became the center of political and economic authority. This is where the solidus was minted.

Mints had been located throughout the empire, but their number diminished dramatically in the seventh century. This coin bears a mint mark at the bottom

reading "CONOB." The first three letters refer to the imperial capital, while the last two are an abbreviation of "obryzum," or gold, as well as the Greek numeral 72 (the coin weighed 1/72 of the original Roman pound). It is unclear which workshop produced the coin, since the so-called *officina* letter that identifies the specific mint is here incomplete. The cross on the reverse also designated the coin's denomination: the least valuable tremissis was marked with a simple cross, the more valuable semissis with a cross on a globe, and the most valuable solidus with a cross mounted on steps, as here. The stepped cross may represent the monumental gem-studded cross erected on the site of the Crucifixion by Theodosius II (d.450), harking back to the "golden" fifth century, when the Roman Empire still had both Eastern and Western halves.

But that time was long gone. Although gold coins continued to be struck and used during most of this depressed period, they were not particularly important for ordinary economic exchange. Far more significant for the empire's fiscal health were copper and bronze coins, whose value was loosely tied to the gold. But during the seventh century, many fewer of these coins were minted. This means that rather little everyday trade was taking place, leading to decreased demand for the coins that oiled the wheels of commerce. Further, the value of the smaller coins gradually diminished over the course of the seventh century. The copper coins lost weight: originally they were eleven grams, then five. After about 658, they stopped being minted altogether. The state was also running out of gold. As it did so, it increasingly made payments to its soldiers in silver and in kind. By the last years of Constans II's reign, the minting of *both* gold and copper coins had virtually ceased. This solidus is a rarity.

At this point, gold coins were little more than ideological statements and objects of numismatic art. But in the eighth century emperors became increasingly worried about the Byzantine emphasis on icons in worship, and this affected coin production as well. As Islamic armies took over their territories, some Byzantines saw this as God's punishment for worshiping "idols": that is, portrait-like images of Christ and his saints. During the first Iconoclastic—literally, "icon-breaking"—period, which began in 726 and lasted until 787, emperors introduced changes in coinage: they portrayed themselves with schematic, generic features on the obverse, and eliminated images of the crosses from the reverse. It was only after the end of the second Iconoclastic period in 843 that images of Christ and true imperial portraits reappeared on Byzantine coins.

29

Bifolium Excised from a Carolingian Gradual, c. 830–860, Germany or northeastern France, gold and silver ink on purple parchment; sheet 29.00 × 10.00 cm (11 ⅜ × 3 ⅞ inches)

T HIS bifolium—a two-page spread—comes from a Carolingian gradual, a book that contains some of the most elaborate choral and solo sections of the Mass. The invention of Western musical notation had only just begun in this period, so the men and women who sang the texts had to memorize (rather than read) all the music. That music—a single vocal line sung without instruments—came to be called "Gregorian chant," an appropriation of the name of the famous sixth-century pope Gregory the Great. Originally the bifolium would have been strikingly beautiful, with its gold and silver inks gleaming against the purple vellum. Although now turned black, the metallic lettering endowed the book with special prestige, appropriately matched by the color purple (today faded to pink)—a color long associated with Roman imperial rule and now, in the ninth century, adopted by Carolingians keen to revive the glory of the Roman Empire.

The gradual was created during a period of political unrest, when several Carolingian kings, heirs of Charlemagne (d.814), were often at war with each other. Even so, all of these rulers and their chief supporters, both lay and clerical, tried to continue the policies of their illustrious ancestor. Crowned emperor by the pope in the year 800, Charlemagne temporarily united the whole of Western Europe—sometimes (anachronistically) called the "Holy Roman Empire"—under his rule. In addition to military conquests, he worked to unify his empire culturally, linguistically, religiously, and even emotionally: he insisted that every male over the age of 12 swear fealty (loyalty) to the emperor himself. At his capital at Aachen—Charlemagne's preferred residence and the site of one of the most important medieval buildings, the Palatine Chapel—the emperor gathered learned men from all corners of Europe to carry

The Carolingian Empire, c. 814.

plicabitur in domo domini
V. Ad adnuntiandum mane
misericordiam tuam et veritatem
tuam per noctem.
[illegible]
Exiit sermo inter fratres
quod discipulus ille
non moritur. V. Sed
sic eum volo manere do
nec veniam tu me sequere.
Hic est discipulus ille
qui testimonium per
hibet de his et scimus
quia verum est testimo
nium eius. [illegible]
Anima nostra sicut pas
ser erepta est de la
queo venantium. V. La
queus contritus est et
nos liberati sumus.
Adiutorium nostrum in no
mine domini qui fecit cae
lum et terram.
[illegible]
Ecce sacerdos magnus
qui in diebus suis pla
cuit deo. V. Non est in
ventus similis illi qui
conservaret legem
excelsi. V. Inveni
david servum meum oleo
sancto meo unxi eum.
[illegible]
Diffusa est gratia in la
biis tuis propterea
benedixit te deus in aeternum.
V. Propter veritatem et
mansuetudinem et ius
titiam et deducet te mi
rabiliter [illegible]

FERIA QUINTA
R. Propitius esto domine peccatis
nostris nequando dicant
gentes ubi est deus eorum.
V. Adiuva nos deus salutaris
noster et propter honorem nomi
nis tui domine libera nos.
FERIA SEXTA
R. Ad dominum dum tribularer
clamavi et exaudivit
me. V. Domine libera animam
meam a labiis iniquis
et a lingua dolosa.
R. Bonum est confiteri domino
et psallere nomini tuo
altissime. V. Ad adnun
tiandum mane misericordiam tuam
et veritatem tuam per noctem.
DOMINICA SEXTA
R. Exurge domine non praevaleat ho
mo iudicentur gentes
in conspectu tuo. V. In con
vertendo inimicum meum
retrorsum infirmabuntur
et peribunt a facie tua.
Ad te levavi oculos meos
qui habitas in caelo.
Ecce sicut oculi servorum
in manibus dominorum suorum
et sicut oculi ancillae
in manibus dominae suae
ita oculi nostri ad dominum
deum nostrum donec misereatur
nobis. Miserere nobis domine
miserere nobis.
R. Deus vitam meam nuntiavi
tibi posuisti lacrimas
meas in conspectu tuo.
V. Miserere mihi domine quoniam
conculcavit me homo [illegible]

out and consolidate his reforms. These included the production of liturgical texts like the gradual, used in the daily lives of monks, nuns, and clerics.

The bifolium illustrated here is written in uncial, a form of capital lettering that was often employed for sacred texts. The first title in silver explains that the ensuing passages are appropriate for the feast of Saint John the Evangelist, while the small silver RG that follows indicates the text (written in gold) to be sung next, and so on. All the chants of the Mass drew on the Vulgate (Latin) Bible, standardized under the Carolingians. Papal Rome was another source of the chants: Carolingian graduals were copied from Roman Mass books, and cantors from Rome were brought north to teach the melodies. The Mass of the Carolingian era consisted of many elements, all sung. It started with introductory chants: the Introit, Kyrie, and Gloria. There followed a service of readings sung on one pitch. Then came the more elaborate musical arrangements that were contained in the gradual book: the gradual chants (which gave the book its name), the Alleluia (or Tract), and the Credo. All but the Credo were responsory chants—that is, the kind that alternated choir and soloists. The Eucharistic sacrifice came next, with offertory rites and prayers. The Mass concluded with more chants. The complexity of this practice explains why it often took many years of education to perform the liturgy properly.

This was one reason for the Carolingian educational reform, which brought about a panoply of changes. Charlemagne called for schools to be established in all bishoprics and monasteries. The ruler wanted instructors "to be zealous in teaching those who by the gift of God are able to learn, according to the capacity of each individual." It is possible that he meant girls as well as boys. Although schools were established only in religious institutions, and books were generally produced in monastic scriptoria, the Carolingians were interested in more than religious learning. Their overarching goal was to continue the glories of the Roman Empire, or at least their idea of this empire. Indeed, the images in Carolingian manuscripts often bear the unmistakable stamp of a classicizing style, discernable especially in the so-called Palace School of illumination. Small wonder, then, that the many books produced during this time included works of ancient authors such as the playwright Terrence, the poet Vergil, and the philosopher Cicero. In 780 the king sent out a directive for his court to acquire rare books. If we have today the works of classical Latin authors, it is largely thanks to the Carolingians—and not only the kings, but also elite women, bishops, and laymen.

Carolingian manuscripts set the standard for literary production for centuries to come, even as book-making spread beyond the monasteries into urban workshops in the later Middle Ages. Medieval books are astonishing for their variety.

Certainly, many of the books produced in the period were religious: the Bible, copied in its entirety or as separate codices; writings of Church Fathers and contemporary theological treatises; service books such as graduals and missals; monastic rules and guidebooks for pastoral care; penitential books and sermon collections. As literacy spread among the laity, books for private devotion became very popular. But there were also encyclopedias and histories; romances and collections of poetry; travel books and world chronicles; treatises on nature and astronomy; manuals on cooking and housekeeping; translations of various works by both classical and Islamic authors; and much, much more.

Throughout the Middle Ages, then, book production continued to be a supremely important endeavor, even though creating a codex was a very laborious process. The papyrus used in antiquity was unavailable, and Europeans did not know how to make paper, a Chinese invention relayed to the West through the Islamic world and widely used only in the thirteenth century. Thus, book-makers used parchment, which was made out of animal skin. The skin was washed, soaked in lime and water, and scraped to get rid of as much hair as possible. Then it was stretched, dried, and buffed. Cut into rectangular sheets, the parchment was folded into bifolia that were pricked and ruled for texts and sometimes images. Subsequently the folia were gathered into quires. The scribe or scribes worked on each quire before binding all of them into the final book. The writers' tools included a quill, a knife, an inkpot, and, of course, ink itself—some of it made from charcoal mixed with gum; some from gall nuts, gum arabic, and ferrous earth; and some, as with this gradual, composed of silver and gold. Different colors were produced from various ingredients: red was made with cinnabar, vermillion with heated mercury, green with malachite or verdigris, yellow with saffron or volcanic earth.

Each manuscript generally began with a title page, or *titulus*. Some books included annotations, rubrics, glosses (on the margins or even in between lines), and decorated initials. Some had a colophon at the end, recording the name of the scribe and the place and date of the manuscript's completion. One scribe used the colophon to memorialize his exhaustion: "Now I've written the whole thing: for Christ's sake give me a drink." Another was disgruntled enough by an improperly scraped quire to write in the margin: "The parchment is hairy." Yet another was displeased with every aspect of the labor before him: "Thin ink, bad vellum, difficult text." But no one complained about copying this bifolium. The scribes of these leaves treated this most musically complex part of the Mass with an appropriately luxurious look: sumptuous and opulent, its form befitting its content of sacred plainsong.

30

Jug, Buyid period, reign of Samsam al-Dawla, 985–998, Iran or Iraq, gold with repoussé and chased and engraved decoration; overall 12.50 × 10.20 cm (4 ⅞ × 4 inches), diameter of base 7.00 cm (2 ¾ inches)

"You are the image of the full moon at night, the first gleam of sun on the horizon of the morning," proclaims the Arabic poetry inscribed on this golden jug. "You are a sword in the times of war, a beneficent rain in times of peace [...] your sword cuts the necks of Buyid enemies in great quantities [...] Glory and prosperity to the just king Samsam al-Dawla [...] May God lengthen your reign!" Samsam al-Dawla (d.998), so exuberantly praised in the inscription, was a Buyid emir whose rule—marked as it was by revolts, betrayals, and civil skirmishes—needed all the good wishes it could muster. Well-wishing aside, it was not uncommon for celestial bodies and great kings to intermingle in poetic imaginations. The great lyricist al-Mutanabbi (d.965), supported by the Buyids, once celebrated one of his patrons by likening him to sunlight: "Glory and nobility were preserved when you were preserved, [...] and light which had left the sun, as though the loss of light were a sickness in its body, returned to it. [...] When you are safe and sound, all men are safe and sound."

The jug itself gleams like the sun. Between four strips of Kufic inscriptions nestle two registers of medallions formed by interlacing bands. On the body of the jug these medallions contain birds, perhaps peacocks; on the neck, each encloses what seems to be a griffin. The spaces between the roundels are filled with vegetal patterns. Although some questions have been raised about the authenticity of this vessel, it is certain that jugs very much like it were produced at this time. The region ruled by the Buyids, right in the heartland of ancient Persia, had long been known for its tradition of ceramics, incised glass, and metalwork. Objects made in expensive materials—ivory, crystal, jade or, as here, gold—bore visual similarity to those made from baser wares. Yet, very few vessels made entirely of precious metals survive. Their rarity might be the result of Islam's suspicion of wealth, or due to the fact that objects in gold or silver were often melted down for coins in times of trouble and privation. Although Christian church treasuries were filled with precious liturgical objects and sacred reliquaries, mosques had little use for lavish displays: this jug is a secular vessel—a very expensive one, to be sure—that would have been used by the wealthy in their daily lives.

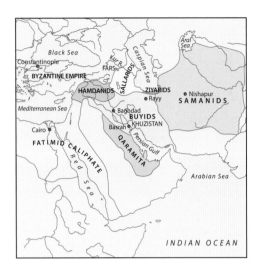

The eastern Islamic world, c. 1000.

The Buyid state was one of many that filled the void left by the decline of the Abbasid caliphs. In the ninth century, the Abbasids had presided over a grand empire stretching from Tunis to Samarkand. Their wealth and prestige were legendary, the stuff of fairy tales later recounted in the "Thousand and One Nights." They guaranteed religious conformity in accordance with Sunni Islam. Sunnism was one of two major branches of the religion that had formed in the seventh century, born out of a dispute over the rightful successor to Muhammad (d.632). The claimant supported by the Sunnis was a member of the Umayyad dynasty, which prevailed until 750, when it was replaced by the Abbasids. The claimant who lost, the Prophet's son-in-law Ali, was killed in 661, and thereafter his followers became the Shi'ite branch. In time, the two developed different spiritual emphases, traditions, and practices, and each considered the other heretical.

And so, when Abbasid power waned—a result of civil war, economic dislocation, and competing local traditions—there was a change in religious culture as well. The Shi'ite dynasties like the Buyids (r.932–1062) came to the fore as local rulers. The Buyids were especially important because they took over Baghdad and, with it, dominated the caliphs, making them into pure figureheads. Originally from the mountains of northern Iran, the Buyids were relatively new converts to Islam when they descended in 945, taking over much of Iran—including the major cities of Isfahan, Shiraz, and Rayy—as well as Mesopotamia. Various branches of the Buyids reigned for over a century, during the so-called Iranian Intermezzo—an interval between rule there by Arabs and Turks. During this time, Shi'ite rituals became interwoven into daily life. They included the public observance of Ghadir Khumm, which celebrated the moment when Muhammad appointed Ali as imam, as well as Ashura, the commemoration of the martyrdom of Ali's son and Muhammad's grandson, imam Husayn (d.680). In 990, Husayn's and Ali's tombs were restored by the Buyid ruler Abdul al-Dawla, and a host of public mourning rituals sprang up around those tombs.

The Iranian Intermezzo was also characterized by a lively pan-Islamic intellectual culture, typified by philosophers like Ibn Sina (d.1037)—known in the West as Avicenna—whose commentaries introduced much of the medieval world to

Aristotle, and physicians like al-Razi (d.925 or 935), who ran two hospitals and advocated an empirical approach to disease. The jug shown here is witness to a different sort of cultural eclecticism. Though a secular object, its bold and angular script in Arabic asserts the inspiration of the Qur'an as the carrier of the very word of God. The inscription itself suggests the work of a poet. Although we do not know about Samsam al-Dawla's own cultural preferences, his vizier (chief minister), 'Abd Allah ibn Sa'dan (d.984/985), was famously surrounded by a coterie of scholars and writers. Certainly in Samsam al-Dawla's day the Buyid dynasty reached its cultural pinnacle. All sorts of public works were being completed, including the building of hospitals and the creation of a dam across the Kur River in Fars province. The dynasty's political connections stretched to the Byzantine Empire and Fatimid Egypt. Its rulers sponsored religious festivals and pilgrimages to holy sites, and they patronized the arts. The exuberant inscription on the jug suggests the taste of an emir keen to be praised. Undoubtedly, al-Mutanabbi's poetry, which was supported by an earlier member of the dynasty, implies the high value placed on encomia and panegyrics on behalf of the ruler.

Both practical and beautiful, precious vessels like this jug were markers of power and prestige. Long before the Buyid period, they were part of the drinking accouterments of the wealthy and noble. Already the Persian court had its cup bearer: while the prince reclined, holding a wine bowl, the cupbearer stood nearby. The tools of his trade included a jug, a sieve to filter the wine, and another jug to receive the purified liquid. Since most ewers of this period were inscribed with blessings for their owners, it is quite possible that this one belonged to Samsam al-Dawla himself.

But if the inscription on the jug expresses the wish that Samsam al-Dawla have a magnificent and long reign, fate decided otherwise. His rule was troubled. Constantly disputing his leadership position with his brother, Sharaf al-Dawla, Samsam al-Dawla had to fight many other challengers as well. From 985 to 986 he was forced to parcel out most of his emirate, holding on only to Baghdad. Soon thereafter his brother seized him, partially blinded him, and threw him into prison. When Sharaf al-Dawla died in 989, however, Samsam al-Dawla's luck turned. Out of prison, he gained a base at Fars, Kirman, and Oman, and, with a well-led army, was able to move into Khuzistan and to take Basrah. The emir came to an unfortunate end soon after the jug glorifying him was made: just as he was beginning to prevail over his enemies, Samsam al-Dawla was assassinated.

31

Lion Aquamanile, 1200–1250, Germany, Lower Saxony, Hildesheim, copper alloy, cast, chased, and punched; 26.40 × 29.00 × 15.00 cm (10 ³⁄₈ × 11 ³⁄₈ × 5 ⁷⁄₈ inches)

Tʜɪs copper alloy lion-shaped jug is an aquamanile—a vessel used for hand-washing, whether by priests in a church or banqueters in an upper-class home. The beast's body, sturdy on its four sparsely decorated legs, is lithe and smooth, but its stylized mane is molded and chased, or grooved. The collar enclosing its neck is a feature of several other lion aquamanilia. The animal's huge, almond-shaped eyes look up with a pleading expression of eager servitude, while the cavities of its two round ears are echoed in the hollow of the spout that emerges from its mouth. Its tail, which serves as a handle, is shaped as a dragon: it is, on further inspection, not so much a lion as a hybrid animal.

Aquamanilia come in a breathtaking variety of forms, although zoomorphic vessels, commonly in the form of a lion, predominate. Other shapes include roosters, unicorns, dragons, griffins, centaurs, dogs, stags, and horses with or without riders. Some of the more ambitious aquamanilia figure known narratives: extant, for instance, are vessels in the form of Samson battling the lion and of Saint George on horseback defeating the dragon. The shape of the vessel might, in some cases, suggest its function. The Samson aquamanile, for instance, would have been particularly appropriate for liturgical use: Samson's combat with the lion (Judges 14:5–9) was seen to prefigure Christ's battle with the devil. Helped by his sub-deacon, the priest would wash his hands before celebrating the Mass, while reciting Psalm 50:6–10, which included the verses "Thou shalt sprinkle me with hyssop, and I shall be cleansed; thou shalt wash me, and I shall be made whiter than snow." The poured water would gather in the basin that accompanied the pitcher; already by the fifth century, subdeacons were supposed to receive both of these vessels when they were ordained. It is notable that the ritual context need not have been specifically Christian: some aquamanilia bear Hebrew inscriptions, suggesting that these vessels were used in Jewish ceremonial settings as well. One such inscription makes clear that the pitcher was used in synagogue services, while another includes the blessing for hand-washing before eating bread.

But other aquamanilia would have been more appropriate in secular contexts. One celebrated example is a pitcher in the shape of the seductive girl Phyllis astride the philosopher Aristotle (d.322 ʙᴄᴇ). Aristotle, the teacher of Alexander the Great (d.323 ʙᴄᴇ), taught his pupil about the wiles of women, and yet even he allowed

himself to be humiliated by the beautiful Phyllis, Alexander's lover: before she would gratify Aristotle's own lustful desires, she insisted on bridling him and riding him around the garden. In this way, Aristotle became no less of a beast than a horse ridden by a knight or a lion defeated by Samson.

The water stored in aquamanilia would have likely been scented: a fourteenth-century handbook on household duties called *Le Ménagier de Paris* suggests that such water be boiled with sage, marjoram, bay leaves, chamomile, or rosemary with orange peel, and then left to cool until tepid. Medieval cookery books called for elaborate creations: cooked chickens mounted astride roasted piglets and topped with gold-plated caps, or a whole foul wrapped in gold or silver leaf. A table with such fare called for an equally extraordinary aquamanile, especially since food was mostly handled with fingers rather than utensils. Indeed, the presence of spigots on some of these pitchers suggests that they were stationary and may have sat on the table for use both during and after meals.

There is no doubt that these zoomorphic and anthropomorphic vessels have a long pedigree, from Roman oil containers to Byzantine lamps to Islamic incense burners and water pitchers. Commercial and cultural exchanges between Europe and the Byzantine and Islamic worlds, as well as a series of military campaigns including the crusades, served to introduce Europeans to a wide variety of cast vessels prevalent throughout the eastern Mediterranean and beyond. Between the twelfth and fifteenth centuries, aquamanilia became very popular in Western Europe, and many surviving examples come from German-speaking lands. This particular one was likely cast in Hildesheim, a celebrated center of production for many marvelous works in bronze. The city, built on very fertile land, was the meeting place of important transportation routes. The Innerste River just below the city supplied the power for the mills needed to support a major manufacturing center. Copper and other mineral ores were available from nearby mines, and wood from neighboring hills provided the fuel for smelting and melting metals.

Hildesheim first became a center of so skilled and specialized a craft in the early eleventh century, when its Bishop Bernward (d.1022) brought his religious, artistic, and architectural ambitions to fruition in what was, at that time, still only a small settlement. He constructed a chapel there as the fitting resting place for a fragment of the True Cross, and rapidly turned it into a grand monastery dedicated to Saint Michael. For it, he commissioned a bronze column with 28 scenes from Christ's ministry and great bronze double doors telling the story of man's Fall and Christ's work of salvation. Solid-cast in a single piece, each door—with its intricate narratives, expressive figures, and delicate, spare landscapes—is a remarkable feat of metalwork mastery.

As the commercial revolution got underway, not long after the time of Bernward, Hildesheim expanded and became part of a far-flung trade network. One of its creations was a huge bronze lion, almost six feet high, commissioned by Henry the Lion (d.1190), the Duke of Saxony. The lion stood guard outside his castle in Braunschweig a symbol of ducal power and authority. The aquamanile pictured here may well have been modeled on Henry's beast, although the process of its manufacture would have been quite different. Because of their function, aquamanilia had to be hollow and cast in the round. First, the core was modeled in clay; it was then covered with sheets of wax of the thickness desired of the eventual metal. Some elements—tails or handles, for example, which did not need to be hollow—were modeled in wax separately, and attached to the main core. The surface was refined and openings were cut in the wax: those were later used to remove the core and/or to fill the vessels with water. The entire ensemble was secured by metal or wood armatures, and a series of wax rods was joined to the surface. Finally, metal pins, inserted through the wax and the core, were used to secure the investment—that is, several layers of clay, usually mixed with sand, which adhered to the wax. Placed near a heat source and turned upside down, the aquamanile released the liquefied wax through the channels formed by melted wax rods. The resultant space was filled with molten metal after the entire ensemble was secured by being placed into well-packed ground. Once the metal cooled, the investment and core were removed, flaws repaired, and the surface finished with filing and engraving.

Saxony, c. 1200.

This so-called lost-wax process of casting, which stands witness to the technical savvy of medieval metalworkers, was described in some detail by one Theophilus in his treatise *On Divers Arts* (c. 1122), which discusses a variety of painting, glass-making, and, finally, metalworking techniques. The last section seems particularly well-informed, and the author of the treatise has been associated with Roger of Helmarshausen, a twelfth-century German Benedictine monk and a celebrated metalsmith, who lived during the time when sumptuous bronze objects—crosses, tomb effigies, baptismal fonts, reliquaries, portable altars, and aquamanilia among them—were produced in impressive quantities throughout Germanic lands. It is from such illustrious ancestors that the Hildesheim lion descends.

32

Luster Wall Tile with a Couple, 1266, Iran, Kashan,
fritware with luster-painted design; 19.50 × 16.00 cm
(7 ⅝ × 6 ¼ inches)

T HIS hand-painted star-shaped tile is dominated by white and copper brown,
with touches of cobalt blue and turquoise. A couple sits cross-legged in
a garden, flanking a cypress tree that grows above a pond. Both have almond-
shaped, narrow eyes, small mouths, and long hair that hangs down in tresses.
Their densely patterned garments nearly melt into a background equally dense
with design; only their round white faces, accentuated by their halos (which do not
indicate sanctity but rather serve as a decorative motif), stand out against the
crowded backdrop. In his right hand the man holds a beaker; his companion's eyes
seem fixed on it. The three plump birds, the tree, and the pond indicate an idealized
garden setting.

The tile was made when the Ilkhanids ruled Iran. They were relative latecomers to
the region, which had been conquered first by Muslim Arabs in the seventh century,
then by Seljuk Turks, also Muslims, in the eleventh. But as the Great Seljuk sultanate
gave way to independent local principalities in the twelfth century, the pagan Mongols
moved into Persia. The Ilkhanids were descendants of Chinghis (or Genghis) Khan
(d.1227) who, forging an empire that extended all the way across Eurasia, came also to
dominate much of the Islamic and Christian worlds. The Ilkhanids, like other
Mongols, were itinerant, moving their
court among different locations according to seasonal changes. When they
encountered the settled way of life in
Iran and Iraq, they adapted to it, building
permanent structures, including grand
palaces. Further assimilation took place
when Ilkhanid Ghazan Khan (d.1304)
broke with the Mongols in China by con-
verting to Islam. He established Tabriz as
his political and administrative capital,
and his successor, Oljeitu, did the same

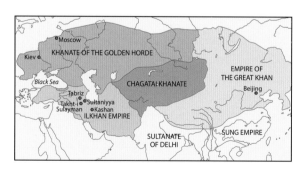

The Ilkhanid Empire, c. 1300.

at nearby Sultaniyya. In the mid-fourteenth century, Mongol rule declined, hit badly
by the plague, and the Ilkhanids were eventually succeeded by rival states, most
importantly that of Tamerlane.

Persia had been famous for its tilework long before Ilkhanid rule. One of the major centers for ceramic production was Kashan, a central Iranian city. In fact, the word "kashi" came to signify "tile" in Persian. Some of the finest luster pottery was produced in Kashan between the twelfth and fourteenth centuries—that is, both before and after the Mongol invasions. Called "enamel of the two firings" by the fourteenth-century Ilkhanid court historian Abu'l-Qasim, luster pottery is a thing of gleaming beauty: first painted with white glaze and fired, the tile was subsequently decorated with metallic pigment and fired again in a special kiln that draws oxygen out of oxides. Often, turquoise and cobalt blue were added before the second firing, as was the case with this tile. The result was a radiant and glossy surface, rich in color and refined in detail. Invented in Iraq in the ninth century for decorating glass, the luster technique turned out to be a perfect medium for pottery, as it mimicked the look of gold and silver without using those expensive pigments. The effect of the glistening surfaces was breathtaking, especially when luster-painted designs were used in wall tile ensembles that would have been lit by candlelight. It is from one such ensemble that the object here undoubtedly hails: its form suggests that it belonged to a larger design of interlocking star- and cross-shaped tiles. Even though the last lines of the inscription on the tile invoke the divine ("May the World Creator preserve this. Wherever you are, offer your gratitude to God"), the subject matter is emphatically secular, and would have been particularly appropriate for a palace setting.

Indeed, similar tiles once decorated the royal residence at Takht-i Sulayman ("The Throne of Solomon"); this tile may possibly come from there. The palace complex was constructed by Abaqa (d.1282), the second Ilkhanid ruler of Persia, shortly after 1265, and it included an audience hall and residential quarters. Built on the site of an ancient fire temple, the complex was meant to serve as a summer resort, one permanent "campsite" for the annual migrations of the Ilkhanid court. Here, as at other campsites, all kinds of social and political rites and ceremonies were carried out—enthronements and appointments of officials, the reception of diplomats and the deputizing of diplomatic missions, marriage and mourning rituals. Ilkhanids were educated at these camps as well: at the age of three, little Ghazan, Abaqa's grandson, came to Takht-i Sulayman to be brought up by Abaqa's favorite wife. Located in a remote, yet strategic, region, Takht-i Sulayman offered good pastureland for animals, a deep thermal lake, and an agreeable climate, as well as a fortress and the perimeter walls left from the ancient Persian occupation. The royal complex was splendidly decorated, and one ensemble of rooms was especially striking. The largest had floor-to-ceiling windows, offering a splendid view of the valley. Along one side were snug chambers,

probably bedrooms for royalty and their guests. The walls here were adorned with tiles—including thousands of luster tiles—carved stucco, and paintings. Most of the tiles were eventually pillaged, but their outlines remain in the plaster. Of the tiles found on site by archaeologists, some feature Mongolian-inspired designs, while others carry images and quotations from Persian poetry.

This tile, too, was inspired by Persian culture, although instead of an epic poem it features an epigraphic band of quatrains that runs along the perimeter of the star. The brown *naskh* script stands out crisply against the white background, calling attention to itself. The verses turn the facial features of the lovers into metaphors—lips become rubies, the pubescent down above the lips is called an emerald, and descending locks of hair are likened to vipers and Zangis, or black slaves. The inscription on the left going down reads: "Your hair, which viper-like is bent on mischief, do you know why it returns behind your back? / When it saw that your ruby has an emerald, it became wild and wanders on the mountain side." The inscription across the top echoes the same idea: "Your tresses, which possess over a thousand Zangis / Are bent on a surprise night-time charge against the Cathay Turks / And that ruby-stealing Zangi in hiding / Have him hanged, for he has plenty of blood on his hands." This last quatrain appears on many other tile pieces from Takht-i Sulayman, and is particularly relevant here, alluding as it does to the dark locks of hair—making a "surprise night-time charge"—that frame the faces of the depicted couple.

The setting of this and similar tiles speaks to the importance of garden parks in medieval Persia. They were conceived as paradisiacal locales, places of escape from the crowded cities—ordered and controlled in contrast with the chaotic world outside of their walls. Ponds and fountains were often focal points of such gardens: they sustained vegetation, delighted the senses, and announced the prosperity of their owners, who spent considerable sums on complex irrigation systems. Conquered by Islamic armies in the seventh century, Persians came also to understand gardens in the light of the Qur'an, making them a metaphor for paradise, with its lush meadows and foliage nourished by flowing rivers and pools. In the *Ilkhanid Book of Ascension* (1286)—a devotional Sunni tale that tells of the Prophet Muhammad's journey to heaven—paradise is described as a magical garden where chrysolite trees with golden trunks "bear silken garments" that guarantee immortality. The paradise garden is filled with birds praising this garden, and from them "a thousand melodies in harmonious verse and with eloquent lyrics are heard." In company with similar tiles, the exemplar here offered both a dream of escape and a foretaste of heaven.

33

Leaf Excised from Henry of Segusio's *Summa Aurea*: Table of Consanguinity, c. 1280, France, Paris, ink, tempera, and gold on parchment; 44.20 × 27.50 cm (17 ⅜ × 10 ¹³/₁₆ inches)

Densely covered with text that seems to strain against both the wide margins and the central image, this folio comes from the so-called *Summa Aurea*, or the *Golden Summa*. It was penned by canon (Church) law professor, bishop, and cardinal Henry of Segusio (or Susa, in northern Italy), best known as Hostiensis (d.1271). The "summa" was the chief form of medieval university scholarship. Our word "summation" derives from the same root and suggests the scope of such treatises, which attempted to cover a huge panoply of knowledge on various topics in a systematic way. Henry's *Summa* took up the many canon laws issued by Pope Gregory IX (d.1241). It was extremely popular, surviving in two versions and many copies, scores of them made after Henry's death. Indeed, it was so highly regarded that in 1477 admirers gave it the moniker "golden," even though Henry called it, quite simply, "my summa."

The page here features a consanguinity tree—a complex diagram that works out degrees of kinship among family members related by blood. In the keyhole-shaped opening, a crowned man stands holding the table filled with roundels that are inscribed with words for blood relations and numbers showing degrees of consanguinity. The man, known as Ego (or "I"), reappears in the central medallion, still crowned, at bust length: he is the anchor in this visual scheme. The roundel above his bust contains the abbreviation for the words *pater* (father) and *mater* (mother), while the medallion below his head is inscribed *filio* (son) and *filia* (daughter). Both roundels are marked with the Roman numeral *i*, which indicates one degree of separation from Ego. To Ego's left and right are the roundels for his (or her) brother and sister, which are marked *ii* to indicate two degrees of separation. The shaft of the arrow-like diagram has medallions that extend vertically, following Ego's direct genealogical line, all the way down to his great-great-grandchildren. Aunts and uncles, nieces and nephews, second and third cousins find their place in this table as well. The family tree thus comprehends a vast array of kinships, each marked by a number used to calculate and regulate proper marital relations. Sometimes such tables of consanguinity were accompanied by or elided with tables of affinity, which featured a couple and listed their relatives by marriage.

Churchmen had two good reasons for controlling marital relationships. One had to do with property, which—along with authority—passed from family members to the next generation. In the early Middle Ages, the custom was for every member of the family to inherit property, even women, though normally their share was lesser. The Church, too, claimed inheritances. It taught that nothing could be better for the wealthy than to give their property to monks, who would pray for the soul of the donor, or to churches where the relics of the holy saints lay, ready to perform miracles.

Most importantly, however, the Church had the moral duty to regulate how the family was constructed. In the early Middle Ages, marriages had nothing to do with the Church—at least from the laity's point of view. There were no "church weddings," and marriages were private family arrangements. But very early on the Church tried to interfere with this. In the first place, it ordered priests to be celibate, though this was not the norm until the twelfth century; and, in the second place, it demanded, often with the support of kings, that certain restrictions apply to marriageable partners. "And we instruct and pray and enjoin, in the name of God, that no Christian man shall ever marry among his own kin within six degrees of relationships," declared the eleventh-century laws of King Cnut, written in the Anglo-Saxon language for even non-Latinate English men and women to read and absorb. Marrying "among kin" within those degrees was considered incest, a terrible sin. The figure in the *Golden Summa* may wear a crown, but one did not need to be a king to be affected by such laws.

While diagrammatic tables were not absolutely necessary to figure out degrees of consanguinity, they were certainly useful and utterly appropriate for books about canon law. The particular laws that Henry commented on had been compiled on directives of Gregory IX in 1230 in order to replace all earlier collections of canons. The section on consanguinity responded to changes in the canon law on that topic introduced by the Fourth Lateran Council in 1215. By then, noble families, who intermarried constantly (not to mention peasants, who were largely rooted to their manor), found it nearly impossible to find mates within the required degrees of separation, which by then numbered seven. A slew of divorces resulted from "sudden" discoveries of forbidden blood relations. To solve these problems, Fourth Lateran changed the number of prohibited degrees of consanguinity from seven to four, returning to the number originally prescribed by Roman civil law. But whereas Romans counted degrees of consanguinity up from the individual all the way to the common progenitor and then back down to the potential partner, medieval canon law calculated the degrees by counting up to the common progenitor for both prospective spouses. What constituted four

degrees of separation for Romans became two for medieval Christians. Marriage between first cousins, in other words, was illegal. In order to safeguard against an accidentally incestuous marriage, noble families were encouraged to keep track of their genealogies.

The man at the center of this consanguinity tree is visually enjoined to be the master—indeed, the king—of self-control and familial organization. He stands tall, with his toes overlapping the frame and with the trefoil inscribed into the circular opening suggesting a halo around his head. Vine tendrils that grow out of the arrow-like chevron allude to the vegetal metaphor of the genealogical tree that was itself an apt metaphor for the fruitful Christian family. And yet, the man does not so much hold the diagram as he is pinned to the background by its upward thrust, rooted in place by its rigid rules of kinship dictated by the canon law.

Such diagrams suggest the pivotal role that the Church played in the everyday lives of medieval Christians. While religion was important to the laity even in the early Middle Ages, the eleventh and twelfth centuries saw a deepened desire on the part of many to conform their lives to that of Christ and to listen ever more avidly to the preaching of the Church. Meanwhile, the Church reformed itself, ending abuses like simony (buying Church offices) and clerical marriages or other carnal unions. New monastic movements offered persuasive models for lives of piety, and scholars of the new universities, just forming at this time, offered good reasons for seeking God's grace through Church sacraments. Canon law was systematized at this same time, the papacy gained new power, the crusades called men (and women too) to give their lives in the service of a Church-sponsored army, and, in short, all the developments of the period made it imperative for the laity to listen to churchmen.

Both the canon law and its diagrammatic depictions hid a tender emotional truth: already in the twelfth century people were praising marriage for love. In the poem *Floris and Blanchefleur* (c.1160s), the two protagonists are brought up together, love one another, are separated, and, after many adventures, wed. In the thirteenth-century Middle English version of the story, "Floris falls at his feet and prays [the emir] to give him his sweetheart. The emir gave him his lover; everyone who was there thanked him then. He had them brought to a church and had them wedded with a ring."

34

Albarello with Two Hares, fourteenth century,
Spain, Paterna, tin-glazed earthenware (maiolica);
22.30 × 9.90 cm (8 ¾ × 3 ⅞ inches)

T HIS jar, used to store dried fruit, honey, medicinal herbs or ointments, is
called an albarello. The term is possibly derived from the Latin adjective
albarius (whitish, referring to the parchment with which the jar was sealed), the
Arabic noun *al-barani* (spice container), or the Spanish *albero* (tree, a reminder of
the wood that was originally used for these jars). Some, like this example, were tall
and slightly curved, allowing them to be grasped easily. Kept in spice shops,
monasteries, hospitals, infirmaries, palaces, and even private houses, albarelli
were items of both healing and luxury. Fourteenth-century author Giovanni
Boccaccio complained about friars who "do not blush to appear fat and florid.
[...] Their cells are full of boxes of ointments and creams, boxes of various
sweetmeats, phials and bottles of distilled waters and oils [...] so that they look
less like friars' cells than the shops of apothecaries and perfumers." The albarello
here belonged to a wealthy family: decorated with two hares flanking a grapevine,
it also boasts the Luna family crest, identifying the jar's provenance as the
municipality of Paterna in Valencia, Spain.

Albarelli were known in Iran and central Asia as early as the ninth century.
By the time this jar was made, their use had spread throughout Islamic territories
and reached southern Europe, primarily Spain and then Italy. Between the thirteenth and the fifteenth centuries, Paterna became known for its ceramic production. Albarelli were among its most popular items, for hospitals alone needed them
in the hundreds to hold balms, oils, and mixtures for every malady: lemon balm
for aches and colds; oils for depression; castoreum to provoke vomiting.

Medieval medicine was both a learned subject and a respected practice.
Countless medical encyclopedias survive from the Middle Ages, along with
herbals that cataloged the medicinal properties of various plants—such as the
ones that would be kept in the albarello. Some books, such as *On the Properties of
Things*, penned by Franciscan friar Bartholomeus Anglicus (d.1272), contained
a wide variety of notes on theology, philosophy, animals, elements, illnesses, and
remedies. Others, like the *Articella*, long the standard textbook, were more
practical. The *Articella* was based on the writings of the second-century Greek
doctor Galen, whose work was translated and compiled by the ninth-century
Baghdadi physician Hunayn ibn Ishaq (Latinized as "Johannitius"). His *Mas'il*

fit-tibb (*Questions about Medicine*), or *Isagoge*, was in turn translated at the end of the eleventh century by Constantine the African, a medical scholar turned monk who spent some time at Salerno: the *Articella* was the result. It also included translations from Hippocrates (d.370 BCE) and from Byzantine treatises on medicine.

Salerno was the chief center of medical studies until the thirteenth century, when universities elsewhere began offering degrees in the field. The curriculum expanded beyond the *Articella* at this point. The 1405 statutes of the University of Bologna for medical students' first year of studies included lectures based on the writings of Galen, Hippocrates, and the eleventh-century Arabic doctor Ibn Sina (d.1037; known as Avicenna in the West). Students also learned anatomy in dissection classes. With proper licenses granted by the rector, human bodies were certainly used for this purpose, although attendance was restricted: according to the statutes, "no more than twenty people may attend any anatomy of a man, and no more than thirty of a woman. And no one may see any anatomy except he be a student who has studied medicine for two whole years." Once finished with their studies, some doctors continued to teach; all did consulting (sometimes by mail) and saw patients.

When doctors visited the ailing, they had to comport themselves properly. There were therefore plenty of advice books about bedside manners. The twelfth-century *Archimatthaeus* was typical of the genre: "Entering the sickroom, do not appear very haughty or over-zealous, and return, with the simple gesture, the greetings of those who rise to greet you. After they have seated themselves you finally sit down facing the sick; ask him how he feels and reach out for his arm." Among doctors' tools were almanacs, or calendars, that contained star charts; flasks that allowed them to examine the patient's urine (a major diagnostic tool); and instruments for bloodletting. Practical physicians' handbooks often featured useful diagrams: a Zodiac Man that correlated planets, stars, and constellations with parts of the human body; a Wound Man that illustrated various weapons and the wounds they inflict; bloodletting diagrams; and urine charts.

A plethora of things, it was believed, influenced human physiology: stars and planets, natural elements (such as earth, fire, water, and air), body fluids called humors, complexions (hot, cold, dry, and wet), and so on. All were interrelated. So, the four humors—blood, phlegm, yellow bile, and black bile—were connected to the four elements, the four seasons, and the four ages of man. Humors had to be kept in balance since they affected one's temperament and might be responsible for physical and mental distress. The need for balance explains the practice of bloodletting: an excess of blood upset the balance among the humors and thus had

to be removed. At the French monastery of Cluny, monks who wished to have their blood let went to the phlebotomist on premises "in silence and with the fear of God." But when Cluny's abbot Peter the Venerable (d.1156) wrote to Master Bartholomaeus of Salerno about his persistent head cold, the doctor advised Peter to wait for a personal visit from his associate and avoid bloodletting in the meantime: "your nature is aggravated more by an excess of phlegm," he wrote, "than an excess of blood."

At times, when an illness was seen as divine punishment, prayer and penance, which could involve a pilgrimage to sacred sites, were in order. Christ himself was conceived of as a physician—as *Christus Medicus*—ready to heal spiritual ailments. Already in the fifth century, Saint Augustine likened Christ to a doctor: "like a skilled physician, the Lord knew better what was going on inside the patient than the patient himself. In the case of bodily infirmities, human physicians do what the Lord also is able to do in infirmities of the soul." By the late Middle Ages, properly educated surgeons and physicians campaigned to distinguish themselves and their noble profession from the shoddy and suspect practice of folk healers, and *Christus Medicus* served as a lofty model for them to emulate and evoke. Perhaps the grapes on the albarello jar, alluding as they do to the wine of the Mass, point to this association. The hares, in turn, may serve simply as a decorative motif, or they may indicate the contents of the jar. Hares were known for their fertility; perhaps the jar held exotic spices such as cardamom and nutmeg, believed to incite desire, cure impotence, and aid in conception.

Certainly conception was a major concern in the period. Three treatises on women's health care were put together at the end of the twelfth century and remained a major source for the treatment of women. Because one of the treatises was by Trota, a female physician at Salerno, the collection came to be called *The Trotula*. It covered menstruation, sexual desire, conception and childbirth, and diseases of the womb: "There are some women in whom the vagina and the anus become one opening and the same pathway. Whence in these women the womb comes out and hardens. We give aid to such women by repositioning [the womb]." After cutting the connection between the anus and vagina, "we heal the rupture with a powder made of comfrey, that is, of bruisewort, and daisy and cumin." Comfrey, made of a hairy root, is just the sort of thing this albarello might once have held.

35

Mirror Case with a Couple Playing Chess, 1325–1350, France, Paris, ivory; diameter 10.20 cm (4 inches)

"I HAVE a daughter who is very beautiful, and so good at playing chess that no man has ever defeated her," says the Saracen emir Ivoryn in the thirteenth-century *chanson de geste* known as *Huon de Bordeaux*. So riled is the emir by the boasting of the young knight Huon that he hopes to see him humiliated and silenced by the princess. "I charge you, by Muhammad, to play the game with her according to this covenant: if she can defeat you, your head will be swiftly cut off. On the other hand [...] if you can defeat my daughter at the game, I will prepare a bed in my chamber, and you will pass the whole night with my daughter and do what you like with her, and in the morning, when you say good-bye to her, I will give you 100 pounds [of silver]." The girl agrees reluctantly. But as she and the knight play the game of chess, it becomes a game of love. Smitten by Huon's beauty, the girl loses, but the chivalrous Huon declines to sleep with her, much to Ivoryn's relief and his daughter's bitter disappointment.

Chess, a game of strategy and patience, was a potent metaphor for courtship. This ivory mirror back shows a courting couple playing chess in a graceful tent. Propped up in the middle by a thin but sturdy pole, it is parted in the front to reveal the pair. The man, slightly smiling and legs crossed, is about to move his piece, while his companion, also faintly smiling, points her right index finger at the board. Another piece, already won, is held in her left hand. The scene appears innocent enough, but all is not what it seems. The young man grasps the pole with his hand, encroaching upon the woman's space. The pole thrusts into the opening folds of the tent, echoing the suggestive folds of the woman's dress, which form a triangle between her legs. In this way the mirror case alludes to what propriety forbids: the sport of love. Ivory—white and smooth and therefore flesh-like—was particularly suitable for images of desire. The sensuous quality of this material, which warms when held, is intimated in this image by the emphatic way the lady cradles her chess piece. The man is about to make his move, and his companion tells him just how to make it.

The mirror itself—missing from this exemplar—would have fitted into the other side of the case. Such mirrors were popular in French and German wealthy households, surviving in large numbers. The subjects carved on their cases were almost always secular, some featuring the God of Love, others the Castle of Love

under attack, still others scenes of courtship and narratives from romances. The game of chess, very popular in medieval literature, was particularly favored for mirrors, which were given as gifts and often formed part of a trousseau. The accounts of the Duke of Burgundy record the following expense for 1367: "Jean de Couilli, comb maker, living in Paris, 5 francs for a case including combs and a mirror of ivory, which he has taken and delivered for Mgr. Guillemin Hannot, his barber and valet de chambre." Frequently, mirrors were sold together with a hair-parter (a sharp stick, rather like a modern letter-opener) and a comb. The ivory was often painted and gilded, though no traces of such decoration remain here.

Paris was a major center for ivory production at this time. The craft was both regulated and protected by guilds. The statutes of one notes that "whoever wishes to be an *ymagier* in Paris—that is, a carver of crucifixes, knife handles, and any other kind of carving, whatever it be that one makes of bone, ivory, wood, and any other kind of materials [. . .] can be so freely, so long as he knows the trade and works according to the uses and customs of the aforesaid trade." Those customs were numerous: an apprenticeship of eight to ten years, stipulations about working hours (carvers could not work at night because the light was insufficient), and taxes owed the king.

In the past, the carving of the couple playing chess would have been taken to suggest an image of "courtly love"—a literary construct, now discredited as having no basis in reality, of an adulterous affair between a lowly knight at court and a lady of high standing. But, in fact, the kind of love most valued at princely and royal courts largely concerned the relationships between the ruler and his (male) allies, followers, and vassals. That is why, for example, Count Raimond VI of Toulouse (d.1222) wrote to his "beloved and faithful men" in one of his towns to authorize them to clear a blockage in a riverbed. Still, troubadours employed by Raimond and his contemporaries made up songs about their love not only for their lords but also for the beautiful women at court. War and love went together in chivalry, as the troubadour poet Peire Vidal made clear: "In daring I equal Roland or Oliver [two famous warriors]. / [. . .] I am the perfect image of a knight; / Indeed that's what I am, for I know the ways of love."

This mirror case seems to capture just such a noble fellow, engaged not only in the game of love but also in the game of war; for chess was also symbolic of warfare—a major preoccupation of the French nobility. At the time that the mirror case was made, France was chronically at war: feuds and rebellions, factional fighting and dynastic instability orchestrated the lives of nobles. Guyenne, the last stronghold of English rule in the hexagon we now call France,

was a perennial thorn in the side of the French king: in 1323 England and France briefly went to war over it, and in 1337, when the French King Philip VI confiscated the duchy, the Hundred Years' War (1337–1453) began. It was treated by the chronicler Jean Froissart (d. after 1404) as the perfect opportunity to demonstrate knightly valor, bravery, and courtesy: "For in all the battles in which they [the English] have taken part, they have achieved renown as the best, by land and sea, and have shown such valor that they ought rightly to be held up as valorous above all other. [. . .] In France there are also to be found strong, robust and vigorous exemplars of chivalry."

Both love and war were noble pursuits; both love and war carried great dangers of sin. This ambiguity is reflected in the very idea of a mirror, which held a multitude of meanings for medieval men and women. Encyclopedic works were often called *specula*, or mirrors, to indicate the way they reflected the world and encompassed the scope of human knowledge. From Albertus Magnus's *Speculum astronomiae* (*The Mirror of Astronomy*) to Vincent de Beauvais's *Speculum maius* (*The Great Mirror*), from *Speculum humanae salvationis* (*The Mirror of Human Salvation*) to *Speculum regale* (*The Mirror of Kings*), the concept of a reflective mirror was employed in political, theological, and philosophical works alike. But mirrors were also symbols of vanity; personifications of Pride were regularly shown carrying mirrors. They distorted and warped the world: convex and concave, with lead backing and uneven color, they served as a fitting embodiment of 1 Corinthians 13:12: "We see now through a glass darkly." Round mirror cases such as the example here were originally squared with images of crawling monsters at the corners—perhaps an implicit reminder of the corrupt and deceptive nature of the beholder's vain gaze.

36

Table Fountain, c. 1320–1340, France, Paris, gilt-silver and translucent enamels; 31.10 × 24.10 × 26.00 cm (12 ¼ × 9 ½ × 10 ³/₁₆ inches)

SILVER-GILT, enameled, and equipped with bells and waterwheels, this stunning three-tiered fountain is an automaton, the only one of its kind to remain largely intact. The fountain works by hydraulic pressure: pumped from below through a central pipe, water spews out of the top turret and side nozzles, setting wheels in motion and bells tinkling. Flowing from one tier to the next through animal- and human-headed conduits, the water finally drains into and then out of a catch basin (now lost). The fountain was made to appeal to the senses—sight by its color and gleam, hearing by the melodious ringing of its bells, smell by its perfumed water.

It was once thought that table fountains were used for ablutions in wealthy households, but that is unlikely. Rather, for practical hand-washing, the rich could choose from a wide variety of water-containers: pouring vessels that came with basins—jugs, ewers, aquamanilia—and stationary lavers with one or multiple spigots. Meals began and ended with hand-washing, which took place at some distance from the table; while dining, people used napkins to keep their hands clean. What were such meals like? Around the time the fountain was made, a well-to-do burger of Paris wrote a guidebook for his young wife, full of instructions about table manners and even menus: when the servants sit down to eat, "have them eat amply of only one kind of dish, rather than several kinds that are fancy or dainty. [. . .] Encourage them to eat heartily and drink well and abundantly, yet it is proper that they finish it all promptly, without sitting too long dallying over their food or lingering at or leaning on the table." Far different were his directives for the meals they would give their upper-class guests: a "sequence of dishes and courses" that might boast as many as 31 dishes and six courses. The menu for one third course alone included "roasted rabbits, partridges, capons, etc., luce [pike], sea bass, carp, and a quartered pottage [a thick stew]."

This fountain was as extravagant and wondrous as such a feast, and hardly more unusual. Automata were beloved at French, Flemish, and Burgundian courts: inventories and literary accounts alike witness to numerous mechanical devices in noble households. They often formed part of the entertainments staged on various important occasions—banquets, weddings, diplomatic receptions. Some of these devices were pneumatic or spring-loaded; others, as here, were hydraulic.

The courts were not the only places for such marvels, however: later medieval Europe was positively awash in articulated sculpture, some of which seems to have been automated. The still-extant thirteenth-century Virgen de los Reyes, a statue of the Virgin and Child from Seville, was equipped with all manner of interior gears and double joints that allowed its arms, elbows, hands, heads, hips, and knees to move. Around the same time, the architect Villard de Honnecourt sketched in his notebook a mechanical bird constructed so that it could siphon wine, and he filled many pages with images of other ingenious mechanical devices. In the fifteenth century, two attendants of Baron Leo von Rozmital described a marvelous automaton, now lost, that they saw at Salisbury Cathedral: it was "worked with weights" that allowed three carved figures of the magi to bring gifts to the infant Christ; for Christ to reach out to those gifts; and for Mary and Joseph to bow to the kings. Anthropomorphic automata also appeared in literature, usually associated with Eastern knowledge and the occult. In the twelfth-century parodic epic *The Journey of Charlemagne to Jerusalem and Constantinople*, for example, Westerners encounter many mechanical wonders, including metal-and-ivory statues of children who blow horns and smile.

While this fountain, like many other automata, is clearly indebted to Eastern—Byzantine and Islamic—antecedents, it is just as clearly an allusion to the French Gothic style of architecture, particularly the *rayonnant*, or radiant, style. Turrets and crenellations, pointed arches and simulated masonry, elegant openwork and enamels that act as stained glass windows all contribute to the sense that this fountain is a Gothic building in miniature. Most of all, it recalls Sainte-Chapelle—a royal chapel built in Paris by Capetian King Louis IX (d.1270) for his newly acquired Passion relics. Although it is unclear whether the fountain was commissioned by a member of the Capetian or the Valois dynasty, its eventual ownership, judging by the telltale eight-point stars on the enamel escutcheons, might be associated with Valois King John the Good's chivalric Order of the Star, founded in 1351.

Both Louis and John considered Paris their royal capital. It was a spectacular city, bustling with commerce and luxury item production. Paris attracted goldsmiths, ivory carvers, enamelers, and manuscript illuminators from all over Europe. It was also the lively site of a university and the home of numerous professors and students. The burger of Paris who instructed his wife about menus also told her how to comport herself on the Parisian streets: "Make sure that you dress decently without introducing new fashions. [...] When walking in public keep your head upright, eyes downcast and immobile ... nor laugh nor stop to speak to anyone on the street. [...] Steer clear of swaggering and idle young men

who live beyond their means and who, possessing no land or lineage, become dancers. [...] Restrain yourself from too much conversation." Alongside these strictures, however, the burger planned to write a whole section on amusements, including games, hawking, and riddles. Perhaps, had he finished his treatise, he might have mentioned fountains as well. While small ones were among the pleasures of wealthy households, large fountains were important urban features. Many, lavishly decorated, still exist in Italy, Germany, France, and Switzerland.

But this object recalls not monumental city fountains but rather those that ruled the medieval imagination. Poets extolled fountains as simultaneously perilous and alluring, sites of both love and loss. The thirteenth-century *Romance of the Rose* has the narrator contemplate the fountain of Narcissus, which "caused the deaths of many valiant men [...] all caught and ensnared here." This fountain reappears one century later in Guillaume de Machaut's *Fountain of Love*, where the dejected Lover comes to an ivory pillar, decorated with the story of Narcissus, and complete with water conduits shaped like a golden serpent with twelve heads. Commissioned by Jupiter and Venus, built by Pygmalion, inhabited by Cupid, and frequented by fairies and nymphs, this fountain is unmerciful to lovers: "It made them love so much / That several have died." Fountains were also potent sites of magic: the northern French *Roman d'Alexandre* has its hero encounter the Fountain of Youth, the Fountain of Resurrection, and the Fountain of Immortality in his travels. In Chrétien de Troyes's romance *Yvain, The Knight of the Lion*, an Arthurian knight named Calogrenant comes across a wondrous fountain in the Broceliande wood: simultaneously cold and hot, it seems to boil and yet remains chilly. As Calogrenant, though advised against it, picks up a nearby golden basin and sprinkles water on a massive emerald stone, he unleashes a tempest.

No such tempest was unleashed by the waters of this delicate fountain. They would have flowed easily and gracefully, encircled by enamels that feature elegant musicians in a garden. One thinks of Giovanni Boccaccio's *Decameron* (1349–1351): there, fleeing plague-ridden Florence, young storytellers gathered around "a fountain of very white marble most marvelously carved." In its center was a figure who tossed the water high, and it "fell back into the crystal-clear basin with a delicious sound," nourishing the countryside garden and diverting the group from their cares. The fountain shown here offered just such a pleasure for the senses and escape from the mundane.

37

Barbute, 1350–1420, Northern Italy, iron; 29.00 × 21.00 × 25.00 cm (11 ⅜ × 8 ¼ × 9 ¹³⁄₁₆ inches), 1.58 kg (3.48 lb.)

WEIGHING about the same as a modern football or army helmet, this iron barbute was forged not in the round shape of a man's head, but rather in a gentle conical form designed to deflect the downward blows of a weapon. The holes lining the edges attached to a chainmail face mask (a camail) that extended down to the neck and shoulders. Probably made in northern Italy, where numerous foundries produced both luxury and workaday items in a variety of metals, it was once worn by a man who defended the Venetian garrison at Negroponte (today Euboea), an island in northern Greece. It bears signs of hard wear, its originally smooth and polished exterior now cratered and worn.

Around 250 pieces of armor were found at Negroponte. They suggest that the warrior who wore this helmet may have also protected himself with a brigandine—a cloth garment with small steel plates riveted to it. If so, he wore it over a shirt of mail. But by the fourteenth century mail was being replaced by plate armor, which consisted of rigid plates of steel. Such plates, first used to protect the knees and lower legs of horsemen, soon came to encase all their limbs and then their entire bodies. Even infantry troops wore versions of such plate armor, which could be transformed and configured for various uses. The shape of plate armor played a decisive role in protecting a soldier by presenting the so-called glancing surfaces that—like those of this helmet—were designed to deflect sword blows.

But why was there so much Venetian armor in Negroponte? The answer lies in the history of Greece, Byzantium, and—above all—Venice. Originally a cluster of nearly uninhabited islands in the middle of a lagoon at the north end of the Adriatic Sea, Venice served as a refuge from Gothic invaders in the fifth century. Yet it grew to become an opulent empire with outposts like Negroponte and even further afield. What distinguished it from other medieval settlements was its access to the sea and, above all, the willingness of its elites to invest not only in land (as was true every-where) but also in overseas trade. In the ninth century, when the rest of northern Italy was under the rule of Charlemagne and his heirs, Venice was effectively independent, though nominally part of the Byzantine empire—the heir of Rome's staunchly Christian eastern half. Gradually Venice came to dominate the Adriatic Sea, its fleets forcing oaths of loyalty from towns all along the eastern coast. It gained trading privileges across the Mediterranean (including the Islamic world), and won

reduced tolls and tariffs as well as special status for its merchants at Byzantium. In exchange for Venetian naval aid, Emperor Alexius (d.1118) granted the Venetians property in Constantinople, the Byzantine capital city; that became the nucleus of a "Venetian quarter"—a self-contained enclave located right along the city docks and a center for overseas trade.

As Venice gained in power, Byzantium lost, buffeted by invasions of Slavs, Bulgarians, Normans (who had taken over Sicily and southern Italy), and various Islamic groups. At the end of the eleventh century, Seljuk Turks entered Byzantine Anatolia, defeating the emperor at Manzikert (today Malazgirt) in 1071 and continuing on toward Jerusalem. Emperor Alexius called on the pope to help supply mercenaries for an army to oppose the Seljuks. Instead of sending troops, Pope Urban II preached the First Crusade in 1095: "From the confines of Jerusalem and the city of Constantinople a horrible tale has gone forth and very frequently has been brought to our ears, namely, that a race from the kingdom of the Persians [...] has invaded the lands of those Christians and has depopulated them by the sword, pillage and fire." The pope then exclaimed: "On whom therefore is the labor of avenging these wrongs and of recovering this territory incumbent, if not upon you?" The excited crowd gathered at Clermont, in southern France, was said to have chanted with one voice: "God wills it." In response to Urban's call, Venice made the crusade a matter of state policy. This was unusual: the other crusade armies were organized not by kings—the heads of state—but by lesser nobles. At Venice, all ships—even merchant ships—were pressed into service for the expedition. In 1099 some 200 ships set sail, carrying around 9,000 crusaders from Venice alone.

The First Crusade resulted in the capture of Jerusalem and the establishment of a thin band of Crusader States along the coast of the eastern Mediterranean. The Venetians took advantage of the new states while they lasted (until 1291), supplying men and ships for their rulers, transporting pilgrims to Jerusalem, and using crusading fervor to advance their own commercial interests. Already in the eleventh century, the Byzantine emperor had given Venice jurisdiction over much of the eastern shore of the Adriatic Sea, tax-free trading privileges in all Byzantine ports, and land in Constantinople itself, the nucleus of the Venetian Quarter there. As new crusades were called to defend the fledgling and weak Crusader States, Venice took an active role. With the Fourth Crusade, called by Pope Innocent III (d.1216), they took over the entire enterprise.

By then, Europe's crusading spirit had waned, while Venice's relations with Byzantium had grown tense. The relatively few crusaders who arrived at Venice in response to Innocent's call did not have the money to reimburse the city's

elaborate advance preparations. Venice had them compensate for the expense by diverting the expedition to loot Constantinople. The army scaled the thick walls of the city in 1204; according to one Byzantine source, "a knight by the name of Peter entered through the gate situated there. He was deemed most capable of driving in rout all the [Byzantine] battalions. [. . .] [He] wore on his head a helmet fashioned in the shape of a towered city. The noblemen about the emperor and the rest of the troops were unable to gaze upon the front of the helm of a single knight so terrible in form [. . .] and took to their customary flight. [. . .] Thus [. . .] the cowardly thousands [. . .] were chased by one man." That helmet was not a barbute, but its importance in battle is here made clear in an unexpected way.

Once Constantinople was taken, the victors divided the spoils. The crusader Baldwin I (d.1205), count of Flanders, was crowned emperor of the Latin Empire. The Byzantines founded successor states. Venice won the harbor at Constantinople, key Greek cities, the island of Crete, all the land along the Adriatic's eastern coast, and rights to various islands, including parts (and later the whole) of Negroponte. In 1261, the Byzantines regained Constantinople, but Venice kept most of its empire. Rivals like Genoa did what they could to weaken it, and the need for defense— against European rivals and Turkic invaders alike—explains Venice's demand for garrisons, such as the one where the helmet pictured here was found. Negroponte was a key site for maritime commerce, forming a bridge between northern and southern Greece.

Venetian territories, c. 1400.

This barbute was made sometime between 1350 and 1420. By then medieval warfare had taken on the more modern form based on artillery. Knights were becoming irrelevant as guns and cannons were taking hold. Helmets still protected soldiers, to be sure, but the garrison at Negroponte was no match for the Ottoman Turks. In 1470 the Ottomans conquered the island and, in the process, destroyed all the written documents there. The barbute remains as a precious witness to a period of Venetian glory.

38

Time, from Chateau de Chaumont Set, 1512–1515,
France, Lyon (?), silk and wool, tapestry weave;
321.80 × 452.00 cm (126 $^{11}/_{16}$ × 177 $^{15}/_{16}$ inches)

Tᴴɪꜱ tapestry, one of a set of four, represents the allegory of Time (others in the set allegorize Youth, Eternity, and Love). It takes place in a lush landscape filled with flowers and fruit-bearing trees. In the foreground, children play in and around a small duck pond. The chateau of Blois provides a suitably impressive backdrop. At the center, a wattle fence separates two groups: three symbolic figures on the right, and several nobles and their entertainers on the left. The nobles are listening to a richly attired man who proffers a bouquet of flowers to them. Formerly interpreted as the personification of Time, he is in fact the French humanist and courtier to three French kings, Pierre Sala (d. 1529).

Sala was a prolific writer. His *Little Book of Love* was an elaborate "valentine," written in both prose and verse. He also composed his own versions of famous medieval romances, including *The Knight of the Lion* and *Tristan*. Born in Lyon, Sala was friends with a fellow Lyonnais, the celebrated painter and architect Jean Perréal, for whom he wrote a treatise on friendship. Although he lived in the age of the printing press—and Lyon was one of the centers of this technology—he insisted that his own works appear in manuscript, almost always richly illustrated. Sala's life and activities show just how porous the borders are between the Middle Ages and the Renaissance. In fact, these terms are simply conveniences for historians, and Sala, along with his contemporaries—the musician Josquin des Prez, the poet Guillaume Crétin, the manuscript illuminators Robinet Testard and Jean Bourdichon—are often appropriated by the scholars of the Middle Ages and early modernity alike.

Here, smartly dressed, Sala discourses on the fleeting nature and changeability of time—the themes addressed in the Old French quatrain woven above his head: "Sometimes we see Time adorned with lush foliage, / as pleasant as an angel. / Then suddenly it changes and becomes most strange. / Never does Time remain in one state." The three nobles accompanied by a jester and two musicians attentively listen to Sala's instruction. The young woman is Sala's daughter, Éléonore, for whom the tapestries were likely commissioned. Her upturned skirt signifies that she is pregnant. She holds a carnation in her left hand, and with her right caresses the chin of a young man next to her. This is her husband, Hector. Another woman, who rests her hand on Hector's shoulder, is his mother, Marguerite, the very

woman to whom Sala sent his "valentine" and whom he would marry in 1519, shortly after these tapestries were woven. The serene scene, framed by other peaceful activities—a man fishing in the moat in the background, a nobleman arriving on his horse up the winding road, a swan staring at its reflection—is disrupted by the commotion beyond the fence. There, a toothless old man in blue is being hit and chased away by a youngster with a heavy stick, while a turbaned woman balances precariously on his shoulders, the tallest figure of all.

The scene ostensibly pictures Youth, ignorant about the passage and complexities of life, assaulting the old man Time; the turbaned woman is the Muse of

History, Clio. The children playing in the stream, the young couple, their older parents, and, finally, the old man himself all gesture to the fleeting nature of time. So does the verdant garden, rendered in radiant color, and reminiscent of backgrounds of many a millefleurs tapestry: the French word "le temps" in the quatrain might mean "time" or "weather" or "season," and its use here suggests the ephemeral quality of the beautiful summer day, "as pleasant as an angel." The little unicorn, who points his spiral horn directly at the Youth's eyes, is usually symbolic of purity and often allegorizes Christ, while his horn is supposed to have both antidotal and aphrodisiacal powers. All in all, the tapestry is reminiscent of an emblem, a genre that flourished in the sixteenth century, and was particularly important to Sala. It combined texts and images to communicate a moral lesson or a philosophical statement: here, it seems, the lesson is to heed time's evanescence and not fall prey to the follies of youth. Emblem books would prove to be an enduring genre; to create a woven emblem, however, was to showcase not only one's wisdom but also one's wealth.

Tapestries—the making of which was laborious, exacting, and very expensive— epitomized the affluence of the European royalty and nobility as well as their tastes. Tapestries were both utilitarian and decorative. Hung on walls, they warmed and insulated otherwise cold stone rooms. Gold and silver threads shone in torch- and candlelight, adding splendor to the already vibrant colors. The dukes of Burgundy had a whole collection of such works of art, allowing them to change wall-hangings as suited the occasion. Tapestries were also portable: they followed wealthy warriors into battle, to be hung up in their tents on the battle-field; they were brought aboard ships when princes took to the sea. For the ceremonial entry of a prince into a city, tapestries were hung on the walls and towers. Nor was Europe the only place where tapestries were prized. When Ottoman Sultan Mehmed II (d. 1481) captured Duke John the Fearless, the duke had to pay for his ransom with tapestries depicting the deeds of Alexander. Kept in treasuries alongside gold and silver objects, aesthetically pleasing and highly functional, tapestries were both symbols of status and markers of their owners' virtue. Nobles took to heart Aristotle's ethical teachings on the moral imperative of magnificence: "The magnificent man is an artist in expenditure: he can discern what is suitable, and spend great sums with good taste. [...] As the object produced must be worthy of the expenditure, so also must the expenditure be worthy of or even exceed the object produced. [...] He will spend gladly and lavishly." Thomas Aquinas (d. 1274) included both "liberality" and "magnificence" among the virtues proper to mankind.

No wonder then that churches, too, commissioned tapestries. Surrounding themselves with elaborate woven depictions of the lives of saints, late medieval clerics demonstrated their authority and moral leadership. An inscription woven into one of a series of panels made for the cathedral of Beauvais in 1460 suggests the close relationship between the beauty of the narrative depicted on the tapestry and the beauty of the church itself: "the venerable pastor [the bishop] had this tapestry made [...] in which is figured the beautiful life of Saint Peter (*Pierre*). It has clothed many stones (*pierre*) in the choir." Taken out and displayed during particular Church feasts, tapestries contributed to the "magnificence" of the Christian religion, as did the splendid embroidered vestments of the clergy who officiated at the altar.

Sala's own tastes were much appreciated by the kings he worked for. This tapestry was at the chateau of Chaumont when Catherine de Medici arrived in France in 1534 to wed the son of Francis I (d. 1547), whom Sala served and to whom he dedicated many of his writings. (Earlier he had been valet to King Charles VIII [d. 1498] and butler for Louis XII [d. 1515].) Considering his love of medieval romances and his rejection of print, Pierre Sala might be thought to have resisted time's passing as depicted in this tapestry. But his interest in and contribution to the new genre of emblems—not to mention the very fact that his "emblematic" tapestry included the hope of a new generation in the form of his grandchild—suggests that he equally welcomed the new.

PART IV

Death and Its Aftermath

39

Columbarium Tomb Plaque with the Monogram of Christ, 500–800, Spanish (Visigothic or Byzantine?), terracotta; 32.40 × 20.80 cm (12 ¾ × 8 3⁄16 inches)

This plaque, made of baked clay, once covered a burial niche in a communal tomb called a columbarium. The tomb itself takes its name from Latin for "dove" (*columba*) because of its resemblance to a compartmentalized dovecot. The image on the plaque is unequivocally Christian. It features an archway resting on stylized pillars and decorated with floral sprays. This architectural motif was often used for the indexes (or canon tables) of early Christian books; it suggests a church apse or perhaps a Paradise. The archway is framed by the Latin inscription "Bracari, uiuas cum tuis" (Bracarius, may you live with your [loved ones]), and contains several Greek letters, which were likely read symbolically. In the middle is the monogram of Christ's name, the so-called chi-rho, composed of the first letters of Christ's name in Greek (X and P). The monogram is flanked by the alpha and omega, the first and last letters of the Greek alphabet, which signify Christ as the beginning and the end of creation.

Because it figured Christ's triumph over death, the chi-rho was a particularly pertinent image for a burial plaque. Yet, aside from tombs, it appeared on many coins, in baptistery and apse mosaics, and in liturgical objects as well. At the roots of its visual history is the conversion of Emperor Constantine at the Milvian bridge in 312. As the Christian apologist Lactantius (d.320) recounted the story of that conversion, the two sides of the civil war at Rome faced one another across the Tiber River: "Constantine was directed in a dream to cause the heavenly sign to be delineated on the shields of his soldiers, and so to proceed to battle. He did as he had been commanded, and he marked on their shields the letter X, with a perpendicular line drawn through it and turned round thus at the top, being the cipher of Christ. Having this sign (☧), his troops stood to arms" and won the battle. Thereafter, Christianity gained in acceptance and popularity, and by the end of the fourth century was the official religion in the Roman Empire. The plaque comes from Spain, one of the Empire's provinces. Although it was largely taken over by the Visigoths in the sixth century, Byzantine pockets remained until the seventh; indeed, the design of the plaque is reminiscent of the altar frontal (see Object 2) produced in a Byzantine context around the same time. The Visigoths were themselves Christians, though until the conversion in 589 of King Reccared (d.601) many—but not all—practiced the variant brand of

Christianity known as Arianism, which held that Christ was distinct from and therefore subordinate to God.

On tombstones throughout the post-Roman world those who mourned the dead—and those who could afford it—paid commercial workshops to carve images and inscriptions to identify the deceased and often to express both sorrow and hope. The practice had deep roots within the ancient world. Mourners during the Hellenistic period (fourth to first century BCE) marked graves with elaborately carved funerary *stelae* and other memorials, often with inscriptions. The Roman and post-Roman worlds continued the custom. The plaque shown here is anonymous, but it was more common practice to identify the names of the deceased. At Trier, a city ruled by the Merovingian Franks after 475, one tomb inscription reads: "Perses rests here in peace; he lived 45 years; his dearest wife put up this epitaph." And on another: "Here Concordia lies in peace, who lived more or less 65 years; Concordius and Concordialis, her very sweet children put up this epitaph." Some inscriptions were long, like this one from Vienne: "Here rests in peace Eufemia of good memory, dedicated to God, adorned with every spiritual grace of which the first is shining charity, [then] virginity, [and] piety. In her 33d [?] year she was lost to death and found life. Because on earth she loved only the author of life, she is joined with Him in heaven. She died in Christ; was resurrected in glory; [and was] buried on the Kalends [the first day] of January or February."

The Goths, of which the Visigoths were one branch (the Ostrogoths were the other), were a multi-ethnic group that initially practiced two sorts of burials: on the one hand cremations, on the other the inhumation of bodies, often with clothing and objects such as fibulae. Jordanes, a rhetorician writing at Constantinople, shaped an account of the history of the Goths in 551 that made their defeat by sixth-century Emperor Justinian a happy event: it allowed the remaining Gothic princess to wed the emperor's son and merge the fate of the Goths with that of the Romans. It is in this light that we should read Jordanes's account of the burial of Alaric—the Visigothic leader whose army pillaged Rome in 410—as a kind of legend: "Turning from its course the river Busentus [. . .] they [Alaric's people] led a band of captives into the midst of its bed to dig out a place for his grave. In the depths of this pit they buried Alaric, together with many treasures, and then turned the waters back into their channel. And that none might ever know the place, they put to death all the diggers." It is noteworthy that Jordanes did not mention arms in the burial: the Goths were fairly unusual in not including weapons among the goods with which they provided the dead. But Alaric was already Christian, and it is thus possible that his grave included no goods at all.

Little specific information is known about Visigothic burial culture, except for its diversity. Some very early Visigothic tombs contained grave goods but others did not; some held ceramics. Some bodies were placed under tiles, some in sarcophagi, some in rock niches, some under rock slabs. But dates and places of burials are conspicuously absent for Visigothic kings, perhaps because the culture was markedly anti-dynastic. Visigothic liturgical texts, for example, contain nothing that describes royal funerals or commemoration of the royal dead. Nevertheless, we do know that Visigothic churches—some converted from Roman mausoleums—contained burials and served as dynastic tombs for certain wealthy families.

Just as wealthy families provided for the dead, so the dying provided for the living. Visigothic law suggests a literate laity, one that drew up wills and valued the written word, though oral wishes were also acceptable: "The last will of a dying person, whether it be signed by his hand and those of witnesses, or confirmed by the seals and signatures of all parties; or even if the testator could not write, or attach his seal [. . .] or if the wishes of said testator should only be expressed verbally, in the presence of others; where any one of the methods above stated is adopted, the will shall be valid in law." Ordinarily, the will was published in the presence of a priest, and this hints at the place of the Church in inheritance practices. In a seventh-century account of one of the bishops of Merida, the story is told of a very wealthy couple desperate for help when the wife "had conceived after her wedding, but the child had died in her belly." The presiding bishop prayed day and night and, instructed "by a divine oracle," operated on the mother to remove the dead fetus. The husband and wife were so joyful that they insisted that the bishop "receive half of all they owned." After they died he "received their entire patrimony." The columbarium plaque, with its emphasis on the life after death promised by Christ, helps explain the couple's bequest.

40

Single-Edged Knife (Scramasax), 600s, Frankish, Burgundy (?),
iron, copper, and gold foil; 36.90 × 4.10 cm (14 ½ × 1 ⁹⁄₁₆ inches)

A scramasax (also called a *seax* and *sax*—the origin of the name of the Saxons) is a broad, short dagger. It features a single sharp edge, flat blade, and a fairly long grip for wielding with both hands. It was both a weapon and a working tool, as useful for cutting wood as for slashing human flesh. Like many other extant Frankish daggers, this one has corroded and lost its component parts—likely because it formed part of a burial hoard and was excavated from a grave. The scabbard (the sheath that once protected the blade) has rusted, and only gold foil bands with beaded ornament remain. Originally, it may have been made of wood, leather, or metal. The hilt of the scramasax is also missing, exposing the original iron core. Its grip would have been fashioned of bone or wood covered with leather, perhaps with silver inlay, and fitted with a small pommel that would have prevented the dagger from slipping out of the soldier's hand. Judging by other scramasaxes that have survived, this one would have featured a fairly short guard between the hilt and blade.

In the seventh century, aristocratic Frankish warriors were equipped with long swords and short daggers, ironbound bucklers, battle-axes, and pikes. Franks may not have worn body armor or helmets, but they protected themselves with shields; their armies consisted, by and large, of footmen, although from the sixth century the Franks steadily added cavalry to their ranks. In such fighting conditions, throwing axes—called *franciscas*—were particularly deadly: hurled from great distances, they were effective and startling weapons. But a scramasax could be equally formidable when used in hand-to-hand combat. Ordinarily, scramasaxes were made of iron, although a few may have been fortified with carbon—which would have made them harder, and deadlier. The Franks were not the only warriors to use scramasaxes, which were common early medieval side-arms, affordable even by the less well-off.

Originally fairly short, in time scramasaxes lengthened, so that by about 700 they became effectively single-edged swords. The importance that swords held in the medieval imaginary is witnessed by an extraordinary number of legends that grew around these weapons. Russian folktales speak of *mech-kladenets*, the unbeatable sword that could fight without its owner's help; Islamic sources praise the scissor-like Zulfiqar given to Muhammad by Jibraeel (Gabriel) on Allah's

order; in Norse mythology, Dáinsleif, a sword made by dwarves, inflicted wounds that did not heal. Arthurian legends describe several swords, including Caliburn, which was pulled from a rock, and Excalibur, given to Arthur by the Lady of the Lake. Welsh versions mention Carnwennan—King Arthur's dagger that had power to shroud him in shadows. Shakespeare's Macbeth saw a spectral dagger as he went to kill King Duncan: "Is this a dagger which I see before me, / The handle toward my hand? Come, let me clutch thee. / I have thee not, and yet I see thee still. [. . .] I see thee yet, in form as palpable / As this which now I draw" (Macbeth 2.1).

Instruments of death, swords also accompanied their owners *in* death: warriors were often buried with their weapons. When Childeric, king of Franks, died in 481 or 482, he was interred at Tournai (today in Belgium) with weapons, including a francisca and gold-and-garnet fittings for a sword or scramasax. A seal-ring within his grave had the inscription "Childerici regis" (belonging to King Childeric) and showed him with long hair, wearing Roman military dress, and carrying a lance. The grave also contained jewelry, coins, and some golden bees that once probably decorated the harness of Childeric's horse. Certainly, we know that near Childeric's grave were three pits, each containing the bones of ten or more horses. It is likely that these were sacrificed in connection with his burial. In the vicinity were many other graves, suggesting that Childeric's burial formed the nucleus of a cemetery that continued in use until the seventh century. Childeric's was a royal burial, and very lavish indeed.

Not all Frankish burials were like his. Poor young men were buried with no grave goods at all, while others were laid to rest with a scramasax alone, and still others with a sword. Aristocratic graves, however, would be richly furnished with horse bits, fibulae (see Object 26), gold rings, decorated wooden buckets, helmets, and other wares. Gender and age mattered. The graves of young and mature women, for example (insofar as the sex may be determined) often contained jewelry. But those of children (both girls and boys) were rarely furnished, and old people in general were buried in small graves with few goods.

What did not seem to affect burial practices was religion. By the time this scramasax was made, Gaul was controlled by the Merovingian dynasty, founded by Merovech, son of a putative union between a Frankish queen and a sea monster. Merovech was a pagan, but his grandson, Clovis I (d.511), converted to Christianity. Whether pagan or Christian, Merovingian graves were provided with goods. These were not necessarily meant to furnish the utensils necessary in the afterlife, but rather may have been part of this-worldly social ceremonies and markers of family prestige. In fact, the greatest number of furnished graves comes

from the period after the Franks converted to Christianity, and the richest among them were placed within or under churches. The Church never condemned such burials, though Caesarius, bishop of Arles (d.542), did rail against "the pernicious error which has developed among Christians [...] of bringing food and drink to the tombs of the dead, as if the souls which had left the body had need of material nourishment." Indeed, directly under a church at Cologne was a tomb containing evidence of just such a meal, including a chicken in a pot and two eggs in a bowl.

Clovis took over much of Gaul. When his grandsons inherited the throne, they divided it among themselves, often clashing in civil wars bemoaned by Gregory, the bishop of Tours (d.594), whose *Ten Books of Histories* are our chief source for the period. Scramasaxes featured in his grim tale of the assassination of Merovingian King Sigibert in 575 by his brother Chilperic. In Gregory's telling, it was Queen Fredegund, Chilperic's wife, who was responsible: "Two young men who had been suborned by Queen Fredegund [...] came up to Sigibert, carrying the strong knives which are commonly called scramasaxes, and which they had smeared

The Merovingian kingdom, c. 600.

with poison. They pretended that they had something to discuss with him, but they struck him on both sides. He gave a loud cry and fell to the ground. He died soon afterwards."

The assassination of Sigibert was a pivotal event in Merovingian history. The heirs of Sigibert, who ruled the eastern Frankish region centered on Metz (later called Austrasia), were unable to prevail over their uncle Chilperic, who ruled Neustria, the region around Paris. Effective rule was thus transferred to Chilperic and his descendants, who eventually took over Austrasia as well. It was one of the Austrasian "Mayors of the Palace" (a sort of prime minister) who eventually ousted the dynasty itself. By the eighth century, the mayor had become de facto ruler of all the Franks. In 751, Pippin III (the Short), father of Charlemagne, was crowned the first king of the new, Carolingian, dynasty. Under the Carolingians, warriors—the wealthy ones on horseback, the lesser fighting as infantry—used swords, spears, and, of course, their handy scramasaxes.

41

Inscribed Tombstone of Shaikh al-Husain ibn Abdallah ibn al-Hasan (d.1110/AH 504), Iran, Yazd, limestone; overall: 65.00 × 42.60 cm (25 9/16 × 16 3/4 inches)

T HIS elegant gravestone overwhelms with its sheer proliferation of inscriptions. They circle it once, twice; they invade the center; they both confirm the
stone's rigid geometry and chafe against its confines. The script—angular,
enhanced with leaf tendrils that crown tall, attenuated letters—is foliated Kufic.
It doubles here as a decorative image and as a text, characteristic for a culture that
viewed images in religious contexts with suspicion and extolled the word above all.
Here, word becomes image: in the Islamic world, calligraphy was seen as the
ultimate, most refined, and sophisticated form of art.

The inscriptions quote the Qur'an, Islam's holy book, understood to be the
words of God as they were revealed to the Prophet Muhammad (d.632) by the
Archangel Gabriel. It is divided into 114 suras (chapters), all but one of which begin
with the *basmala*—"In the name of God, the Merciful, the Compassionate." Such
recitations are invoked on al-Husain's tombstone, where the *basmala* recurs at the
beginning of two inscriptions along the stone's border. The outer inscription
quotes from the sura "The House of Imran": "Every soul shall taste of death;
you shall surely/ be paid in full your wages on the Day / of Resurrection.
Whosoever is removed from the Fire and Admitted to Paradise, shall / win the
triumph" (3:183). The inscription on the inner border, from the sura
"Distinguished," continues to affirm Paradise as the destiny of the deceased:
"Those who have said, 'Our Lord is God' / then have gone straight, upon them
the / angels descend, saying, 'Fear not, / neither sorrow; rejoice in Paradise / that
you were promised'" (41:30). At the bottom of the tombstone are the names of its
carvers.

In the center of the stone is a pointed, ogive arch, decorated with fine arabesques and standing on two column volutes. The shape of the arch in the middle
evokes a *mihrab*: a niche in the *qibla* wall of the mosque—the wall that indicates
the direction of Mecca and therefore the direction of the daily ritual prayer.
Muhammad lived in Mecca when he first heard the recitation that became the
Qur'an, but when few Meccans converted, Muhammad left for the more welcom-
ing Medina in 622 (this was the *hijira*, year 1 of the Islamic calendar). Initially, he
instructed his followers to pray facing Jerusalem, but soon thereafter he changed
his mind and designated Mecca—the city where the main Islamic sanctuary of the

Ka'ba is located—as the focus of devotional exercises. Even the deceased were to be buried in such a way that their bodies face Mecca—that is, on their side, parallel to the *qibla*. Because the wall with the *mihrab* marked the *qibla*, the niche was one of the most important architectural elements of a mosque, shrine, or tomb, often intricately and profusely decorated with inscriptions as well as with floral and geometric designs. The shape of the *mihrab* is a frequent feature of prayer rugs, turned so as to point to Mecca, but it also took on funerary and commemorative connotations: the stylized form of the niche appears in mausoleums, on ceno-taphs, and on tombstones. Here, the inscription within the arch commemorates the name of the deceased—Shaikh al-Husain ibn Abdallah ibn al-Hasan—and the date of his death in the year 504 of the Muslim calendar, equivalent to 1110–1111.

The tombstone comes from the city of Yazd in central Iran, and this date means al-Husain lived under the rule of the Great Seljuk sultans. Originally from the Eurasian steppe, the Seljuk Turks were a nomadic people that gradually took on linguistic and cultural identity as they moved west seeking pasture for their sheep, camels, and horses. Passing into Muslim regions like Khurasan, they converted to Islam. Eventually they conquered Baghdad and ruled alongside the Abbasid caliphs, adopting not the Shi'ite form that had dominated the Islamic world since the tenth century, but the Sunni brand instead. This made them champions of the caliphs at Baghdad and allowed them to cast their further conquests as a form of jihad. This word, literally meaning "striving [in the ways of God]," was often put into practice via holy war. Gradually also adopting the sedentary ways of those whom they vanquished, the Seljuks became builders: they commissioned new mosques and rebuilt others. They raised free-standing towers and minarets, some used to call worshipers to prayer and others simply marking the piety of their builders.

They also built tombs. Muslims had built mausoleums from the earliest days of Islam, but the practice became especially widespread in the tenth century, when the Shia form of Islam predominated. When the Seljuks arrived, they repurposed such monuments, shifting the objects of their commemoration from descendants of the Shi'ite martyr Ali to Companions of the Prophet and Old Testament prophets. Yet, despite their conversion to Islam, the Seljuks seem to have kept a few pre-conversion burial practices. Funerary rituals detailed in the Hadith (accounts of the sayings of Muhammad) require corpses to be washed, wrapped in a plain shroud, and buried directly in the ground, and yet some excavated tombs have been found to have silk garments in place of simple shrouds, and some contain coffins.

The Seljuks also constructed splendid mausoleums for themselves, modeling them on the older monuments—either towers or square buildings topped by domes—but also introducing some innovations. In particular, they built whole funerary complexes, which incorporated a palace, a mosque, and often school-rooms as well. Sometimes round, at other times polygonal, many featured highly decorative brickwork, and some were adorned with a high, formal gateway. Those who, like al-Hussain or his family, could not pay for such grand complexes but were nevertheless well-to-do, ordered tombstones. It is unlikely that they were used as headstones, but some were instead set into the walls of a funerary complex or a religious building at some remove from the body buried in the crypt of the same building. In that way, the tomb-stones served to commemorate the dead rather than mark their graves.

By the time al-Husain died, the Seljuks had split, the two most impor-tant groups being those of Anatolia, who took over much of the eastern Byzantine empire, and the Great Seljuks who ruled Iraq and Iran. For the Christians living at the time, the

The Seljuk Empire, c. 1090.

triumph of the Seljuks was a period of apocalyptic crisis and resulted in the First Crusade. Western armies departed in the summer of 1096, and by 1099 a narrow strip of land along the coast from Edessa to Gaza was in the hands of the Crusaders. The Iraqi poet Abu l-Muzaffar al-Abiwardi (d.1113) lamented the swift advances of the Franks and excoriated his contemporaries: "We have mingled blood with flowing tears [. . .] Dare you slumber in the blessed shade of safety, / where life is as soft as an orchard flower?" Yet, notwithstanding the loss of Antioch and Jerusalem to the crusaders, much of the Islamic world, including Iran, was unaffected. It took a delegation from Syria to the caliph's court to rouse the sultan, and even then the response was tepid: the chief envoy from Damascus "made a speech which made the assembled company weep. Someone was appointed from the [caliphal court] to go to the sultan's camp and inform them of this disaster. Then apathy reigned." We do not know whether al-Husain's life, to borrow from al-Abiwardi, was "soft as an orchard flower." But "shaikh" was the honorific for an elderly man; at the very least, al-Husain seems to have lived in "the blessed shade of safety" and died at a venerable age.

42

Condemnation and Martyrdom of Saint Lawrence, c. 1180, Germany, Lower Saxony (Hildesheim?), gilded copper, champlevé enamel; 9.55 × 20.80 × 0.16 cm (3 ¾ × 8 ³⁄₁₆ × ¹⁄₁₆ inches)

EARLY Christian saints were tortured and martyred in a wide variety of painful and inventive ways: they were eaten by lions, torn apart by horses, skinned alive, broken on wheels. Not many, however, died in as grisly a manner as Saint Lawrence did. According to the story of his life and death as told in the *Golden Legend*, a collection of saints' lives gathered by Jacobus de Voragine about a century after this plaque was made, Lawrence was subjected to many different kinds of tortures for his faith. Beaten with clubs and burned with hot blades, he was then flogged with whips and finally roasted on an iron grill. Jacobus was amazed by the horrors, observing that there never was their equal in the history of martyrdom. Because of "the bitterness of his sufferings [...] their effectiveness [...] his constancy or fortitude [...] his wonderful fight and the mode of his victory," Lawrence was "sublime in glorification [...] [and] crowned unto eternal rest in heaven." He seemed to welcome his torments: as the coals burnt him, the saint turned cheerfully toward his tormentor, Emperor Decius (d.251), and said, "Look, wretch, you have me well done on one side, turn me over and eat!"

The plaque most likely comes from a reliquary shrine that held some of Lawrence's charred remains. Against a fine blue ground, two scenes unfold in succession. On the left, the enthroned Decius hands a scroll to Lawrence—undoubtedly, his death sentence. Lawrence, a third-century deacon, is charged with being a Christian, and a cheeky one at that: when ordered to turn over the Church treasures to the Crown, goes the story, he assembled the poor and the infirm and presented them to the emperor as the Christian treasure. On the plaque, the tonsured Lawrence is attired as befits his office, in a dalmatic and an alb, and identified also by a halo preemptively encircling his head. He is being led away by an attendant dressed in a conspicuously Roman garb: a pagan, a non-believer. Little did the emperor know that Lawrence's martyrdom, as was proper for a good Christian saint, would trigger a whole set of conversions from among the military rank, most notably that of the local prefect Hippolytus—who would later be torn asunder by horses.

On the right, Lawrence is stretched on the grill, his hands and feet tied together, his elaborate dalmatic stripped from his now naked body. Two executioners wield long poles to hold the saint down—or else, indeed, to turn him over. An angel, peeking from the cloud in the upper right corner, stretches out his arms to receive Lawrence's soul. The entire scene is framed by a golden border with two inscriptions separated from one another by small crosses. One inscription identifies the main protagonist of the plaque as S[AN]C[TU]S LAURENTIUS, and another provides a narrative context for the scenes, enjoining the viewer to look: ECCE DEI MILES SUP[ER]AT LAURENTIUS IGNES ("Behold the soldier of God, Lawrence, defeats fire"). The defeat in question is spiritual rather than physical. Early Christians turned Roman values inside-out, so that the active soldier so praised by pagan Romans was said to be bested by the passive martyr, whose praises were sung by the angels.

The image is well served by the enameling technique of champlevé ("raised field" in French) in which the metal plate is incised and depressions are filled with the enamel fused to the metal surface during the firing process. The object is then slowly cooled, smoothed, and polished. The plaque's beauty lies both in its expressive figures and in its limited use of vivid color: the red ground behind the gilded copper of the grill echoes glimmers of red in the etched figures; the

white block of the throne enlivens the scene of condemnation; and the rich blue of the backdrop holds the composition together. Blue was a color with many symbolic meanings, the most important being heaven. It was used liberally in contemporaneous manuscripts and stained glass alike. But if a manuscript illuminator required the costly lapis lazuli to achieve such brilliant color, both enamelers and stained glass-makers had a much cheaper substance to use: they could attain the same effect by mixing cobalt into a base flux made of flint or sand, potash or soda. The most famous enamels were made in the twelfth and the thirteenth centuries in areas around Limoges (France) and the river Maas (Meuse), as well as in Silos (Spain) and Cologne (Germany). This plaque may have been manufactured in Hildesheim, a place known for its stunning metalwork production.

A product of the twelfth century, the plaque comes from a place and time when few Christian deacons were subject to martyrdom. Nevertheless, many other people in that period were indeed tormented and put to death by flames for their beliefs. These were the heretics, who lived mainly in highly urbanized areas—including the Rhineland, Italy, and the south of France. Chafing against the centralized organization of the Church and its doctrinal strictures, some of them elaborated a variant theology. At a meeting in 1165 in Lombers (southern France), the "good men" and "good women" (as they called themselves) were questioned by the presiding bishop. One issue concerned the Eucharist—the bread and wine that was believed to become the body and blood of Christ when consecrated by the priest. Was the Eucharist salvific? "They answered that whoever consumed it worthily was saved [that is, would go to heaven], but the unworthy gained damnation for themselves; and they said that it could be consecrated by a good man, whether clerical or lay." The Church condemned this notion as heretical: the "good men" were labeled "Cathars"—a term used long ago for some heretics in the early days of Christianity—and the whole machinery of the Church was marshaled against them and other apostates. The first time Cathars were burned was at Cologne in 1163, and from then on various groups of heretics, including some churchmen who ran afoul of the Church, were subject to punishment and sometimes death by fire. For the heretics themselves, however, this fate did not mean exclusion from the heavenly afterlife. After a woman named Astruga was burned at Lunel in 1321, for example, one of the onlookers turned to her friends to declare that she was surely "Saint Astruga the Martyr."

Most Christians did not think that heretics like Astruga were in heaven. But they were anxious to ensure the salvation of their own souls, a destiny not entirely certain. Lay people often got their assurance by proxy through the prayers of the men and women who lived according to a rule—canons and monastics. Theirs was

considered to be a living martyrdom, a sacrifice of their own wills in obedience to a rule and an earthly superior, whether abbot or prior. This most pious way of life gave these religious specialists fair assurance of going to heaven and at the same time the right to intercede with God, Christ, the Virgin, and the saints on behalf of the souls of others. Thus, donations poured in: laypeople gave land and money— and sometimes their children—to the Church in return for prayers for their souls. Some donated costly reliquaries to churches. Women offered their labor in making the precious vestments worn by priests—like the dalmatic and alb on the plaque, which the artist depicts as richly decorated from head to toe. If the plaque comes from Hildesheim, it was very likely presented as a pious gift to the reformed cathedral church there and the canons who served it.

43

Leaf from a Psalter, The Crucifixion, c. 1300–1330, Flanders, Liège, ink, tempera, and gold on vellum; 9.4 × 7.3 cm (3 $^{11}/_{16}$ × 2 $^{13}/_{16}$ inches)

THE central episode in the Christian narrative of salvation, the crucifixion of Jesus of Nazareth, is described as a crowded affair in all the four gospels written by Christ's disciples. Matthew and Mark recall busy throngs milling about the cross: soldiers dividing Christ's garments and crucifying two thieves on either side of him, the scornful passers-by, the mocking officials who call out to Jesus to come down from the cross to prove his royalty and divinity. Luke has Christ's followers standing "afar off" (23:49), but John brings them near, to the foot of the cross, and singles out the Virgin Mary, her sister Mary of Cleophas, Mary Magdalene, and himself—the beloved disciple. Christ, according to John, commends the Virgin to John ("Behold thy mother") and John to the Virgin ("Woman, behold thy son"). He then drinks the vinegar given him by Roman soldiers and dies.

It is, ostensibly, this narrative that is suggested here, in a Crucifixion miniature excised from a fourteenth-century Mosan psalter. Often sumptuously illuminated, psalters were used as devotional books before the advent of Books of Hours; they included the full complement of 150 Psalms, commonly accompanied by a calendar and a litany of the saints. In this vivid image, Christ hangs limply on a green cross, whose color evokes the tree of life. Abundant blood streams down his arms, spreads like a star around his side wound, and trickles down his feet to the hillock where the cross stands—the Golgotha, or the Calvary. Nailed to the cross is the titulus, which derisively announces the charges against the crucified man: the abbreviation INRI stands for "Jesus of Nazareth, King of the Jews." A cruciform halo frames Christ's handsome face and wavy hair; a loincloth cascades down his elegantly curved body. He is flanked by Mary, who lowers her head and folds her hands in prayer, and John, who turns to the Virgin and gestures toward Christ's body and, specifically, his side wound. Christ's eyes are closed: he has given up the ghost.

But the busy crowds are nowhere to be found in this miniature. The three figures are alone; even the landscape has been lost to the golden background. Above, the scene is framed by a tall pointed trefoil arch in the center, itself crowned by a small red trifoliate leaf, and flanked by two pinnacles. The visual insistence on the number three—altogether, there are three arches, and tripartite

leaves burst outward from the corners and the sides of the frame in bunches of threes—undoubtedly refer to the Trinity. The scene seems to unfold within a celestial realm figured as a Gothic church. This was a familiar visual trope in later medieval Europe, when such churches dominated the urban landscapes with their soaring steeples, elaborate sculptural programs, and tall lancet windows filled with stained glass. The scene here, in fact, is reminiscent of a stained glass panel, or else of an enameled reliquary box, resplendent with brilliant blues and reds that, thickly outlined, stand out against the gold. This, then, does not simply illustrate a narrative but recalls instead liturgical, cyclical time, appropriate for a devotional book that was read at specific hours of the day, and in which images served as foci of contemplation and prayer.

Christ's tormented and bleeding body provided one such focus of pious meditation. Right around the period this image was created, a new cult focused on Christ's wounds and blood took root in northern Europe. In the wake of the fourteenth-century plague epidemic, the practice of self-flagellation (whipping) became popular: people united themselves to Christ not just through prayer, communion, and relics, but through their own suffering and wounded bodies. The flagellant movement began in Italy, but it soon became even more prevalent in Germany and Belgium. While the Gospel of John is the only one that mentions the piercing of Christ's side—doing so, moreover, in just one terse line—the emphasis on Christ's blood was given an extra push at the Fourth Lateran Council in 1215. The Council declared that as part of the sacrament of the Mass, the wine and bread on the altar were quite literally "transubstantiated" by the priest (acting by God's grace): although they still looked like bread and wine, they became in fact the very body and blood of Christ. Stories began to circulate of the host itself bleeding. The new focus on the Real Presence of Christ in the Eucharist spilled into Jewish–Christian relations, culminating in the Blood Libel: an accusation that Jews sacrificed a Christian boy every year in order to use his blood in their Passover rituals.

The ruling of 1215 also resulted in changes to the Mass. In order to emphasize the preciousness of the Eucharist, giant rood screens and chancels were built to separate the altar from the laity. The effect was to withhold the sacred host at the moment it was the most longed for. Women suffered doubly because they were denied communion from the cup (so, too, were men in Bohemia), preventing them from taking communion with Christ's blood. Some women compensated: when the Dutch Cistercian nun Beatrice of Nazareth (d.1268) received only the wafer, even so (wrote her hagiographer), "it seemed to her that all the blood which flowed from [Christ's] wounds was poured into her soul, and that all the drops of

that precious liquid were so sprinkled on it [her soul] that it was wholly washed by these drops and most perfectly cleansed from all the dust of sin." The intimacy of the Crucifixion scene shown here—the way its architectural elements break through the frame and the way it brings the crucified body into the reader's space—is telling, suggesting how fully people wished to have access to Christ's sacramental blood. It is not certain whether this book came from a monastic community or was used by a lay reader, but a female patron seems likely. It was made in the diocese of Liège, where the production of illuminated manuscripts—particularly of psalters and psalter-hours—flourished during the thirteenth and fourteenth centuries. Nearly half of these books seem to have belonged to women, witnesses to their fervent devotional life, whether within marriage, in nunneries, or in Beguinages—houses for pious laywomen who, unlike nuns, did not take permanent vows.

Men, too, focused their devotions on the blood of Christ as the fullest symbol of his sacrifice and thus as the means of mankind's ransom from death—or, put another way, as the guarantee of human resurrection. Even though dead bodies do not bleed, in this miniature Christ's dead body oozes blood, the flow not only watering the ground beneath the cross but also fertilizing it with its life-giving properties. When in 1247 the English King Henry III acquired a relic containing Christ's blood for the church of Westminster, the bishop of Norwich preached a sermon, "in which he stated," according to the Benedictine monk Matthew Paris (d.1259), "that, of all things held sacred amongst men, the most sacred is the blood of Christ; for it was the price of the world, and the shedding of it was the salvation of the world. [. . .] In truth, the cross is a most holy thing on account of the more holy shedding of Christ's blood made upon it, not the blood-shedding holy on account of the cross." This miniature brings home the point: Christ's blood seems to flow through the ground and out of the page, toward the reader-viewer. The patterns of use evident on the page suggest it was understood in precisely this way: the green hillock and the trefoil leaves directly below have been smudged, probably by desirous lips and eager fingers.

44 Diptych with Scenes from the Life of Christ, c. 1350–1375, Germany, Thuringia or Saxony, ivory; 20.7 × 11.1 cm (8 ⅛ × 4 ⅜ inches) (each panel)

THIS small diptych—a two-part panel—features four scenes from the life of Christ: the Raising of Lazarus, the Entry into Jerusalem, the Crucifixion, and the Entombment. Carved in fairly high relief, the scenes were meant to foster meditation on Christ's ministry and death. The preciousness of the ivory, with its diminutive and elegant figures moving about with frenzied passion under an architectural canopy, belies the grim subject matter of the diptych.

Arranged to be read from left to right, top to bottom, the four scenes establish a thematic conversation across the panels. On the top left, Christ is raising the dead Lazarus straight from his tomb. The story is recounted in the Gospel of John 11:1–44. Jesus is beseeched by Lazarus's sisters, Mary and Martha, to save their sick brother. He delays until Lazarus has died, for, as he tells his disciples: "Lazarus is dead, and for your sake I am glad I was not there, so that you may believe. But let us go to him." In the panel, Lazarus's stinking corpse is indicated by one of Christ's disciples, who covers his mouth and nose. The wondrous miracle of Lazarus's resurrection, John explains, spreads Christ's fame and guarantees that there will be crowds on Palm Sunday, when Christ arrives in Jerusalem. That very arrival is depicted on the adjoining panel on the right. Again, Christ is surrounded by an excited, adoring crowd—some line the road with their cloaks laid out for the donkey's hooves to step on; others climb into trees to better see their savior. Jerusalem is turned into a medieval fortified city, with telltale crenellations and turrets flanking the central grated gate.

In the ivory, the miracle of Lazarus's resurrection is directly linked to Christ's own demise. It is ultimately this transgression of the norm—the return of the dead—that upsets the Sanhedrin (the council) of Jerusalem, leading the high priest Caiaphas to send Christ to Pontius Pilate, who sentences him to death. The Crucifixion, with Christ's emaciated body stretched out on the cross, is placed directly below the Raising of Lazarus, and the two are in this way set in direct contrast. The one who brought life now dies himself. To his right, the Virgin Mary is held up by her supporters, her eyes closed; to his left, excited onlookers point at the cross. One might expect the final panel to show the Resurrection—and so to echo the raising of Lazarus—but this is not the case: instead, the scene at the

bottom right represents the Lamentation and Entombment. Christ's body is laid atop the sepulcher, the mourners tenderly grasping his torso, head, and feet. Angels grieve in heaven, and Saint John falls on his knees before the coffin, clutching Christ's right arm. This is unusual: ordinarily it is Mary Magdalene who is represented kneeling before Christ's corpse.

The stress here is on the bodies: the body of Lazarus, fetid but revivified; the body of Christ, living and dead; and the hyperactive bodies of his followers. This is no accident: ivory, with its smooth surface, its milky color, its quality of warming under human touch, was understood to be akin to skin. Devotional subjects carved in ivory, therefore, often foregrounded Christ's humanity, placing emphasis on the man of flesh and blood rather than the distant and invisible god. This particular diptych, like many of its kind, was made for private meditation, likely for an aristocratic—or at least wealthy—owner. Ivories were expensive, the material hard to procure and even harder to carve without damaging. Carvers worked with elephant or (more rarely walrus) tusks, suiting their work to the size and natural curve of their materials. Sometimes ivories were painted and/or gilded, although this example does not bear any traces of polychromy. It may have worn off, or the diptych may have been conceived to emphasize the natural qualities of the material. The size of the diptych assured its portability while at the same time highlighting its exquisiteness and its association with jewelry and pocket-sized devotional manuscripts. The ensemble begs close and repeated viewing: one imagines the owner studying the miniature figures, tracing their movements, meditating on the vanities of flesh while handling the flesh-like material.

The era between the first third of the thirteenth century and the last decades of the fourteenth century is often seen as the golden age of ivory. Its popularity was due to the confluence of two developments: the increasingly personal religiosity of the laity, who sought objects on which to focus their pious meditation; and new trade routes, which made it possible for elephant tusks from Africa to travel some 10,000 miles by land and sea to reach Germany, where this and many similar ivories were made. But getting the goods to European markets was difficult. Overland routes were slow and dangerous. The most direct route, westward through the Straits of Gibraltar, was almost impossible for sailing ships driven only by the wind. Once on the Atlantic, moreover, hostile regimes in the Maghreb, Balearic Islands, and Iberian Peninsula made voyages hazardous. By cultivating good relations with those regimes and developing new ships powered by oars as well as sails, the Genoese overcame these difficulties. The Venetians generally used another route, over the Alps to Germany.

Yet another, northerly route was employed by Scandinavian traders to import walrus ivory along with furs from Iceland or Greenland.

One way that elephant tusks made the trip from Africa to Europe was by piggy-backing, as it were, on the alum trade. Alum was a necessary compound for cloth-making, and by the thirteenth century the cities of northern France and Flanders had flourishing textile industries. Wool was imported from England, turned into cloth, and sold in markets across Europe and beyond. The best alum, used in the dyeing process, came from North Africa and Egypt. Genoese and Venetian merchants were the major intermediaries between Egypt, the shipping center for goods from Africa, and the north. From the north, the Italians brought to Alexandria cloths of various quality as well as wood, iron, and pitch (all needed for shipbuilding). They returned north with ships that carried alum, along with luxury goods such as spices, dates, figs, silks, gold, coral, and precious stones—and elephant tusks. Relatively light, the ivory was worth many times its weight and thus was extremely profitable.

Ivory was widely used: extant are small statuettes of the Virgin and Child and sculptures of the crucified Christ; croziers and low-relief plaques sometimes assembled into larger altarpieces; and secular pieces such as combs and mirrors, caskets and hair-parters. Multi-part devotional objects like this diptych became particularly popular and, by the fourteenth century, were produced in great numbers. Because master carvers used a limited number of models in various arrangements, the quality was uneven and the iconography often lacked originality. Still, different combinations of familiar scenes allowed each piece to have its own emphasis according to the owner's tastes and needs: some focused on Christ's childhood, while others—like the example here—highlighted his suffering and the promise of resurrection. That devotional objects carved in ivory were highly prized is witnessed by the legend of Saint Hedwig, Duchess of Silesia (d.1243). Hedwig owned an ivory statuette of the Virgin and Child, and the legend recounts that she carried it with her everywhere and that she clutched the ivory in her hands as she died.

Major western trade routes, c. 1300.

45

Master of Heiligenkreuz, Death of the Virgin, c. 1400,
Austria, tempera and oil with gold on panel; 66.00 × 53.30 cm
(25 $^{15}/_{16}$ × 20 $^{15}/_{16}$ inches)

THE New Testament does not say very much about the Virgin Mary, one of the most beloved saints of the later Middle Ages. When the devout wished to know more about her childhood, her parents, her life after Christ's death, and, indeed, about her own death, they turned to the apocrypha—stories about biblical characters found outside of the accepted canon of texts such as the Gospels. In his tremendously popular collection of saints' lives, *The Golden Legend*, the thirteenth-century friar Jacobus de Voragine codified a variety of narratives about the Virgin that came from apocryphal sources. This painting is based on one such narrative, which was visualized in a broad variety of contexts: portal sculpture, manuscript pages, and, as here, painted panels. It depicts the death, or—since some stories suggested that she was not dead but merely asleep for three days until Christ came to collect her—the so-called "Dormition (Sleep)" of the Virgin.

Here, Mary is propped up in a bed, covered with an ornate brocaded throw. She is young, dressed in blue, her golden hair streaming down her back under a white headdress. She is thin and pale in death, her hands piously crossed over the coverlet. These hands, with their tremendously long and thin fingers, are echoed in the spindly digits of the apostles variously arranged around the deathbed. At the center, Saint Peter is performing the last rites. Resplendent in his papal tiara and white robes, he sprinkles Mary's body with holy water, while another apostle helpfully holds up a codex inscribed, undoubtedly, with the Office of the Dead. The young John, dressed in green, carries a lighted candle, as does the apostle directly behind him. Another one, probably Saint Andrew, stands at the foot of the bed, censing the air. Two apostles sit on a wide bench in front of the bed, reading. The one on the right is turning pages of his book while wiggling his toes in seeming impatience. His companion on the left presses the rivet of his spectacles to his forehead and brings the book close to his eyes in an attempt to see the text— very likely the prayers for the dead—a bit better.

Above the apostles, engraved on the gold background, angels emerge from scalloped clouds. On the left are two singers and two instrumentalists, one playing a triangle and another shaking hand bells. On the right are more musicians: a singer, a figure playing a psaltery, another beating a string drum and, at the very back, a wind instrument player. Other angels carry banners. The golden

clouds part at the top to reveal Christ, crowned as the ruler of heaven. He holds a small figure dressed in white, her hands folded in prayer: this is Mary's soul. Just barely visible within the blue backdrop are faint figures of other angels extending their attenuated hands toward Christ and Mary in adoration. Engraved into the background is a tooled frame enclosing the upper part of the painting as well as the saints' halos.

One man, however, lacks a halo. He stands nearest the Virgin, bringing his face very close to hers. With his left hand, he touches her shoulder; with his right, he grasps her pillow from behind. Some faux Hebrew script is inscribed on his left sleeve. The man's appearance is as distinctive as his garment and different from all the others: he has a very large hooked nose, a full head of dark curly hair, and a long, forked beard. This appears to be no one other than Judas, shown with the exaggerated features that medieval artists reserved for the Jews. His presence is troubling; it contradicts the Gospel accounts, which say that by the time of Mary's death, Judas was already dead and had been replaced by another apostle, Matthias. The other apostles, conversely, are exactly where they should be. As the *Golden Legend* recounted, they were gathered around the bed of Mary by the will of God, miraculously brought there from the faraway lands where they had been preaching. John, for example, was in Ephesus when he heard "a clap of thunder, and a shining cloud picked him up and whisked him to Mary's door." John, Christ's beloved disciple, was delivered there first, but then all the others "were snatched up into the clouds from wherever they were preaching, and deposited" in the same place.

The painting suggests that its beholders need to be similarly "snatched up." Between the two apostles in the foreground is a conspicuously empty space, alleviated only by a green pillow: an invitation for the viewer to enter the scene, to kneel on the cushion, and to pray together with the holy men. This visual injunction is echoed in contemporaneous devotional instructions to the pious. The immensely popular fourteenth-century treatise *Meditations on the Life of Christ* enjoined the reader to imagine herself participating in key moments in the sacred narratives of Christ's life, "feeling yourself present in those places as if the things were done in your presence." Addressed to an unnamed nun in the order of the Poor Clares, the treatise was likely penned by a Franciscan.

Indeed, this panel was originally part of a diptych, its pendant representing the death of Saint Clare (now at the National Gallery of Art in Washington, DC). Although we know nothing about the Master of Heiligenkreuz (his name refers simply to the place where another diptych of his once belonged), it appears that he was commissioned to paint panels for various religious houses in Europe. It is

likely, therefore, that the Virgin-Clare diptych was made for a convent of Poor Clares, generally called the second order of Saint Francis. Founded by Saint Clare—an early follower of Francis—along with other women and their clerical sponsors, the Poor Clares lived strictly enclosed in their convents, followed a rule, and dedicated themselves to poverty, penance (particularly fasting), and prayer. In much of this they were typical of many female religious of their day, not quite nuns but not quite laywomen either. The formula was so popular that by the time of Clare's death in 1253, there were 110 houses of Poor Clares in Italy and many others elsewhere in Europe. Clare was canonized very quickly, and in general the Poor Clares excelled in producing saints as well as in composing songs, prayers, and long poems about them.

The sophisticated style of the painting, its resplendent surface decoration, and its air of courtly refinement betray the taste of its patrons. Though dedicated to poverty, the Poor Clares right from the start generally came from aristocratic, noble, and even royal families, and by 1400 their poverty was no more than symbolic. The abbesses (heads) of rich houses patronized the arts. Cities vied for these houses, whose wealth and cachet added luster to the urban landscape. Many such nunneries served in effect as family mausoleums, where chanting prayers comprised a major part of the nuns' daily occupations. While Clare had prohibited her nuns from singing, many houses soon adopted a new and more liberal rule. Some sang their prayers polyphonically, with two or more independent melodies, and the nuns spent considerable time preparing for their musical performances. Colette of Corbie led a reform of the order c. 1400, but she did not adhere to Clare's prohibition about music. Rather, she asked that the nuns pray with angelic voices, "pleasing and melodious." Though we do not know exactly what she meant, this painting suggests the choirs of angels as a model for such prayers, guided here by Saint Peter in singing the Office of the Dead.

46

Claus de Werve, Mourner from the Tomb of Philip the Bold, Duke of Burgundy, 1404–1410, Champmol, Vizille alabaster; 41.1 × 17.6 × 11 cm (16 ⅛ × 6 ⅞ × 4 ⁵/₁₆ inches)

Hᴀɴᴅs clasped, head sharply turned, lips pursed, and eyes narrowed, this alabaster mourner, or *pleurant*, from the Tomb of the Duke Philip the Bold (d.1404) possesses a formidable physique that seems to reveal his personality. The man's mouth is downturned and his massive chin is covered in stubble; the closely cropped hair emphasizes the roundness of his skull, and the furrowed brows crease the forehead with deep folds. In his original place on the tomb, this mourner stood under one of the central arches that lined the perimeter of the structure, among other alabaster *pleurants* (forty-one in all). The man's fur-lined garment with wide sleeves falls in heavy folds down his rotund body, revealing but a tip of one shoe. Despite his cowl-like garb, he is not a monk but a layman, meant to remind viewers of the real *pleurants* who accompanied the duke's funerary procession from Halle (in Brabant, where he died unexpectedly) to Dijon, the duchy's capital, and ultimately to the Chartreuse de Champmol. The Chartreuse was a Carthusian foundation endowed by Philip and his wife Margaret (d.1405), and meant to double as a ducal necropolis. Begun in 1383, it was unusually large, housing double the usual twelve monks and offering guest rooms for pilgrims. Much of the monastery was adorned with various family symbols of the duke and duchess, making it quite clear on whose behalf the monks were supposed to pray. Champmol's church was dedicated in 1388 and there, right in the monks' choir, stood Philip's tomb before it was destroyed during the French Revolution.

Rather small—a bit more than 16 inches in height—the mourner statue nonetheless appears monumental, as do all the other carved figures that once formed part of the tomb. The tomb itself was a grand affair, unusual in conception and much imitated by the duke's successors. Originally designed by Jean de Marville, the court sculptor who died in 1389, the monument was then continued by the celebrated sculptor Claus Sluter, who himself died in 1406; finished by Claus de Werve in 1410, some six years after Philip's death, it has been reconstructed at the Musée des Beaux-Arts de Dijon. The tomb was conceived as a two-deck structure defined by slabs of black marble. Atop the upper slab was the recumbent effigy of the duke—hands folded, feet resting on a golden-maned lion, with two angels kneeling by his head and holding his helmet. Between this and the lower slab, a refined openwork arcade revealed the figures of the mourners, turning and

gesturing, frozen in mid-motion. Among them were a bishop and a deacon, a priest and choirboys, cantors and monks; the rest were meant to suggest the members of the duke's family and his court. They echoed in alabaster the real *pleurants*, accompanying the duke in perpetuity, implying the funerary cortege as an eternal performance of sorts. The tomb was conceived to be looked at from all sides, to be experienced kinesthetically, as the mourners glided in and out of view between the arcaded galleries.

The Duchy of Burgundy, c. 1400.

This dramatic monument was of a piece with Philip's political strategy: he held his patchwork duchy together largely by tireless travel from one end to another, impressing his subjects with grand processions, lavish banquets, ceremonial entries into cities, and choreographed presentations of manuscripts and tapestries. He financed much of this by canny manipulation of his brother, Valois King Charles V of France (d.1380), diverting royal wealth into Burgundian coffers. Philip's funeral employed sixty torch-bearing weepers all along the some 360-mile route from Halle to Dijon. Philip's son broke away from the French crown to ally himself with England during the Hundred Years' War (1337–1453), but he followed his father in commissioning a near copy of the Champmol tomb for himself.

Though more extravagant than most, the Burgundian duke's tomb, decorated with a procession of *pleurants*, was deeply rooted in the ambivalent traditions of medieval mourning practices. Death evoked two conflicting emotions: sorrow for the loss of the living person and, in the context of Christian belief, joy at the soul's eternal redemption. When the Florentine Dominican Remigio dei Girolami (d.1319) delivered a sermon upon the death of Beatrice of Anjou, wife of Bertrand de Baux, he admonished Bertrand to grieve properly by citing Ecclesiasticus 22:11: "Cry but little." At the end of the thirteenth century, the city statutes of Valréas (a commune in southeastern France) railed against the cries and lamentations "of those following the body of the dead in the streets, in the church or at the cemetery." At the same time, however, Christians—from theologians to simple confessors—were increasingly valorizing the shedding of tears. Tears of penance were seen as cleansing; tears poured forth during prayer were considered a grace; inability to weep was deemed deeply suspect. Tears were treated as a "gift of God," especially by women who sought an emotional mode of devotion. But men wept too. At the end of the

thirteenth century, William of Tocco reported that whenever the Dominican theologian and Saint Thomas Aquinas (d.1274) "wanted to study, dispute, read, write or dictate, he first went to a secret place of prayer and prayed, covered with tears, in order to learn in truth the divine secrets." Around the same time, the Dominican Thomas de Cantimpré (d.c.1270), who lived and wrote in the northern half of what would later be Philip's duchy, asserted that tears shed for the dead counted as precious intercessions on behalf of their souls. As the doctrine of purgatory became precise, defining a special place where the souls of the dead were cleansed of their sins for a fixed period of time, so did the role of the living in hastening that purification via "good deeds" on behalf of the dead. Tears became assimilated to prayers.

The traditional specialists in prayer were the monks. The Carthusians—a particularly austere order, focused on reclusion, contemplation, and penitence—were considered outstandingly powerful advocates before God, their intercessory prayers deemed especially effective. At the same time, since the tears of the mourners were now themselves considered akin to prayers, the image of the mourner came to look more and more like that of a monk. In fact, the monastic habit—sober in color, covering the body like a shroud—was itself meant to signify social death. While monks retreated from the world, the mourners made the essential link to the streets. The laymen who attended the ducal funeral, be it members of his family or the poor, were required to wear the black hooded cloaks that were distributed to all participants. Garbed like monks, the mourners were suspended between the contemplative life of the recluse and the active life to which they would return.

At the time of Philip's death, so somber and sober a funeral procession was only a bit more than a century old. Earlier funerals had been noisy affairs (and many still were), with professional women mourners hired to weep, tear their hair and clothing, and cry out as the body went to the grave. In the mid-thirteenth century, women mourners and their dramatic behaviors were gradually suppressed, at least in the new "ideal" of the funerary procession. Now the mourners hardly glanced at the corpse; they kept their heads bowed or turned away; their hands were hidden in voluminous gowns, kept clasped, or used to worry rosary beads or prayer books. The *pleurant* seen here—sheathed in a thick cloak, hands held tight—stands as the epitome of this new griever.

47

Master of Guillebert de Mets and Workshop, The Last Judgment, Leaf from a Book of Hours, 1430s, Flemish, ink, tempera, and gold on vellum; 12.60 × 8.50 cm (4 $^{15}/_{16}$ × 3 $^{5}/_{16}$ inches)

THAT the world will end, inevitably, dramatically, and imminently, was a given for medieval Christians. Time was linear: it started when God created the world out of nothing, and it will come to its spectacular conclusion when that same God so ordains. Saint John was told as much when in exile on the island of Patmos: a visionary witness to the future, he was shown the Antichrist's advent, the Four Horsemen of the Apocalypse, angelic trumpets that sounded destruction, a whore of Babylon riding a dragon, and many other such questionable delights and blood-chilling horrors. In his Book of Revelation, John put down every key event of the world's end, including the Resurrection of the Dead and the Last Judgment. Revelation chapters 20 and 21 describe these events as a grand spectacle in which God appears on a great white throne that seems to take up the entire world, and the dead are coughed up by the earth, water, and hell itself. They are judged according to their deeds, either saved or thrown in a pool of fire if their names do not appear in the Book of Life. Thereupon a new heaven and a new earth form, and a new Jerusalem descends from heaven. Here God will dwell with his people and "death shall be no more."

Visions of the Apocalypse inspired some of the most striking representations in the long Middle Ages. *The Commentary on the Apocalypse*, penned by the Spanish monk Beatus of Liébana (d.c.798), was lavishly and vividly illustrated for centuries to come, and is preserved in many visually arresting manuscripts. Images of the Last Judgment and of the Second Coming greeted the beholders from the portals of great Romanesque and Gothic churches: in Laon and in Moissac, at Saint-Denis and at Chartres. Thirteenth-century England produced remarkable illustrated Apocalypses, filled with detailed and inventive visual narratives. In the later Middle Ages, the Last Judgment became a staple image in Books of Hours where it regularly accompanied the Office of the Dead.

The devotional book from which this folio comes shows Christ as the Man of Sorrows. His wounds displayed, he sits on a rainbow and presides over the resurrection of the dead within an arched window. On either side, the Virgin and Saint John intercede on behalf of humanity. The earth opens up, and naked men and women prepare to climb out of their graves just as two angels sound their

long golden trumpets. These trumpets break the bounds of the arched image and end up in the wide margin, where two odd creatures cavort among the elegant foliage. The sound of the trumpets, it seems, is all encompassing, reaching not just the known world but also its unruly edges. Saint Michael, kneeling on the ground at the center, is busy weighing the souls of the dead. A deformed devil pulls at one side of the scale, attempting to upset the balance and condemn the soul to hell by tricking Michael into believing that the soul's bad deeds outweigh the good. But Michael is ever vigilant, striking the devil with his cross-topped staff and ready to send him tumbling into the disorder of the margin.

This illumination is attributed to the workshop of Master of Guillebert de Mets, an artist likely trained in Paris, or at least by Parisian painters, and who worked in Flanders in the 1430s, in the middle of the Hundred Years' War. The war itself was fought between England and France (1337–1453), but Flanders, too, was much affected, for it depended on English wool for its weaving and other cloth-making industries. When, during that war, the Duchy of Burgundy was created by the Valois dukes— a branch of the French royal dynasty—Flanders, whose cities prized their self-governing independence, became the core of its restive northern branch. The workshop of the Master of Guillebert de Mets worked for the ducal court even as it gained commissions from citizens in the rich Flemish cities of Ghent and Bruges and produced books for the open market.

The Duchy of Burgundy, c. 1477.

The historical moment provided plenty of dramatic events that could rightfully be construed as apocalyptic. The Hundred Years' War was one; constant outbreaks of bubonic plague another; and the expansion of the Ottoman Turks into what had once been Byzantium (and beyond) was yet a third. They provided preachers with much fodder for sermons on the world's demise. But in point of fact, John's Revelation had a long afterlife in medieval thought and speculation. Interest in the date when the world would end abounded, even though theologians frequently warned against such predictions. After all, Scripture straight-out said that this time "the Father has fixed by his own authority" (Acts 1:7). Still, calculations began already in the second century, while in the fourth century Bishop Martin of Tours thought that the Antichrist was already born and the Apocalypse imminent. In 398, crowds in Constantinople were terrified by pre-Apocalyptic prodigies; the fall of Rome in 410 was seen as the sure sign of the end. Anxieties similarly arose around the year 500, then again

around the year 800, and then more certainly around the year 1000: after all, John's Revelation spoke of Christ's 1,000-year-long reign, although it was unclear whether one had to begin counting from the time of the Incarnation or the time of the Crucifixion. In the twelfth century, the Italian theologian Joachim de Fiore prophesied that his current epoch (which he called "the Age of the Son") would end in 1260, and usher in the new era ("the Age of the Holy Spirit") in which God would become directly accessible to humanity.

The events of the late Middle Ages added still more portents of the world's demise. In April of 1429, the Franciscan friar Richard arrived to preach his apocalyptic sermons at the Parisian Cemetery of the Holy Innocents. He spoke daily for over a week and was heard by thousands of people who gathered to learn his prophecies of the marvelous and terrible things to come in 1430. In an act of contrition, his listeners destroyed their finery by throwing it into a bonfire. There is little doubt that countless sermons just like Richard's rang throughout late medieval cities, rallying the pious to repent, and warning them of the inevitable end.

But clearly not everyone was casting goods into the flames: this Last Judgment folio from a Book of Hours serves less as a witness to such fervent sentiment than to the taste for luxury. This was an expensive prayer book, pocket-sized, lavishly illuminated, designed to help the wealthy laity combine their piety with obvious aesthetic pleasures. Such opulent objects were snapped up by members of the Burgundian elites: rich burgers, ecclesiastical dignitaries, and members of the court. The dukes legitimized their rule by surrounding themselves with splendid tapestries, tableware, books, costumes, dramas, and music. That same taste for luxury was shared by everyone who could afford it. Courtiers commissioned ivory game boards, belts with fancy money pouches, and fine clothes made of patterned silks and velvet. In addition to sumptuous liturgical vessels, brocaded vestments, and reliquaries, Flemish churches ordered grand altarpieces, painted in the newest medium—oil. Among them was the famous Adoration of the Mystic Lamb, produced by Jan and Hubert van Eyck for the Ghent's Church of Saint John. Dedicated on May 6, 1432, the image refers, in part, to the liturgy for All Saints' Day—and so to readings from the Book of Revelation included therein.

48

Initial T from a Choral Book with Isaac and Esau, c. 1460–1470, Northern Italy, ink, tempera, and gold on parchment; sheet 18.00 × 16.00 cm (7 ¹⁄₁₆ × 6 ¼ inches)

T HE story of Isaac and his sons, Esau and Jacob, was fraught with meaning for both the Christians and the Jews in the Middle Ages. Esau and Jacob were twins who struggled already in their mother Rebecca's womb. Esau was born first, hairy and red, while Jacob came right after, holding onto Esau's heel. Genesis 27 tells the story of Isaac, going blind in his old age, who summons Esau, his favorite, and sends him off to hunt: "Thou seest that I am old, and know not the day of my death. / Take thy arms, thy quiver, and bow, and go abroad: and when thou hast taken some thing by hunting, / Make me savoury meat thereof, as thou knowest I like, and bring it, that I may eat: and my soul may bless thee before I die" (Genesis 27:1–4). The conversation is overheard by Rebecca, who hastens to warn her own favorite, Jacob, and they hatch a plan. Rebecca helps Jacob dress into Esau's smelly hunter's garments, wraps his hands in lamb skin, cooks up Isaac's favorite meal, and sends Jacob to see Isaac in his brother's stead. So deceived, the unseeing Isaac blesses Jacob instead of Esau, discovering the deception only when Esau returns from the hunt. But it is too late. Distraught at his brother's deception, Esau exclaims: "Hast thou only one blessing, father? I beseech thee bless me also." And Isaac, who has just appointed Jacob Esau's lord, pronounces the fateful words: "In the fat of the earth, and in the dew of heaven from above / Shall thy blessing be. Thou shalt live by the sword and shalt serve thy brother: and the time shall come, when thou shalt shake off and loose his yoke from thy neck" (Genesis 27:38–40). Jacob, fleeing Esau, goes into exile but returns triumphant, the father of the twelve tribes.

This historiated T initial presents a pivotal moment in the story. Isaac, who towers over his son, lies in an enormous bed. His eyes are closed, to indicate his blindness, and he turns away from Esau, his right hand resting on top of the red coverlet, his left ostensibly touching Esau to ascertain his identity. Isaac's head is framed by a halo; his hair is well-coifed, his beard neatly parted and curling at the ends, his skin white and unblemished. Esau, by contrast, is hairy and scruffy, his hands, face, and neck covered in stubble. He kneels before the bed, his bow in a sling at his back. The blue of Esau's cloak stands out against the red coverlet, itself set in contrast with the green wall behind Isaac. The stem of the letter T, painted with white floral motifs, serves to accentuate Esau, as does the blue flourish below his feet.

The narrative was understood as a tense religious struggle by both Christians and Jews, although the two groups interpreted it quite differently. For Christians, the triumph of the young Jacob over his older brother was the victory of the New Testament over the Hebrew Scriptures. Jews, conversely, conceived of Esau as the embodiment first of Edom, then of Rome, then of Christians as a whole, while Jacob symbolized Israel and Judea. The episode spoke particularly strongly to the late medieval European Jewry, banished from England in 1290, from France in 1306, from Spain in 1492, and from many cities everywhere else in Europe. For Jews, Jacob signified redemption, the ultimate triumph of the chosen people. To such a beholder, any image of Esau and Jacob—and these images appeared frequently in the illuminated Haggadot, the ritual books for the Passover—was pregnant with messianic meaning, with the promise of deliverance.

But the book that included the image pictured here was neither made nor used by a Jewish community. A large illuminated initial, here incised from a choral manuscript, it was doubtless painted by one of the many professional Christian artists working in northern Italy at this time. Books such as these were quite enormous in order to allow all the members of a choir to see the words and music. The large T in this miniature marked the beginning of the first word, "Tolle," in a chanted response for the matins of the second Sunday in Lent: "Tolle arma tua," or "Take up your weapons." All antiphonaries contained these words and music for that day, and some featured illustrations, like this one, of the moment when Isaac calls on his firstborn to take his weapons and go out to hunt. Just as the liturgy was made up primarily of psalms that were understood as prefigurations of the Christian message, so too was this passage from Genesis.

Although neither the artist nor the users of this book would have cared much about the Jewish significance of Isaac and Esau, the artist was obliged to imagine how to reconstruct the scene. That may not have been as difficult as it sounds. Although the fifteenth century saw a proliferation of laws to keep Christians and Jews apart, many Jews lived in (or, rather, on the outskirts of) northern Italian cities, where they were appreciated for their economic contributions and were allowed to observe their religious practices, build synagogues, construct cemeteries, and celebrate their holidays. Christians consulted Jewish doctors and borrowed from Jewish money-lenders (along with pawn-brokering, money-lending was one of the very few professions that Christian communities left open to Jews). The creator of this initial, in other words, may have known something about local Jewry and their death rituals.

Some of these were described in an account by Elijah Capsali (d.1555), who studied in Padua with Rabbi Judah Mintz. When the rabbi lay dying in 1509, writes

Capsali, he summoned "all the rabbis of Padua, among them my teacher Rabbi Isserlein, and these brave men of Israel gathered around his bed [. . .] Then in their presence he conferred rabbinical ordination upon Rabbi Isserlein and ordered them to do him honor. He laid his hand upon him, blessed him and commanded him saying: 'Now I am dying. May the Lord be with you' [. . .] Rabbi Abba Shaul [del Medigo] and I also were there to receive his blessing. After which, his son Rabbi Abraham Mintz approached, with his own children. The dying man had them come next to him on the bed, placed his hands upon their heads, kissed them and embraced them. When he had finished blessing his descendants, he composed his feet upon the bed and died."

The death of Rabbi Mintz (on Friday) was followed by burial (on Sunday). The whole community of the synagogue fasted, suspended work, constructed a coffin, and began the burial rites at the home of the dead man. There "the rabbis and notables stepped to the fore, raised up the deceased, and carried him on their shoulders to the room in the courtyard, whose walls had been draped in black." After stacking up holy books next to the bier, the men (including young Capsali) lit torches and listened to a long homily. Then they processed to the cemetery, during which all the men "considered worthy" took turns carrying the coffin. Once at the grave site, "Rabbi Hirtzen then came forward, recited the prayer, and raised up a great lamentation." At last, the body was transferred to the grave, its head placed on a special copy of the Torah, the first five books of the Hebrew Bible. Rabbi Mintz was a great man in the eyes of his community, a righteous man in the mold of Abraham and Isaac; were Isaac to have lived and died in late medieval Italy, he would undoubtedly have merited an equally elaborate ritual.

49

A Bridal Couple, c. 1470, southern Germany, oil on panel; unframed 62.30 × 36.50 cm (24 1/2 × 14 5/16 inches)

NOTHING, at first glance, is more innocuous than the image of an aristocratic bridal couple standing together against a background of dense foliage. Stylishly dressed, they wear matching colors, matching beaded chaplets, and matching rings as unequivocal signs of their engagement. The young woman has just given her beloved a chicory sprig, now fastened to his chaplet, and he is offering another sprig to her. Tethered by gaze and touch, the two appear enraptured with each other: he gently holds her waist, she looks into his eyes. But all is not well in this deceptively idyllic world. The forest is a living shadow, menacing and dark; the flowers droop and fade; the wilting grass turns yellow at the lovers' feet. This subtle hint of ominous decay is magnified on the back of the panel, where the couple is represented as a pair of corpses, putrefied and riddled with vermin.

Deceased Lovers, reverse of the Bridal Couple panel

At some juncture, the panel was sawed lengthwise and separated into two paintings. But they are meant to be read as one: on the reverse, the figures change places, and so each appears to be joined at the back to its ghastly double. Their flesh seems to metamorphose directly through the wood of the panel. The elegant young man has turned into an untidy corpse, his clothes replaced by a shroud, the circlet just below his left knee echoed by the coiling serpent at his feet and flies alighting on his legs. The woman's body, also decayed, is no longer clothed in a graceful dress but in a winding sheet; her necklace and the pearly chaplet have turned into a slimy noose-like serpent. She lays a reassuring hand on her companion's shoulder, but the man turns away, as if repulsed by his corpse-bride's touch. Ashamed of his rotting naked body, he tries to lift his shroud to hide his genitals; those of his companion are barely concealed by a repugnant toad.

The doubling of the bodies—whole and decaying, sound and rotten—is a defining characteristic of late medieval macabre art, here taken to its extreme. But here each corpse—bigger than its living counterpart and therefore somewhat distinct from it—suggests Death personified, a didactic figure who prompts beholders to contemplate their own

inevitable demise. This contemplation, moreover, had to take a kinesthetic form: because one image hides the other, to fully comprehend the painting, one has to walk around the panel or else to physically grasp and turn it around. The painting is a resounding example of a universal *memento mori*—a reminder of death, of the fleeting nature of human existence. It is also a reminder of the Original Sin. The mirrored poses of the bridal couple, decomposition hidden within their living flesh, and the futile attempt of the male corpse to cover his shame—all suggest that the two are meant to call to mind Adam and Eve, the first couple, whose disobedience brought death into this world.

The obverse of the painting, then, implies a verdant Eden. Its flowers—cherry blossoms and clover, valerian and cowslip—are fragrant symbols of love and fecundity. But the back of the painting upends these expectations, featuring barren and fractured rock at the corpses' feet and a spectral void behind their backs. Like the flesh of the two hapless lovers, the woods and grass have died away, their nearly palpable smell dissipating, replaced by the implied stench of aged and rotting bodies that attract snakes, scorpions, and flies. The liminal locale and the equally liminal nature of the macabre couple—they are neither truly dead nor truly alive—evoke the concept of purgatory where souls await their final judgment.

Not heaven, not hell, but something in-between, purgatory was a waystation en route to the ultimate reward. Only saints could gain heaven right away. Saintly bodies were believed to triumph over decay—despite any sensory evidence to the contrary. That is why their relics could rightly be encased in gold and why those relics, though only bits and pieces of their bodies, contained, in the words of Victricius of Rouen (d.c.404–409), "the truth of the whole of their bodily passion." Those who committed mortal sins were sent directly into hell, to be eternally tormented by its horrific denizens. Dante Alighieri's famous vision of nine concentric circles of hell was but one literary incarnation of this idea among many; the late twelfth-century vision of the Monk of Eynsham memorably describes the place as "inaccessible to all except to torturing devils and tortured spirits," chaotic and malodorous, where vipers, "dreadful beyond belief, monstrously large and deformed [. . .] exhaling execrable fire from their nostrils [. . .] lacerated the crowds of wretched beings." But heaven and hell were not the only otherworldly destinations: there was a place reserved especially for those who were neither saints nor irredeemable sinners.

In the eleventh century, there was only a vague notion of such a "third place" where the souls of the dead might go. The Cluniac monk Jotsaldus recounted hearing of a place of belching fire "in which the souls of sinners undergo diverse

punishments for a fixed time by the manifest judgment of God. Indeed, a multitude of demons were appointed ever to renew their torments. They, restoring [the souls'] punishments from day to day, heap up more and more intolerable sorrows. Nevertheless, [the demons lament that] due to the prayers of religious men and almsgiving to the poor [. . .] often the souls of the damned were being freed from their punishments through God's mercy." But later, in the city schools, more precise ideas took shape. Thomas Aquinas (d.1274) wrote that purgatory exists in two places: in one "the place of purgatory is situated below and in proximity to hell, so that it is the same fire which torments the damned in hell and cleanses the just in purgatory." The other place is on earth, where punishments remind the living of God's plan and inspire them to pray for the release of those below. Thomas described a complex hierarchy of intercessory prayer—prayer on behalf of others—with the saints near the top (just under Mary and Christ) because "the more closely they are united to God, the more are their prayers efficacious."

Certainly, the bridal couple appear in need of intercession. Double macabre portraits like this were made for lay patrons, offering them a way to think about what happens after life's quick passage. Not just physical decomposition and bodily torment awaited the deceased; they had to brace for spiritual suffering as well. The panel was a forceful reminder to a married couple to confess their sins and do penance for them. By the late fifteenth century, there were numerous ways to carry out penance and thereby avoid or lessen the punishments of purgatory: pray, fast, go on pilgrimage, give alms, and buy an Indulgence—a sort of promissory note of time remitted from purgatory in return for a pious act or payment for one. Although Martin Luther (d.1546) famously objected to the sale of Indulgences, thereby launching the Reformation, they were so popular in Germany—where this panel was made—that early printers like Johannes Gutenberg (d.1468) made them in quantity, with spaces left blank for the date and the name of the purchaser. But one could hardly buy one's way entirely out of the agonies of post-mortem cleansing—at least, not this aristocratic pair. Putrid, decaying, these living corpses stand in a desolate place that forcefully echoes Dante's description of purgatory as "a level place more solitary than roads through deserts."

50

Hans Holbein, Dance of Death, The Pope, cut c. 1526–1527, Germany, woodcut; trimmed sheet 7.0 × 4.8 cm (2 ¾ × 1 ⅞ inches)

THE Pope sits enthroned before the crowd, his splendid seat overhung with an embroidered baldachin. Climbing on the baldachin, his back to the viewer, is a deformed little devil with clawed feet, scaly legs, and pointed ears. Another devil swoops down from the sky, tail curled, tongue out, holding what seems to be a papal bull. The armrests of the throne are supported by cherub-like grotesques with demon's wings and vegetal tails. Cradling and kissing the papal feet is a kneeling emperor. Behind the ornate throne, convivially putting its bony arm around the Pope's shoulder, a grinning skeleton cranes its exposed vertebrae to stare right into the man's weary face. Another skeleton stands in the crowd behind a cardinal, parroting him. It has donned the cardinal's hat, taken a cross-topped staff, and is clutching its shroud in imitation of the cardinal who grasps his cope. The knotted string of the cardinal's hat is mirrored uncannily in the long worm that writhes inside the skeleton's hollow body.

Such a spectacle of decaying flesh, juxtaposed with its living double, marks the late medieval art of the macabre, a genre of sorts that put decomposition on display. There was the *Encounter of the Three Dead and the Three Living*, which featured noblemen who stumble upon animated corpses, their very doppelgangers, during a hunt. There were the *transi* tombs, which paired an idealized effigy of the deceased with an image of his decaying corpse. And there was the Dance of Death, or *la danse macabre*, which—in its emphasis on death's oppressive physicality—stands as the culmination of the macabre aesthetic. Wildly popular across medieval Europe, the Dance of Death proclaimed the inevitability of death as well as its equalizing force. The medieval *danse macabre* takes the form of a dejected throng: men (and sometimes women) of various classes, hieratically arranged and interspersed by grinning skeletons, move inexorably toward their death. Indeed, the skeletons are Death: death personified, repeated again and again, grabbing laymen and clerics, mocking them in biting verse and ugly jig. Accompanying the image is the text: a dialogue between Death and the living. Monumental paintings in particular often included the image of a Preacher standing at the beginning of the procession, and, in a sense, directing it. One painting—made for the city of Reval (modern-day Tallinn, Estonia) by the great German artist Bernt Notke (d.1509)—has the Preacher exclaim: "O, reasonable

creature, whether poor or rich! / Look here into this mirror, young and old, / and remember all / that no one can stay here / when death comes as you see here." In fact, such an image itself could be conceived as a visual sermon. In Paris, the *danse macabre* mural was painted at the Cemetery of the Holy Innocents, and at least on one occasion a mendicant friar came to preach his terrifying apocalyptic sermons in front of it. The Dance of Death also appeared in prints, none better known than those designed by Hans Holbein the Younger and subsequently cut by Hans Lützelberger. The original impressions of these designs—the so-called "proofs"—were made around 1526 or 1527; this print is one such "proof."

Extraordinarily popular in the later Middle Ages, macabre images have generally been linked to the effects of the plague—especially the so-called Black Death, which killed off a good half of the European population during 1346–1353. This explanation, however, is hardly apt: one finds very few *transi* tombs or Dances of Death in Italy, the initial locus of the plague; the *Encounter* images appeared long before the plague struck; and the Dance of Death gained popularity in the fifteenth century, when the epidemics had subsided considerably. Especially pertinent for the Dance of Death imagery, which hails the leveling force of death, is the fact that by the time of its appearance the plague stopped being the ultimate equalizer: the epidemics struck mainly children and spared adults, who developed some immunity to the disease.

Instead, the popularity of the Dance—which dramatized individual confrontations between mankind and mortality—is more likely informed by anxieties about the nature of bodily death and its spiritual consequences. In the fourteenth century, the Church was split by the Great Western Schism (1378–1417), and suddenly Europe had two popes: one in Avignon, another in Rome. Trust in religious institutions declined, while the popularity of mendicant preachers and of lay religious movements soared. The pious were urged by both to assume responsibility in their relationship with God: death was inevitable, and Christians were encouraged to forge their own path to salvation. The Preacher in the Dance of Death frequently enjoined his audience to look into the painting as if into a mirror, a familiar sentiment that appears in late medieval sermons. For example, a fourteenth-century Franciscan preaching handbook, *Fasciculus Morum*, claims that death is "like a mirror because in it all men are seen without differences, the rich as well as the poor, the old as well as the young; in the same way, death spares no one." Mendicant preachers were also well known for infusing their sermons with shockingly graphic descriptions of bodily death, to bring home the point about the necessity of leading a proper life. The *Fasciculus Morum*, for instance, revels in its description of signs of death: "the nose grows cold, the face turns pale,

the eyes darken, the ears grow deaf, nerves and veins snap, and the heart is split in two. There is nothing more base or abominable than a corpse," the author concludes. The Dance of Death, this macabre societal mirror, extols such spectacles of decomposition, all with a healthy dash of satire directed at the unwilling dancers.

In Holbein's woodcuts, the dancing procession has been replaced by a series of narrative vignettes. Each print shows a different hapless victim—the Sailor, the Monk, and the Rich Man, among many others—approached and snagged by the frightful skeletal specter. Ecclesiastics in particular fare poorly in Holbein's woodcuts: Death steals the miter and the crozier from the fat Abbot, peeks over the Cardinal's shoulder as he sells indulgences, drags the Bishop away from the field where confused sheep and an equally confused congregation are scattered. It is the Pope, however—the leader of the Church, its rock and its shepherd—who is derided above everyone else. He is the only one in the series accompanied by two skeletons; a suggestion, perhaps, that the Pope is dying a physical and a spiritual death both. The Pope, however, seems oblivious, as he is poised to crown the man groveling at his feet. This figure is familiar from one of the tracts penned by Martin Luther (d.1546), a German theologian who stood at the origins of the Protestant Reformation movement. Luther once described the Antichrist, who—unlike Christ who washed his disciples' feet—makes a pagan prince kiss his feet. Holbein's scene is an obvious reference to Luther's words.

Indeed, Holbein's prints were created during the Reformation, when the Church split yet again, this time into Catholic and Protestant movements. Protestants contested papal authority with their belief that the Bible was the only legitimate source of divine knowledge. Still, aside from the image of the Pope, Holbein's designs betray no clear anti-Catholic or pro-Protestant sentiment. Indeed, the cycle was issued by both Catholic and Protestant printers within the span of four years. It was rather the texts that were published alongside the woodcuts that gave them a denominational flavor. Catholic printers like the Brothers Trechsel accompanied Holbein's images with the verses of a Catholic poet, Gilles Corrozet, which considerably softened visual criticism of the Pope. Conversely, in the edition published by the Protestant brothers Frellon, Holbein's designs were accompanied by various essays that were distinctly Protestant in tone. Religious affiliations may have changed, but the popularity of Holbein's designs endured. They continued to be reprinted for centuries, arresting and visceral, showing Death as the ultimate force: inevitable, inexorable, relentless.

Illustrations

The following objects are from the collections of the Cleveland Museum of Art; all photos © The Cleveland Museum of Art.

1. Jonah Cast Up, c. 280–290, Asia Minor (?), marble; 41.50 × 36.00 × 18.50 CM (16 5/16 × 14 1/8 × 7 1/4 inches). John L. Severance Fund 1965.238
2. Altar Front, c. 540–600, Constantinople or Ravenna, marble; 101.00 × 169.50 × 25.50 CM (39 3/4 × 66 11/16 × 10 inches). John L. Severance Fund 1948.25
3. Pilgrim's Flask with Saint Menas, sixth–seventh century, Egypt, terracotta; 10.00 × 6.40 CM (3 7/8 × 2 1/2 inches). Gift of Bruce Ferrini in memory of Robert P. Bergman 1999.231
4. Calyx (Chalice), 900s–1000s, Byzantium, Middle Byzantine, blood jasper (heliotrope) with gilt-copper mounts; height 7.70 CM (3 inches). John L. Severance Fund 2013.49
5. Christ's Mission to the Apostles, c. 970–980, Ottonian, Milan, Italy, ivory; overall: 18.20 × 9.90 × 1.00 CM (7 1/8 × 3 7/8 × 3/8 inches). Gift of the John Huntington Art and Polytechnic Trust 1967.65
6. Feline Incense Burner, 1100s, eastern Iran, western Afghanistan, or Turkmenistan, Khurasan, copper alloy, cast and chased; 35.50 × 11.00 × 32.50 CM (13 15/16 × 4 5/16 × 12 3/4 inches). John L. Severance Fund 1948.308
7. Leaf from a Qur'an, 1100s, Iran, opaque watercolor, ink, and gold on paper; 32.00 × 21.30 CM (12 9/16 × 8 3/8 inches). Purchase from the J. H. Wade Fund 1939.507
8. Arm Reliquary of the Apostles, c. 1190, Lower Saxony, Hildesheim, Germany, gilt-silver, champlevé enamel, oak; 51.00 × 14.00 × 9.20 CM (20 1/16 × 5 1/2 × 3 9/16 inches). Gift of the John Huntington Art and Polytechnic Trust 1930.739
9. Virgin and Child, late thirteenth century, Liège (?), wood (oak) with polychromy and gilding; 83.00 × 24.00 × 20.00 CM (32 5/8 × 9 7/16 × 7 13/16 inches). John L. Severance Fund 2014.392
10. Christ and Saint John the Evangelist, early fourteenth century, Germany, Swabia, near Bodensee (Lake Constance), polychromed and gilded oak;

92.71 × 64.45 × 28.84 CM (36 1/2 × 25 5/16 × 11 5/16 inches). Purchase from the J. H. Wade Fund 1928.753

11. Master of Rubielos de Mora, The Coronation of the virgin with the Trinity, c. 1400, Spain, oil on panel; 144.60 × 91.40 CM (56 7/8 × 35 15/16 inches). Gift of the Hanna Fund 1947.208

12. Christ Carrying the Cross (panel from an altarpiece), 1400s, England, Nottingham, painted and gilded alabaster; 47.00 × 28.30 CM (18 1/2 × 11 1/8 inches). Andrew R. and Martha Holden Jennings Fund 1969.296

13. Leaf from an Antiphonary, Initial H with the Nativity, c. 1480, South Germany, Augsburg (?), ink, tempera, and gold on vellum; leaf 62.50 × 41.00 CM (24 9/16 × 16 1/8 inches). The Jeanne Miles Blackburn Collection 2014.25

14. Adam and Eve, Fragment of a Floor Mosaic, late 400s to early 500s, northern Syria, Byzantine period, marble and stone tesserae; 142.90 × 107.30 × 5.72 CM (56 1/4 × 42 3/16 × 2 1/4 inches). John L. Severance Fund 1969.115

15. Curtain Panel with Scenes of Merrymaking, sixth century, Egypt, tapestry weave with supplementary weft wrapping, undyed linen and dyed wool; 144.20 × 26.70 CM (56 3/4 × 10 1/2 inches). Purchase from the J. H. Wade Fund and Gift of the Textile Art Alliance in memory of Robert P. Bergman 2000.5

16. Plaque from a Portable Altar Showing the Crucifixion, 1050–1100, Germany, Lower Rhine Valley, walrus ivory; 5.10 × 9.55 CM (2 × 3 3/4 inches). Gift of Arnold Seligmann, Rey and Company, Inc. 1922.359

17. Dragon's Head, 1100–1150, Anglo-Norman?, walrus ivory; height 6.40 CM (2 1/2 inches). Gift of Thomas P. Miller in memory of James J. Rorimer 1975.258

18. Bowl with Engraved Figures of Vices, 1150–1200, Germany, bronze, spun, hammered, chased, and punched; 6.05 × 28.95 CM (2 3/8 × 11 3/8 inches). Purchase from the J. H. Wade Fund 1987.61

19. Engaged Capital with a Lion and a Basilisk, 1175–1200, northern Italy, Emilia (Bologna?), marble; 30.20 × 33.00 × 29.25 CM (11 7/8 × 12 15/16 × 11 1/2 inches). Purchase from the J. H. Wade Fund 1972.20

20. Leaf from a Cocharelli Treatise on the Vices, Acedia and Her Court, c. 1330, Genoa, ink, tempera, and gold on vellum; sheet 16.30 × 10.30 CM (6 3/8 × 4 inches). Purchase from the J. H. Wade Fund 1953.152

21. Miniature from a Mariegola, The Flagellation, 1359–1360, Venice, workshop of Lorenzo Veneziano, tempera and gold on parchment; sheet 29.50 × 21.00 CM (11 9/16 × 8 1/4 inches). Purchase from the J. H. Wade Fund 1950.374

22. The Madonna of Humility with the Temptation of Eve, c. 1400, Italy, tempera and gold on wood panel; framed 191.50 × 99.00 × 11.00 CM (75 3/8 × 38 15/16 × 4 5/16 inches). Holden Collection 1916.795

23. Zebo (Zecho) da Firenze, Grotesques from the Hours of Charles the Noble, King of Navarre (1361–1425), c. 1404, France, folio 22, ink, tempera, and gold on vellum; codex 20.32 × 15.71 × 6.98 cm (8 × 6 1/8 × 2 11/16 inches). Mr. and Mrs. William H. Marlatt Fund 1964.40.11.b

24. Günther Zainer, The Virgin Mary Overcoming a Devil, from *Speculum Humanae Salvationis/Spiegel menschlicher Behältnis*, c. 1473, Germany, Augsburg, hand-colored woodcut, 7.4 × 12.0 cm (2 15/16 × 4 3/4 inches). Gift of Leonard c. Hanna, Jr. 1928.762

25. Demon in Chains, illustrated single page manuscript, c. 1453, style of Muhammad Siyah Qalam (Iran?), opaque watercolor and gold on paper; 25.70 × 34.40 cm (10 1/16 × 13 1/2 inches). Purchase from the J. H. Wade Fund 1982.63

26. S-Shaped Fibula, sixth century, Frankish, silver with garnets; 2.20 × 2.80 × 0.80 cm (13/16 × 1 1/16 × 5/16 inches). Gift of Joe Hatzenbuehler 2007.225

27. Button, 500s, Byzantium, rock crystal, garnet, granulated gold; diameter 3.05 cm (1 3/16 inches). Gift of Mrs. Horace Kelley 1946.259

28. Solidus with Busts of Constans II and Constantine IV (obverse), 659–661, Byzantium, gold; diameter 1.90 cm (11/16 inches). Gift of Dr. Norman Zaworski 2012.22

29. Bifolium Excised from a Carolingian Gradual, c. 830–860, Germany or northeastern France, gold and silver ink on purple parchment; sheet 29.00 × 10.00 cm (11 3/8 × 3 7/8 inches). Purchase from the J. H. Wade Fund 1933.446

30. Jug, Buyid period, reign of Samsam al-Dawla, 985–998, Iran or Iraq, gold with repoussé and chased and engraved decoration; overall 12.50 × 10.20 cm (4 7/8 × 4 inches), diameter of base 7.00 cm (2 3/4 inches). Purchase from the J. H. Wade Fund 1966.22

31. Lion Aquamanile, 1200–1250, Germany, Lower Saxony, Hildesheim, copper alloy, cast, chased, and punched; 26.40 × 29.00 × 15.00 cm (10 3/8 × 11 3/8 × 5 7/8 inches). Gift of Mrs. Chester D. Tripp in honor of Chester D. Tripp 1972.167

32. Luster Wall Tile with a Couple, 1266, Iran, Kashan, Ilkhanid period, fritware with luster-painted design; overall: 19.50 × 16.00 cm (7 5/8 × 6 1/4 inches). Gift of the John Huntington Art and Polytechnic Trust by exchange 1915.524

33. Leaf Excised from Henry of Segusio's *Summa Aurea*: Table of Consanguinity, c. 1280, France, Paris, ink, tempera, and gold on parchment; 44.20 × 27.50 cm (17 3/8 × 10 13/16 inches). Purchase from the J. H. Wade Fund 1954.1

34. Albarello with Two Hares, fourteenth century, Spain, Paterna, tin-glazed earthenware (maiolica); 22.30 × 9.90 CM (8 3/4 × 3 7/8 inches). In memory of Mr. and Mrs. Henry Humphreys, gift of their daughter Helen 1943.276

35. Mirror Case with a Couple Playing Chess, 1325–1350, France, Paris, ivory; diameter: 10.20 CM (4 inches). Purchase from the J. H. Wade Fund 1940.1200

36. Table Fountain, C. 1320–1340, France, Paris, gilt-silver and translucent enamels; 31.10 × 24.10 × 26.00 CM (12 1/4 × 9 1/2 × 10 3/16 inches). Gift of J. H. Wade 1924.859

37. Barbute, 1350–1420, northern Italy, iron; 29.00 × 21.00 × 25.00 CM (11 3/8 × 8 1/4 × 9 13/16 inches), 1.58 KG (3.48 LB.). Gift of Mr. and Mrs. John L. Severance 1923.1065

38. Time, from Chateau de Chaumont Set, 1512–1515, France, Lyon (?), silk and wool, tapestry weave; 321.80 × 452.00 CM (126 11/16 × 177 15/16 inches). Leonard C. Hanna, Jr. Fund 1960.176.3

39. Columbarium Tomb Plaque with the Monogram of Christ, 500–800, Spanish (Visigothic or Byzantine?), terracotta; 32.40 × 20.80 CM (12 3/4 × 8 3/16 inches). Gift of John D. Rockefeller, Jr. 1938.160

40. Single-Edged Knife (Scramasax), 600s, Frankish, Burgundy (?), iron, copper, and gold foil; 36.90 × 4.10 CM (14 1/2 × 1 9/16 inches). Purchase from the J. H. Wade Fund 1926.429

41. Inscribed Tombstone of Shaikh al-Husain ibn Abdallah ibn al-Hasan (died d. CE 1110/AH 504), 1110, Iran, Yazd, limestone; 65.00 × 42.60 CM (25 9/16 × 16 3/4 inches). Edward L. Whittemore Fund 1950.9

42. Condemnation and Martyrdom of Saint Lawrence, C. 1180, Germany, Lower Saxony (Hildesheim?), gilded copper, champlevé enamel; 9.55 × 20.80 × 0.16 CM (3 3/4 × 8 3/16 × 1/16 inches). Purchase from the J. H. Wade Fund 1949.430

43. Leaf from a Psalter; The Crucifixion, C. 1300–1330, Flanders, Liège, ink, tempera, and gold on vellum; 9.4 × 7.3 CM (3 11/16 × 2 13/16 inches). The Jeanne Miles Blackburn Collection 2011.54

44. Diptych with Scenes from the Life of Christ, C. 1350–1375, Germany, Thuringia or Saxony, ivory; 20.7 × 11.1 CM (8 1/8 × 4 3/8 inches) (each panel). Andrew R. and Martha Holden Jennings Fund 1984.158

45. Master of Heiligenkreuz, Death of the Virgin, C. 1400, Austria, tempera and oil with gold on panel; 66.00 × 53.30 CM (25 15/16 × 20 15/16 inches). Gift of the Friends of The Cleveland Museum of Art in memory of John Long Severance 1936.496

46. Claus de Werve, Mourner from the Tomb of Philip the Bold, Duke of Burgundy (1364–1404), 1404–1410, Champmol, vizille alabaster; 41.1 × 17.6 × 11 CM (16 1/8 × 6 7/8 × 4 5/16 inches). Bequest of Leonard C. Hanna, Jr. 1958.67

47. Master of Guillebert de Mets and Workshop, The Last Judgment, Leaf from a Book of Hours, 1430s, Flemish, ink, tempera, and gold on vellum; 12.60 × 8.50 CM (4 15/16 × 3 5/16 inches). The Jeanne Miles Blackburn Collection 1999.130

48. Initial T from a Choral Book with Isaac and Esau, C. 1460–1470, northern Italy, ink, tempera, and gold on parchment; sheet 18.00 × 16.00 CM (7 1/16 × 6 1/4 inches). Purchase from the J. H. Wade Fund 1949.535

49. A Bridal Couple, C. 1470, southern Germany, oil on panel; unframed 62.30 × 36.50 CM (24 1/2 × 14 5/16 inches). Delia E. Holden and L. E. Holden Funds 1932.179

50. Hans Holbein, Dance of Death, The Pope, cut C. 1526–1527, Germany, woodcut; trimmed sheet 7.0 × 4.8 CM (2 3/4 × 1 7/8 inches). Dudley P. Allen Fund 1929.147

The following object is from Le Musée de l'Œuvre Notre-Dame, Strasbourg.

49. Inset: Deceased Lovers, C. 1470, southern Germany, oil on panel. Work in public domain.

List of Maps

References

Introduction

Stephen N. Fliegel and Elina Gertsman eds., *Myth and Mystique: Cleveland's Gothic Table Fountain* (Cleveland/London, 2016).

Remigius of Auxerre, *Commentum in Martianum Capellam*, quoted in *Medieval Grammar and Rhetoric: Language Arts and Literary Theory, AD 300–1475*, ed. Rita Copeland and Ineke Sluiter (Oxford, 2009), 49.

1

The Bible translation used here and throughout this book is from Douay-Rheims Bible, accessible at www.drbo.org.

2

Procopius I.1.46 , trans. Cyril A. Mango at www.learn.columbia.edu/ma/htm/or/ma_or_gloss_proko.htm.

Saint Justin Martyr, *Dialogue with Trypho* 40 in Ante-Nicene Fathers, vol. 1, at http://st-takla.org/books/en/ecf/001/0010501.html.

4

Psellus, *Chronographia*, I, 117, trans. E.R.A Sewter (New Haven, 1953) at http://sourcebooks.fordham.edu/basis/psellus-chron001.asp.

Isidore of Seville, *Etymologies: Complete English Translation*, XVI.vii.8, trans. Priscilla Throop, 2 vols. (Charlotte, VT, 2005), 1:xvi.7.8.

Nicetas Choniates, *Historia*, in *Translations and Reprints from the Original Sources of History*, vol. 3 (Philadelphia, PA, 1907), 15–16.

5

Widukind of Corvey, *Deeds of the Saxons*, trans. Bernard S. Bachrach and David S. Bachrach (Washington, DC, 2014), 62–64.

Otto III, *Diplomata*, ed. Teodor Sickel, *Die Urkunden Otto des II*, Monumenta Germaniae Historicae, Dip. regum 2.1 (Hanover, 1893), 775, trans. BHR.

Sean Gilsdorf, *Queenship and Sanctity: The* Lives *of Mathilda and the* Epitaph *of Adelheid* (Washington, DC, 2004), 132.

6

The Qur'an translation used here and throughout this book is from *The Koran Interpreted*, trans. A. J. Arberry (New York, NY, 1955).

7

Abu Hayyan at-Tawhidi, "Epistle on Penmanship," in *Four Essays on Art and Literature in Islam*, ed. Franz Rosenthal (Leiden, 1971), 24, 34, 36.

8

Ottonian Germany: The Chronicon of Thietmar of Merseburg, trans. David A. Warner (Manchester, 2001), 265.

Bernard of Clairvaux, *Apologia for Abbot William*, in *The Cistercian World: Monastic Writings of the Twelfth Century*, ed. and trans. Pauline Matarasso (London, 1991), 56.

"*Translatio*: The Translation of Sainte Foy, Virgin and Martyr, to the Conques Monastery," in *The Book of Sainte Foy*, ed. and trans. Pamela Sheingorn (Philadelphia, PA, 1996), 266.

10

Aelred of Rievaulx, *A Rule of Life for a Recluse*, in *The Works of Aelred of Rievaulx*, vol. 1: *Treatises; The Pastoral Prayer*, trans. Mary Paul Macpherson (Spencer, MA, 1971).

Henry Suso, *The Life of the Servant*, trans. James M. Clark (Cambridge, 1952), 18–19.

Margaret Ebner, *The Revelations*, in *Major Works*, trans. and ed. Leonard P. Hindsley (New York, NY, 1993), 125.

11

Council of Lyon II, *Constitution on the Procession of the Holy Spirit*, quoted in Edmund J. Fortman, *The Triune God: A Historical Study of the Doctrine of the Trinity* (Grand Rapids, MI, 1982, reprint 1999), 218–219.

Pedro López de Ayala, *Rimado de Palacio*, quoted in Joseph F. O'Callaghan, *A History of Medieval Spain* (Ithaca, NY, 1975), 631.

Saint Vincent Ferrer, O.P., *Sermon for Trinity Sunday* (1), trans. Albert G. Judy, O.P. at www.svfsermons.org/B294_Trinity.htm.

Hildegard of Bingen, *Scivias*, trans. Mother Columba Hart and Jane Bishop (Mahwah, NY, 1990), 161.

12

John Leland, *Itinerary in England and Wales; Parts I–III* (London, 1907), 38.

"Trial and Flagellation; Crucifixion," Play 15, Chester Cycle 1572/2010, ed. A. F. Johnston, p.7, at http://groups.chass.utoronto.ca/plspls/wp-content/uploads/2015/09/chester15.pdf.

13

The Rule of the Franciscan Order, trans. David Burr at https://sourcebooks.fordham.edu/source/stfran-rule.html.

David of Augsburg, *De exterioris et interioris hominis compositione*, quoted in Peter V. Loewen, *Music in Early Franciscan Thought* (Leiden, 2013), 95, n. 10, trans. BHR.

14

Tertullian, *Disciplinary, Moral and Ascetic Works*, trans. Rudolph Arbesmann, Emily Joseph Daly, and Edwin A. Quain (Washington, DC, 1959), 117–118.

"Adam lay ybounden," in *Songs and Carols from a Manuscript in the British Museum of the Fifteenth Century*, ed. Thomas Wright (London, 1856), 32–33, trans. EG.

15

Eusebius, *Church History* 2.16.1, in *Nicene and Post-Nicene Fathers* 2nd series, vol. 1 (New York, NY, 1890), 116.

16

Robert the Monk, *Urban II's Sermon at Clermont* in *Urban and the Crusaders*, ed. Dana C. Munro (Philadelphia, PA, 1895), 7.

Solomon bar Samson, *Hebrew Chronicle*, in *Jews in Christian Europe: A Source Book, 315–1791*, ed. Jacob Rader Marcus and Marc Saperstein (Pittsburgh, PA, 2015), 77.

Rabbi Eliezer ben Nathan, "O God, Insolent Men," trans. Susan L. Einbinder, in Barbara H. Rosenwein, ed. *Reading the Middle Ages: Sources from Europe, Byzantium, and the Islamic World*, 2nd ed. (Toronto, 2014), 269.

17

Aberdeen Bestiary, University of Aberdeen Library, Special Collections, MS 24 at www.abdn.ac.uk/bestiary.

18

Abelard, *Letter 7* (to Heloise), in *Guidance for Women in Twelfth-Century Convents*, trans. Vera Morton and Jocelyn Wogan-Browne (Cambridge, 2003), 67.

Thomas Aquinas, *Summa Theologica* [henceforth ST] II-II, Q.94, art.4, at www.newadvent.org/summa/3094.htm#article4.

Tertullian, *On Idolatry* 1.1, in *Tertullianus: De idololatria*, ed. and trans. J. H. Waszink and J. C. M. van Winden (Leiden, 1987), 23.

Tertullian, *The Apparel of Women* 1.1, in *Disciplinary, Moral, and Ascetical Works*, trans. Rudolph Arbesmann et al. (Washington, DC, 1959, reprint. 2010), 117–118.

19

Bernard of Clairvaux, *Apology*, trans. David Burr at http://sourcebooks.fordham.edu/source/bernard1.asp.

The Rule of St. Benedict, ed. and trans. Bruce L. Venarde (Cambridge, MA, 2011), 3.

Jotsaldus, *De vita et virtutibus sancti Odilonis Abbatis* 2.13, *Patrologia Latina* 142:926, trans. BHR.

Third Lateran Council, Canon 27, quoted in R. I. Moore, *The War on Heresy* (Cambridge, MA, 2012), 205.

20

Thomas Aquinas, ST II-II, Q.77, art.4 and Q.35, art.3, at www.newadvent.org/summa/3077.htm#article4 and www.newadvent.org/summa/3035.htm#article3.

Domenico Cavalca, *Specchio de' Peccati* (Florence, 1828), 37.

Dante Alighieri, *Purgatory* 18:100–104, in *The Divine Comedy*, trans. Charles S. Singleton (Princeton, NJ, 1970–1975), 195.

Dante Alighieri, *Inferno*, 7:118–124, in *The Divine Comedy*, 77.

22

Sister Bartolomea Riccoboni, *Life and Death in a Venetian Convent: The Chronicle and Necrology of Corpus Domini, 1395–1436*, ed. and trans. Daniel Bornstein (Chicago, IL, 2000), 47.

24

Thomas Aquinas, ST I, Q.63, art.3 and art.8, and Q.64, art. 4, at www.newadvent.org/summa/1063.htm and www.newadvent.org/summa/1064.htm.

Fourth Lateran Council, *Select Canons*, 1215, Canon 1, trans. H. J. Schroeder at http://sourcebooks.fordham.edu/source/lat4-select.asp.

26

Pactus Legis Salicae, in *The Laws of the Salian Franks*, trans. Katherine Fischer Drew (Philadelphia, PA, 1991), 73, 91.

Beowulf (bilingual edition), ed. Seamus Heaney (New York, 2001), 213, lines 3163–3168.

Einhard, *Vita beati Karoli magni* 23, Monumenta Germaniae Historica, Scriptores 2, ed. G. H. Pertz (Hanover, 1829), 456, trans. BHR.

Notker, *Gesta Caroli Magni* 2.17, quoted in Rachel Stone, "The Emperor's New Clothes: Moral Aspects of Carolingian Royal Costume," Paper presented at International Medieval Congress, Leeds, July 2011, p.1 at www.academia.edu/3630842/The_emperors_new_clothes_moral_aspects_of_Carolingian_royal_costume.

27

Odo of Deuil, *De profectione Ludovici VII in Orientem*, quoted in A. P. Kazhdan and Ann Wharton Epstein, *Change in Byzantine Culture in the Eleventh and Twelfth Centuries* (Berkeley, CA, 1985), 76.

29

Charlemagne, *De litteris colendis*, trans. D. C. Munro at http://sourcebooks.fordham.edu /source/carol-baugulf.asp.
Scribal complaints quoted in Leila Avrin, *Scribes, Script, and Books: The Book Arts from Antiquity to the Renaissance* (Chicago, IL, 1991), 224.

30

Abū al-Ṭayyib Aḥmad ibn al-Ḥusayn al-Mutanabbī, *Poems of Al-Mutanabbī*, ed. and trans. A. J. Arberry (Cambridge, 1967), 29.

32

The Ilkhanid Book of Ascension: A Persian-Sunni Devotional Tale, trans. Christiane J. Gruber (New York, 2010), 70, 72.

33

Laws of King Canute, 1.7, trans. A. J. Robertson, in *Love, Marriage, and Family in the Middle Ages: A Reader*, ed. Jacqueline Murray (Toronto, 2010), 40.
Floris and Blanchefleur, at http://faculty.virginia.edu/OldEnglish/enmd885/floris.html.

34

Giovanni Boccaccio, *The Decameron*, trans. Richard Aldington (New York, 1930), 409.
Bologna statutes in *Medieval Medicine: A Reader*, ed. Faith Wallis (Toronto, 2010), 203.
Archimatthaeus, trans. Henry E. Sigerist, in *Reading the Middle Ages: Sources from Europe, Byzantium, and the Islamic World*, ed. Barbara H. Rosenwein, 2nd ed. (Toronto, 2014), 346.
Master Bartholomaeus of Salerno, in *Medieval Medicine: A Reader*, trans. Faith Wallis (Toronto, 2010), 409.
The Trotula, trans. Monica Green, in *Medieval Medicine: A Reader*, 189.
Saint Augustine, *Sermones Guelferbytani* 17.1, trans. Rudolph Arbesmann in "The Concept of 'Christus Medicus' in St Augustine," *Traditio* 10 (1954), 19.

35

Huon de Bordeaux: Chanson de Geste, in *Les anciens poetes de la France*, ed. F. Guessard and C. Grandmaison (Paris, 1860), 221–222, trans. BHR.
Peire Vidal, *Drogoman senher, s'agues bon destrier*, in *Troubadour Poems from the South of France*, trans. William D. Paden and Frances Freeman Paden (Cambridge, 2007), 134.

Froissart, *The Online Froissart: A Digital Edition of the Chronicles of Jean Froissart*, fol. 2r, trans. Keira Borrill, at www.hrionline.ac.uk/onlinefroissart.

Inventaires mobiliers et extraits des comptes des ducs de Bourgogne de la maison de Valois (1363–1477), ed. Bernard Prost (Paris, 1902), 266, no. 1460, trans. in Richard H. Randall Jr., "Popular Romances Carved in Ivory," in *Images in Ivory: Precious Objects of the Gothic Age*, ed. Peter Barnet (Princeton, NJ, 1997), 70.

Titre LXI.1, in *Les métiers et corporations de la ville de Paris: XIIIᵉ siècle. Le livre des métiers d'Étienne Boileau*, ed. René de Lespinasse and François Bonnardot (Paris, 1879), 127, trans. in Elizabeth Sears, "Ivory and Ivory Workers in Medieval Paris," in *Images in Ivory: Precious Objects of the Gothic Age*, ed. Peter Barnet (Princeton, NJ, 1997), 20.

36

The Good Wife's Guide: Le Ménagier de Paris, A Medieval Household Book, trans. Gina L. Greco and Christine M. Rose (Ithaca, NY, 2009), 57, 59, 94, 142, 222, 253, 257.

The Travels of Leo of Rozmital through Germany, Flanders, England, France, Spain, Portugal and Italy, 1465–1467, ed. and trans. Malcolm Henry Ikin Letts (Cambridge, 1957), 57.

Guillaume de Lorris and Jean de Meun, *The Romance of the Rose*, trans. Frances Horgan (Oxford, 1994), 25.

Guillaume de Machaut, *The Fountain of Love*, in *The Fountain of Love (La Fonteinne Amoureuse) and Two Other Love Vision Poems*, ed. and trans. R. Barton Palmer (New York, 1993), lines 1418–1419.

Giovanni Boccaccio, *The Decameron*, trans. Richard Aldington (New York, 1930), 173.

37

Robert the Monk, *Urban II's Sermon at Clermont* in *Urban and the Crusaders*, ed., Dana C. Munro, University of Pennsylvania, Translation and Reprints from the Original Sources of European History, vol. 1, no. 2 (Philadelphia, PA, 1895), 8.

O City of Byzantium, in *Annals of Niketas Choniates*, trans. Harry J. Magoulias (Detroit, 1984), 313.

38

Aristotle, *The Nicomachean Ethics* 4.2, trans. H. Rackham (Cambridge, MA, 1932), 207.

Woven inscription quoted in Laura Weigert, *Weaving Sacred Stories: French Choir Tapestries and the Performance of Clerical Identity* (Ithaca, NY, 2004), xvii, trans. BHR.

39

Lactantius, *Of the Manner in which the Persecutors Died* cap. 44, trans. William Fletcher, 2 vols. (Edinburgh, 1871), 2:203.

Epitaphs in *Recueil des inscriptions chrétiennes de la Gaule*, vol. 1: *Première Belgique*, ed. Nancy Gauthier (Paris, 1975), nos. 49 and 13b; vol. 15: *Viennoise du Nord*, ed. Henri I. Marrou and Françoise Descombes (Paris, 1985), no. 112, trans. BHR.

Jordanes, *The Gothic History*, trans. Charles Christopher Mierow (Princeton, NJ, 1915), 95.

Visigothic Code 2.11, ed. S. P. Scott in *The Library of Iberian Resources Online*, at http://libro
.uca.edu/vcode/vg2-5.pdf.

Lives of the Visigothic Fathers, trans. and ed. A. T. Fear (Liverpool, 1997), 59–61.

40

Caesarius of Arles, quoted in Edward James, *The Franks* (Oxford, 1988), 140–141.

Gregory of Tours, *Ten Books of Histories* 4.51, in Gregory of Tours, *The History of the
Franks*, trans. Louis Thorpe (London, 1974), 248.

41

Abu l-Muzaffar al-Abiwardi, *Poem*, in *Arab Historians of the Crusades*, trans. from Arabic,
Francesco Gabrielli, trans. from Italian, E. J. Costello (Berkeley, CA, 1969), 12.

Report on envoy's speech quoted in A. C. S. Peacock, *The Great Seljuk Empire* (Edinburgh,
2015), 83.

42

Onlooker of Astruga's execution quoted in Louisa Burnham, *So Great a Light, so Great
a Smoke: The Beguin Heretics of Languedoc* (Ithaca, NY, 2008), 77.

Jacobus de Voragine, *The Golden Legend: Readings on the Saints*, trans. William
Granger Ryan (Princeton, NJ, 2012), 453, 456–457.

43

The Life of Beatrice of Nazareth, 1200–1268, trans. Roger De Ganck with J. B. Hasbrouck
(Kalamazoo, MI, 1991), 279.

Matthew Paris, *English History from the Year 1235 to 1273*, trans. J. A. Giles (London, 1853),
2: 241.

45

Jacobus de Voragine, *The Golden Legend: Readings on the Saints*, trans. William
Granger Ryan (Princeton, NJ, 2012), 464–465.

Meditations on the Life of Christ, An Illustrated Manuscript of the Fourteenth Century
(Paris, Bibliothèque Nationale, MS ital. 115), trans. and ed. Isa Ragusa and Rosalie
B. Green (Princeton, NJ, 1961), 387.

De B. Coleta Virgine [Colette of Corbie], *Acta sanctorum quotquot toto orbe coluntur*, vol. 6
(Antwerp, 1643), 555, quoted in Mary Natvig, "Rich Clares, Poor Clares: Celebrating the
Divine Office," in *Women & Music*, 4 (2000): 59–70 at 69.

46

Remigio dei Girolami, *Sermo in morte di Beatrice d'Angiò*, ed. and trans. (into Italian) at
www.e-theca.net/emiliopanella/remigio/8150.htm, trans. BHR.

Statute of Valréas quoted in Jacques Chiffoleau, *La Comptabilité de l'au-delà* (Rome, 1980), 139.

William of Tocco, *Ystoria sancti Thome de Aquino de Guillaume de Tocco (1323)*, ed. Claire le Brun-Gouanvic (Toronto, 1996), 157, trans. BHR.

48

Elijah Capsali, *Seder Eliyahu Zuta*, quoted and translated in Robert Bonfil, *Jewish Life in Renaissance Italy*, trans. Anthony Oldcom (Berkeley, CA, 1994), 268–269.

49

Victricius of Rouen, *De laude sanctorum*, in *Christianity and Paganism, 350–750: The Conversion of Western Europe*, ed. and trans. J. N. Hillgarth (Philadelphia, PA, 1986), 25.

Vision of the Monk of Eynsham, in *Visions of Heaven and Hell before Dante*, ed. Eileen Gardiner (New York, 1989), 197–218, 209.

Jotsaldus, *De vita et virtutibus sancti Odilonis Abbatis* 2.13, Patrologia latina 142:926, quoted in Barbara H. Rosenwein, "Cluniac War and Monastic Peace: Cluniac Liturgy as Ritual Aggression," *Viator* 2 (1971), 129–157.

Thomas Aquinas, ST(Appendix II), at www.newadvent.org/summa/7001.htm and ST II-II, Q.83, art. 11, at www.newadvent.org/summa/3083.htm#article11.

Dante Alighieri, *Purgatory* 10, in *The Divine Comedy*, trans. Charles S. Singleton (Princeton, NJ, 1970–1975), 99.

50

Fasciculus Morum, a Fourteenth-century Preacher's Handbook, ed. and trans. Siegfried Wenzel (University Park, PA, 1989), 101–102, 718–719.

Index